Mini G

to North Ea

Editor: Robert Meddes
Assistant Editor: Jonathon Lewins
Contributors: Hannah Layford, Terri Eaton, Hayley Ramage Design: Joseph White
Photography: Phyllis Christopher, Helen Collard, Sally-Ann Norman, Dan Civico, Joseph White.

Advertising: Mandy Baxter, Jane Stafford

Published by The Crack Ltd.
Unit 1, Woods Pottery, Stepney Bank, Newcastle upon Tyne NE1 2NP
Copyright 2011 The Crack

ISBN 978-1-897706-14-5

Hello and welcome to The Crack Guide To The North East, a book that will take you rather merrily on a journey through the best of what the region has to offer. If you intend to visit for a weekend - or even if you're upping sticks and decamping to Newcastle, Sunderland, Durham, Tees Valley (or surrounding areas) - then this definitive guide will tell you everything that you need to know about enjoying yourself while here. Dive in.

Durham Brass Festival

We've heard it rumoured that the good folk of the north-east occasionally likes to have a pint. (It's true. We'll admit it.) Thankfully, such passions are well catered for with plenty of places on hand to help us slake our thirsts. These run from old-fashioned boozers which have remained unchanged for years on end, to swanky luxe-bars that are populated by punters showing off their expensive new haircuts.

The Tanners

BIGG MARKET

Featured in countless 'young people looking very drunk and showing their knickers' style documentaries, The Bigg Market is very nearly all wall-to-wall fun-pubs and hen/stag parties a-go-go.

BALMBRAS
5 The Cloth Market, Newcastle,
0191 222 3131 **M** *Monument*
The pub will forever be associated with the Geordie anthem, "The Blaydon Races", which was first sung here back in the day. (The song includes the line: "We took the bus from Balmbras".) However, it's as far removed from a traditional pub as you can get and packed out with young revellers.

BAR 24
24 the Cloth Market, Newcastle
M *Monument*
Regular music, live sports and house trebles. No doubt one for the party-seekers. Open from about 5pm.

THE BEE HIVE
2 High Bridge, Newcastle
0191 2325017 **M** *Monument*
Nice little traditional boozer attracting a range of clients from 18 to 80. House trebles start from £1.95 and there's plenty of other drinks to keep you happy.

THE BLACKIE BOY
11 Groat Market, Newcastle
0191 232 0730 **M** *Monument*
One of our favourite Bigg Market establishments. You'll find a slightly older crowd with everyone from be-suited businessmen to hearty party types mingling happily. Now connected to the swanky Perdu bar - double the fun.

CIRCUIT 1
32-36 Cloth Market, Newcastle,
M *Monument*
Not much in the way of seating in this loud and lairy establishment which pumps the decibels and lager out in equal measure. Not the place for discussing the finer things in life.

CITY VAULTS
11-13 Bigg Market, Newcastle
0191 221 0850 **M** *Monument*
One of the busiest establishments in the Bigg Market, City Vaults is a large bar that's very popular with visiting stag and hen parties. Great spot for football fans with over 30 HD screens. They also do £1 drinks on Wed all night, Thurs 9pm-10pm and 12-1am, and Sun 11pm-1am.

Lady Grey's

The Duke of Wellington

COSY JOE'S
31 Groat Market
0191 232 2234 **M** *Monument*
Attracting an older crowd at the moment, this lively bar is a hot spot for karaoke nights. They've even got something called Party Pods which is basically a room you can hire to sing karaoke with your mates. Sounds fabulous doesn't it... open Thurs and Sun 8-late, Fri 5pm-3am and Sat 12-3am.

KISS
18 Cloth Market, Newcastle
0191 221 0530 **M** *Monument*
Part of the posse of Bigg Market pubs that form the bedrock for the city's daftie revellers. Come 11pm on a Friday night you'll begin to wonder why they didn't name it 'Snog'...

FLARES
31-33 Mosley Street, Newcastle
0191 261 1029 **M** *Monument*
As you can probably guess, this is a 70s theme pub with the staff all dolled-up in stupid wigs and the like. Why does the 1970s always equate to the cheesier side of disco in these type of places? No matter, it can get very full, with people boogie-ing their hearts out.

OHSO
7-9 Groat Market, Newcastle
0191 231 2913 **M** *Monument*
One of the more swanky places in the Bigg Market area this place bills itself as a deluxe bar and they also have a cellar club if you feel in need of throwing a few dancefloor shapes.

THE OLD GEORGE INN
Cloth Market, Newcastle
M *Monument*
One of Newcastle's oldest licensed premises, dating from the time of King Charles I (who is reputed to have had a pint here). It's reached by a narrow, cobbled walkway (off the madness that is the Bigg Market) and gets a big thumbs up all round for its olde worlde, split level quaintness. There's plenty of room and loads of tables and chairs and the music is kept to bearable levels.

CENTRAL STATION
Clustered loosely around Newcastle's main train station, make tracks towards some of the coolest bars in the north as well as the Pink Triangle (cluster of gay and gay friendly bars).

BABY LYNCH
28-32 Collingwood Street, Newcastle
0191 261 6386 **M** *Central Station*
A longish bar which has a retro, but well done, 70s theme with a mixture of exposed brickwork, old portraits and flying ducks... Plenty of seating, some booths and a nice vibe.

The Bodega

Tilleys Bar

BAR FLEET STREET
16 Pudding Chare, Newcastle
0191 232 0253 Ⓜ *Central Station*
A modern looking bar which still retains a homely touch. Genuinely appeals to customers of all ages from loyal regulars to those hankering after fun and excitement (let your hair down on Friday and Saturday nights with some DJ action).

THE BODEGA
125 Westgate Rd., Newcastle
0191 221 1552 Ⓜ *Central Station*
The Bodega always scores highly when the real ale organisation, CAMRA, comes a-calling (often claiming 'best pub'). As you'd expect then, the foamy stuff served up here is always top of the hops with nine real ale pumps that are regularly changed. They even do carry-outs for your beer. And it's not just the ale that is a thing of beauty: check out the gorgeous glass dome ceilings, which create a light and airy atmosphere. Very friendly place to have a pint.

THE BRIDGE HOTEL
Castle Square/Garth, Newcastle
0191 232 6400 Ⓜ *Central Station*
An excellent place to slake your thirst. There's plenty of room and loads of tables, so you should always be able to grab a seat and when the sun's out there's an excellent little beer garden with smashing views of the Tyne Bridge.

The Bridge has an excellent reputation for live music and you'll hear everything from indie to folk to poetry. Slightly older clientele, no doubt attracted by the good beer (particularly their hand pulled ales) and canny grub.

CENTURION
Central Station, Neville St., Newcastle
0191 261 6612 Ⓜ *Central Station*
Formerly the first class lounge for the train station, this establishment is a bar/ delicatessen and is something of a looker with the beautifully tiled and high glass ceiling giving the whole place a sense of grandeur. A cut above.

DESTINATION
Neville Street, Newcastle
0191 260 6305 Ⓜ *Central Station*
Near to the Station, this attracts many a passer-by before they hop on their train. But there's also something for the locals, with resident DJs on every night and decent drink prices. Plus there's a nice little outdoor area for enjoying the Newcastle sunshine. Ahem.

THE DOG
15 Malborough Crescent, Newcastle
0191 221 0775 Ⓜ *Central Station*
Friendly pub with a mixture of gay and straight punters. Not the biggest, but has a loyal following.

The Dog & Parrot

The Empress

Floritas

Head of Steam

THE DOG & PARROT
52 Clayton St. West, Newcastle
M *Central Station*
Friendly and popular pub with a nice cosy atmosphere. They always have a fine and varied selection of real ales on offer.

THE EMPRESS
1 The Side, Newcastle
0191 221 1173 M *Central Station*
Caught betwixt the Bigg Market and the Quayside route, The Empress is a canny little boozer that attracts those heading between the two who fancy a breather (it's on a steep hill).

FLORITA'S
28-32 Collingwood St., Newcastle
0191 261 8271 M *Central Station*
This hangout for the trendier haircuts around town consists of The Tropical Garden (oversized outdoor garden complete with cocktails, beats and cold beers); The VIP Suite (with no joining fee!); The Main Room (big sounds, big sound system, sun-drenched anthems); Club Tropicalia (lounge and dance to cool and kitsch sounds). Good stuff.

THE FORTH
Pink Lane, Newcastle
0191 232 6478 M *Central Station*
The Forth has had a great reputation for a long time and justifiably so. It has a make-yourself-at-home feel with plenty of great seating and the cracking atmosphere is always bubbly and friendly. Their food is a tad more expensive than the usual pub stuff but the quality more than justifies this. They've also got an upstairs terrace area. Unreservedly recommended.

GOTHAM TOWN
Neville Street, Newcastle
0191 233 1471 M *Central Station*
Holy gargoyles Batman! Dark and loud, with plenty of gothic flourishes and hidden nooks and crannies. You're more likely to find pastel shirted punters than Goths pressed to the bar, however. House trebles are £2 weekdays and £2.50 on a weekend.

HEAD OF STEAM
2 Neville St., Newcastle
0191 232 4379 / 230 4236
M *Central Station*
Practically opposite the Central Station, this is a top pub. Set over two levels and with a wide range of European lagers and real ales you'll find the clientele made up of the cooler end of the market, drawn no doubt by the music policy which consists of funk, soul, dub, indie and alternative. A good 'un and a superb venue for live music as they host the best up and coming bands around.

Town Wall

Revolution

THE LONG BAR
39/47 Westgate Road, Newcastle
M *Central Station*
Named after the bar that used to be directly opposite the train station and the first port of call for Michael Caine in Newcastle gangster flick, Get Carter. Narrow (and long) and with plenty of lounge-like seating, this place can get pretty busy with punters enjoying sundry happy hours.

THE LOUNGE
8 Neville St., Newcastle
M *Central Station*
A light, airy and comfortable place. They also have a downstairs club area where you can dance yourself dizzy to chart fodder and hits from the past. During the day it also attracts plenty of punters, especially if it's warm as they have an outdoor seating area.

MADAME KOO
36 Collingwood Street, Newcastle
0191 261 8271 **M** *Central Station*
Various different nights on offer here with a multitude of music types. Plus there's some funky décor to go with it.

THE MILE CASTLE
19-25 Grainger Street, Newcastle
M *Central Station*
Wetherspoons pub with three bars, loads of

seats and widescreen TVs. Can't go wrong with the prices here either.

MIMO
8 Pudding Chare, Newcastle
0191 340 8198 **M** *Central Station*
New to town and a funky place to get a drink (including shooters, wine and champagne) and a bite to eat (try the buffalo chicken wings, ribs, hot dogs or burgers – scrummy).

NORTH
Neville Street, Newcastle
M *Central Station*
This small but perfectly formed bar is surely the cutest in town and offers an excellent range of premium beers & spirits and also an extensive cocktail list. Great, unpretentious service and quality DJs every evening (playing stuff you're not likely to hear elsewhere) prove that it's glam up North.

O'NEILLS
38 Neville St., Newcastle
M *Central Station*
Another Irish theme pub (i.e. distressed walls, loads of muck and tat plastered over the walls and more than one Guinness pump) handily placed opposite the Central Station, which means that during the day you'll often be tripping over loads of luggage and groups of lads who've come to Newcastle for a stag do.

THE OTHER ROOMS
Times Square, Newcastle
0191 232 1122 M *Central Station*
The sister bar/club to mega club Digital, The Other Rooms is part of the hip end of the Newcastle scene. This is a great place to catch live bands and has a pleasingly intimate atmosphere.

TOWN WALL
Pink Lane, Newcastle
0191 232 30000 M *Central Station*
Town Wall is a relatively new pub to the Toon with smart décor and a no-nonsense attitude. They specialise in real ales, world beer and good grub.

PERDU
20 Collingwood Street, Newcastle
0191 260 3040 M *Central Station*
One of the sleekest members of Newcastle's swank quota and it's all chandeliers, round booths and fancy-dan cocktails. It's connected to the Blackie Boy, which is reached through a lovely alley if you fancy some alfresco drinking (and a ciggy).

RAFFERTY'S
29-31 Pink Lane, Newcastle
0191 232 3269 M *Central Station*
A bar for old blokes who are more than willing to forgo those designer chairs and pine floors for an old fashioned boozer dispensing dirt cheap beer. The bar is split between regulars and a student side, they also so student night on Monday and Thursdays offering a whole range of cheap drinks.

REVOLUTION
Collingwood St., Newcastle
0191 261 8901 M *Central Station*
A beautiful looking interior (just check out those high ornate ceilings) this is a bar that stocks a multitude of flavoured vodkas (and a range of beers and lagers naturally). Loads of comfortable chairs and settees, DJs and a nice vibe make this one to check out.

THE STAR INN
79 Westgate Road, Newcastle
0191 261 4343 **M** *Central Station*
Something of a traditional boozer with an older clientele, although it's right opposite the Academy (live music venue) so great place for a pre- post-gig pint.

THE TELEGRAPH
Orchard St., Newcastle
0191 261 8991 **M** *Central Station*
Just behind the central train station, The Telegraph is a cool joint with plenty of booths and seating downstairs and a room upstairs where DJs go through their paces. The beer garden on the roof is one of the best around when the sun's got his hat on.

TILLEY'S
105 Westgate Rd., Newcastle
0191 232 0692 **M** *Central Station*
Great real ale can be had at this popular bar which has plenty of modern seating, a good vibe and lovely, really inexpensive food served up during the day. Definitely worth checking out: a real goodie and the regular local DJ nights draw in the crowds. They'll even let you buy a bowl of chips for £1 with any drink after 5pm.

TOKYO
17 Westgate Rd., Newcastle
0191 232 1122 **M** *Central Station*
If it's elegance you're after, then look no further. Tokyo - all candles & chandeliers – fits the bill. It exudes a knowing decadence, and what's more, there's three intimate floors of it. The top floor opens out into a glorious rooftop terrace with lovely exposed bricks.

TUP TUP PALACE
7 St. Nicholas St., Newcastle
0191 261 8579 **M** *Central Station*
Another pub to file under the luxe-bar banner (whatever they are). It's dark, has a sunken bar, plenty of unusual fixtures and fittings and a roster of DJs doing their thing. Tuesday is student night with 69p drinks. Ooh la la.

TWIST
Times Square, Newcastle
M *Central Station*
Situated next to the Life Centre, this funky place attracts a decent mix of folk attracted by the modern furnishings and bright and breezy vibe that it exudes.

UNION ROOMS
48 Westgate Rd., Newcastle
0191 261 5718 **M** *Central Station*
This J.D. Wetherspoons pub is situated in one of the grandest looking buildings in Newcastle. They have numerous bars set over two floors and it's pretty packed whenever you choose to venture. Plenty of food offers if you get peckish.

YATES'S
30 Grainger St., Newcastle
M *Central Station*
Housed in one of Newcastle's most beautiful buildings, Yates's is a huge bar set over three levels and attracts a wide mix of punters. Attractions include: cheap beer, plenty of seats and a pool table on the top floor.

HAYMARKET
Close to both universities, the Haymarket area attracts its fair share of students, who rub shoulders with a mainly older clientele.

THE CROW'S NEST
Percy Street, Newcastle
0191 261 2607 **M** *Haymarket*
After going through plenty of name changes The Crow's Nest returns to its original moniker and the decor is suitably unflashy. Plenty of seating and tables, dark woods, carpets etc and after a refurb there's now big screens for watching your team fritter away that two-goal advantage.

THE FIVE SWANS
14 St Marys Place, Newcastle
0191 2111140 **M** *Haymarket*

One of JD Wetherspoon's newest additions to the city. Deceivingly big pub taking up a full corner, with all the expected food and drinks from other pubs in the chain. Very student friendly and right next to the university campuses.

GOOSE
Eldon Garden, Percy Street, Newcastle
0191 221 2208 **M** *Haymarket*
This is a dead popular pub with pretty much everyone. It's right near the shops and it's pretty massive. Plus there's some cheap deals on food and drinks.

THE HANCOCK
2a Hancock Street, Newcastle
0191 281 5653 **M** *Haymarket*
Near both the universities this pub has long been a favourite with students and workers from the nearby Civic Centre. Decent food and the beer garden tends to get packed at the merest hint of sun.

THE HOTSPUR
103 Percy St., Newcastle
0191 232 4352 **M** *Haymarket*
The epitome of your decent town centre pub, with loads of blackboards detailing the strength of the beer, bare floorboards and a frothy collection of cask ales and continental bottled beers on offer. Worth checking out.

LYH
10 Northumberland Rd., Newcastle
0191 232 1308 **M** *Haymarket*
This is a fantastic, traditional looking boozer taking all the things that are good about pubs and doing them very well indeed. They stock a large range of real ales and world draught beers, have an excellent kitchen, plus all Newcastle United games, home and away, are screened. The first floor area is also available for private hire.

Hootie Coochie

The Forth

PACIFIC
12-22 Northumberland Rd., Newcastle
0191 245 0440 **M** *Haymarket*
This modern looking bar is split over a couple of levels and is a good place to chill or catch some sporting action (they've got lots of screens). Great drinks promos too and is one of the few places around with a pool table.

PERCY ARMS
83 Percy Street, Newcastle
0191 222 1412 **M** *Haymarket*
Musical trends come and go, but the Percy remains resolutely heavy metal. A legend in its own opening time; it has big screen TV, bags of real character and they have a great retro night on a Friday and it's rock on a saturday. At £1.89 for a pint, the prices will definitely keep your wallet happy.

THREE BULLS HEADS
57 Percy Street, Newcastle
0191 260 2984 **M** *Haymarket*
Often gets very busy attracting lunchtime shoppers dropping in for a bite to eat, students, football fans and anyone else who doesn't fancy paying through the nose for an over-priced pint of fizzy. It has a Cheers-esque bar structure and they usually have plenty of staff on, making it relatively easy to get served.

TRENT HOUSE SOUL BAR
1-2 Leazes Lane, Newcastle
0191 261 2154 **M** *Haymarket*
A firm favourite with students, locals, footie fans and just about everyone else, this ahem, 'world famous' bar, has long enjoyed a reputation as one of the best in Newcastle. Friendly atmosphere, outstanding jukebox, and a tuck-shop style array of sweets are some of the delights on offer.

WEST COAST GRILL BAR
Percy Street, Haymarket, Newcastle
0191 230 3344 **M** *Haymarket*
Has recently underwent something of a re-fit and remains a canny place for decent and filling grub. Specials on burgers (Monday), ribs (Tuesday), fajita (Thursday). You can also get two for one on Wednesday on food if you show your cinema ticket... If you don't want food – just grab a drink and watch the sport on Sky.

MONUMENT
The centre of town, and home to a mixture of pubs which attract shoppers in need of a cuppa, real ale fans and trendy types alike. This is also the place you'll find The Gate complex.

1 GREY STREET
1 Grey Street, Newcastle
0191 230 0455 **M** *Monument*
Small but rather lovely place that is a
great place to grab a glass a wine. Really
handy for the Theatre Royal which is just
up the bank.

ALVINOS BAR
88 Pilgrim Street
0191 261 5656 **M** *Monument*
Marvellous, Italian-owned bar which is open
from 10am for lovely coffees and a great
place to get imported bottled and draught
beer. They also do great cocktails and food
is also available (from snacks to pasta/pizza
dishes). Oh – they have an outdoor terrace
upstairs, too. We like.

THE BACCHUS
34 High Bridge, Newcastle
0191 261 1008 **M** *Monument*
A very traditional pub environment here: all
dark woods and courteous bar staff. Good pub
food and a fine selection of wines and spirits
along with plenty of comfortable seating
for you to relax and enjoy it all. Great pub
specialising in real ales and to prove it they're
winners of CAMRA's Real Ale Pub of the Year
three years running.

BAR 42
16-18 Hood Street, Newcastle
0191 232 4365 **M** *Monument*
Cheap trebles and a very popular student
venue, there's often a queue of people here.
It's a dark basement bar, with plenty of booths
and in a central location.

BANNATYNE BAR & BISTRO
The Gate, Newgate St., Newcastle
0191 261 9666 **M** *Monument*
Refurbished with space-age white Bannatyne's
is a chic, modern venue with an upmarket feel.
Stylish decor, a relaxing vibe where you can
sit with your pint and enjoy the mood lighting.

BARLUGA
35 Grey St., Newcastle
0191 230 2306 **M** *Monument*
Barluga is surely one of the most sumptuous looking bars in town. Everything is chic and 'just so', and there is plenty of plush seating plus they do rather lovely food, too.

BEYOND BAR & GRILL
The Gate, Newgate St., Newcastle
0191 222 1113 **M** *Monument*
Beyond Bar and Grill is a stylish bar/restaurant with chic décor, canny chefs and live DJs (seven nights a week), giving it a fantastic atmosphere for drinking, eating and socialising.

THE BLACK GARTER
31 Clayton St., Newcastle
0191 260 2099 **M** *Monument*
Once you get past all the people standing in the doorway smoking Woodbine's you'll find a boozer full of older punters watching the racing on telly. They start serving beer at 9am...

BABYLON
14-16 Newgate St., Newcastle
0191 261 8701 **M** *Monument*
A nineties theme bar. Oh. My. God. A shrine to all things rubbish with a soundtrack by Oasis.

BIJOUX
36 Mosley Street, Newcastle
0191 260 2378 **M** *Monument*
Bright and trendy place with some canny offers on and a good time feel.

THE CHARLES GREY
118 Grey St., Newcastle
0191 261 5587 **M** *Monument*
Situated slap bang in the centre of town next to Grey's Monument, the bar is reached by ascending a couple of flights of stairs. It's tasteful enough with lots of little cosy booths overlooking the folk milling around below. Canny outside seating area, too, beside the famous monument.

THE DUKE OF WELLINGTON
High Bridge, Newcastle **M** *Monument*
Tucked down High Bridge, this is a very comfy little boozer renowned for its excellent ales. Due to its proximity to the Bigg Market it gets very busy over Fridays and Saturdays but no one would ever really describe it as a Bigg Market type venue as you get a very mixed (older) crowd passing through its door. We love it.

FITZGERALD'S
60 Grey Street, Newcastle
0191 230 1350 **M** *Monument*
This largish pub has a mixed clientele including

Crown Possada

No.28

business people, students and those of us who consider a seat and a table as a good thing. A canny meeting place to start the night's proceedings.

HOOCHIE COOCHIE
54 Pilgrim Street, Newcastle
0191 222 0130 **M** Monument
The newest bar in town and what do you know, it's swiftly become one of our favourites. It's got that luxe/bar feel without being in any way pretentious, with loads of delectable booths to park yourself in. Great range of drinks available too and their music policy is fabulous, playing the kind of funk and soul that always hits the spot. What's more, they also play host to some incredible gigs (see Music Venues section for more on this).

IDOLS
Newgate Shopping Centre, Newcastle
0191 232 3887 **M** Monument
If the phrase 'Toon Tottie' sets your pulse racing, make a bee-line for this place on match days where their collection of 'erotic dancers' go through their scantily clad paces. Basement bar reached by descending a flight of stairs (like Dante's eighth circle of hell).

THE KEEL ROW
The Gate, Newgate St., Newcastle
0191 229 9430 **M** Monument
Part of the Lloyds No.1 chain, which means the drink prices are kept on the low side. The lighting is dimmed to create a nice, cosy feel and there's always plenty of seating too.

LADY GREY'S
20 Shakespeare Street, Newcastle
0191 232 3606 **M** Monument
What a beauty this place is. It's not been in town long, but is very traditional with great real ales (six of which are from the fabulous local brewers Hadrian and Mordue). Superb range of bottled stuff too and their pub grub is top drawer. The supper menu runs from sirloin

steaks to proper pies and beer battered fish and chips with plenty of sandwiches, snacks and sharing plates also available. A winner!

THE LIVING ROOM
2-12 Grey Street, Newcastle
0870 220 3172 **M** *Monument*
With gold-framed paintings lining the walls, modern chandeliers, and extravagantly upholstered seating, The Living Room certainly makes quite a swanky splash. There's sparkle to go with the class, however, with superb cocktails very much a feature of any evening here. There's a canny restaurant adjoining the bar, too, serving everything from breakfasts to full-blown evening meals. They have a basement bar with DJs on Friday and Saturday night which is also available for hire.

THE LODGE
26 Mosely St., Newcastle
0191 230 5413 **M** *Monument*
One of the city's larger establishments, this bar/cafe is situated in one of the many beautiful buildings on Grey St. (on the corner of Grey St. and Mosley St.) and has a laid-back air, despite its size. Big screen action is manna from heaven for football fans. They're big on pizzas and appear to be very proud of their 100% fresh dough...

THE MARKET LANE
72-74 Pilgrim Street, Newcastle
0191 232 0251 **M** *Monument*
This traditional bar has a loyal band of regulars, a fair few of whom are now going bald but spunkily still sport daft ponytails. Commonly known as the Monkey Bar, it's packed with old rockers, blokes trying to watch the racing on TV and those in need of a good natter. Love it.

MOOD
The Gate, Newgate St., Newcastle
M *Monument*
This modern and vibrant venue offers great menus in their restaurant section and plenty of entertainment elsewhere. DJs play hits from the 60s to now while the country's best cover bands, themed nights and special events mark it down as a place to truly let your hair down.

THE MUSHROOM
82 Grainger Street, Newcastle
0191 261 9990 **M** *Monument*
The Mushroom is reached by descending a flight of steps which leads you into one of the top trebles bars around (cheap, too!). DJs every night of the week, great sound-system and light-show, very comfy booths and open late too.

Centurion

Tup Tup Palace

NO. 28
27-29 Nelson Street, Newcastle
0788 612 6409 **M** *Monument*
Tucked away down one of the alleys that leads to the Grainger Market (and then up some stairs) this is a very funky new addition to Newcastle's laid-back quota. Well worth hunting out as they do delicious food and hold a variety of club nights, too. Salubrious without pretension – hooray!

THE NORTHUMBERLAND ARMS
Prudhoe Chare, Newcastle
0191 261 7582 **M** *Monument*
Situated just off Newcastle's main shopping area, Northumberland Street, this is a basement joint which is popular with all during the day (the food's locally sourced and lovely) and at night check out some hot sounds, chilled vibes and some of the best real ale around. Plenty of seating, too, so get yourself parked.

OPERA
The Gate, Newgate St., Newcastle
0191 222 1113 **M** *Monument*
Opera is a swanky establishment at The Gate serving the finest cocktails, champagne, spirits and health boosting juices, surrounded by the ambient atmosphere of guest pianists. This intimate venue is the perfect environment for a private party, business meetings or corporate lunches.

POPOLO
82-84 Pilgrim Street, Newcastle
0191 232 8923 **M** *Monument*
A lovely horseshoe bar takes centre stage in an elegantly styled interior, reminiscent of a classic US car with a streamlined red, black and cream décor. Industry renowned for its cocktail expertise, continental beers, award-winning bartenders and intimate leather sofa booths, all of which make this cool joint one of the best bars in town.

PLAYERS
The Gate, Newgate St., Newcastle
0191 260 2233 **M** *Monument*
Big student bar but also one for the sports types. They've got podiums for their "all-star" dancers to put on shows for your pre- and post- match entertainment...

SAM JACKS
Newgate St., Newcastle
0191 261 8982 **M** *Monument*
Bucking bronco anyone? This US themed bar is the ideal place to party, with themed nights, live entertainment, drinks promos and yes, a bucking bronco...

SINNERS
63 Newgate Street, Newcastle
0191 232 6440 **M** *Monument*
You know where sinners end up don't you? Hell, and this is it.

TIGER TIGER
The Gate, Newgate St., Newcastle
0191 235 7065 **M** *Monument*
Set over several floors, the individually designed rooms and musical styles include the laid-back Lounge Bar, funky Kaz Bar, contemporary restaurant and up-beat club.

TRILLIANS ROCK BAR
Princess Square, Newcastle
0191 232 1619 **M** *Monument*
Journey down the hallowed stairs to this legendary jumpin' joint which has always been a hit with the rock crowd. A variety of live bands often play here (both local and well known national acts) on a stage that is extremely well equipped for a pub venue. Late opening, great beer, and drinks offers all week mark it down as a real belter.

QUAYSIDE
Undoubtedly one of the most popular drinking circuits in town and a hit with everyone from casual drinkers to hard-core stag and hen parties...

AKENSIDE TRADERS
Akenside House, The Side, Newcastle
0191 260 3175 **M** *Central Station*
All dark wood & brass, this is one of the Quayside's most popular pubs during the week when they've got some of the most attractive happy hours around pulling in the thirsty punters by the score. You can usually get a good view of the footie for midweek games too. They have some great offers on food like two meals for £5.99 all week and DJs Friday and Saturday night.

BALTIC BAR
South Shore Road, Gateshead Quays
0191 440 4948 **M** *Central Station*
Situated within the stunning, BALTIC, The Centre for Contemporary Art, this is a great

Fluid

Rosie's Bar

place to relax in chilled surroundings and discuss the merits of installation art, or simply enjoy the fine range of quality beers on offer. When it's hot grab an outdoor seat and enjoy the views of the river Tyne.

BAR 38
Exchange Buildings, Lombard St.,
Newcastle 0191 261 6463
M *Central Station*
Newly reopened, refurbished and with plenty of drinks offers, Bar 38 is bound to resume its status as one of the top student trebles bars in the Toon.

BOB TROLLOP
32-40 Sandhill, Quayside, Newcastle
0191 261 1037 **M** *Central Station*
Veggies should make a beeline for this place as they consistantly win awards for the vegetarian pub food it specialises in. It's one of the less frantic bars on the Quayside, which means that with its comfortable atmosphere, it's one to check out, even if you are a meat eater. They offer 15% student discount on food and have plenty good drinks offers.

CHARLIE'S BAR
57-60 Sandhill, Newcastle
0191 222 0164 **M** *Central Station*
Just before you head over the Swing Bridge across to Gateshead is Charlie's (on the corner) which is a decent place to grab a cocktail or continental beer. Comfy seating is a plus.

CHASE
13-15 Sandhill, Newcastle
0191 245 0055 **M** *Monument*
A place to drink, a place to eat, and a place to dance. Chase pulls in a younger crowd who are generally "up for it". They also host the official warm up to the popular Vice City Friday and the warm up to Voodoo Project club night at The Riverside on a Saturday.

THE COOPERAGE
32 The Close, Quayside
M *Central Station*
The Cooperage has one of the most arresting facades in Newcastle, nay, the country, being as it is hundreds of years old and retains all its original features. And it's a brilliant pub too, serving up some of the best cask ales around. Don't miss.

THE CROWN POSADA
31-33 The Side, Newcastle
0191 232 1269 **M** *Central Station*
A fun pub: that is if your idea of fun is sitting in an old fashioned beer vending emporium, quietly supping a pint without the distraction of blaring music, TVs or video games in comfortable snug like areas with maybe the company of a dog. We do.

EYE ON THE TYNE
11-17 Broad Chare, Quayside, Newcastle 0191 261 7385
M *Central Station*
This used to be The Bonded Warehouse, now it's got a much slicker feel with loads of comfy seating etc. It all feels a bit identikit though...

FEVER
Akenside Hill, Quayside, Newcastle
0191 232 6778 **M** *Central Station*
Situated directly under that symbol of Geordie pride, the Tyne Bridge, Fever strives for a reputation as a fun pub, but feels like the Quayside's little brother.

JIMMYZ BAR
48-52 Sandhill, Newcastle
0191 230 1619 **M** *Central Station*
Lovely leather seats and big windows let you watch the hub-bub outside. It's something of a party place for the Quayside and very popular with stag and hen parties (and people who spend every weekend as if they were on a stag or hen party).

MARTHA'S
Lower Dean Street, Newcastle
0191 233 1010 **M** *Central Station*
Smartish bar, famed for its courtyard area, which is a great place to be on those balmy nights. Inside there's a canny conservatory (ideal place to quaff those cocktails); they also have a big screen for sports and an upstairs bar.

OFFSHORE 44
40 Sandhill, Quayside, Newcastle
0191 261 0921 **M** *Central Station*
Located in an ancient, beautiful and indeed historic building. Inside, and in keeping with the riverside location, the pub has a decidedly nautical theme; quite dark and intimate with some of the most comfortable Chesterfields around. A good 'un.

Cumberland Arms

PITCHER & PIANO

108 Quayside, Newcastle
0191 232 4110 Ⓜ *Central Station*
The Pitcher has long been one of the most popular bars on Newcastle's vibrant Quayside scene and is handily situated near several of the nicer restaurants down there. Its huge glass facade offers stunning views of the river and the Millennium Bridge as well as the BALTIC art gallery.

THE QUAYSIDE

35 The Close, Quayside, Newcastle
0191 221 0828 Ⓜ *Central Station*
Situated right on the banks of the Tyne in an old stone building this is another of the Lloyds No.1 chain of pubs. They also have beer gardens front and back.

QUILTED CAMEL

36 Sandhill, Quayside, Newcastle
0191 221 1885 Ⓜ *Central Station*
Reached through a small doorway and up a flight of stairs, Quilted Camel is actually one of the Quayside's most idiosyncratic establishments with a quite unique interior, which is as lavish as they come. One of the best bars down the Quayside and great for cheap trebles.

RED HOUSE

32-40 Sandhill, Quayside, Newcastle
0191 261 1037 Ⓜ *Central Station*

Cosily done out with plenty of flagstones and almost hidden nooks and crannies. There's offers on trebles all day, everyday and you can get cheap pints too. Great views of the busy Quayside nightlife in varying stages of inebriation if you can grab a window seat. They also offer 15% student discount on food and have plenty of good drinks offers.

SLUG & LETTUCE

Exchange Buildings, Quayside,
Newcastle 0191 261 7196
Ⓜ *Central Station*
Part of the national chain and a good looker. Plenty of seating, a fine wine list and a canny food menu, which changes with the seasons.

THE WATERLINE

96 East Quayside, Newcastle
0191 230 5531 Ⓜ *Central Station*
One of the very best pubs you'll find down the Quayside, they offer a delicious gastro pub menu which is one of the best you'll find anywhere. In the summer months, when the sun is glinting off the Tyne, there's not many better places to be than seated outside around one of their many wooden tables. A real winner!

ST. JAMES/CHINATOWN

St. James' Park is home to Newcastle United and the pubs nearby get packed out on match days. On other days the clientele

Opera

Mood

is generally a little older or people having a drink before/after a meal in nearby Chinatown.

BARKOLLO
22 Leazes Park Road, Newcastle
0191 232 5871 M *St. James*
This is a pretty new addition to the scene and is something of musical restaurant (see restaurants for more information on this) but is also a really cool joint to call in for a Peroni or an Amstel, too. Make sure that you seek it out for good vibes aplenty.

FLUID
17-25 Gallowgate, Newcastle
0191 221 2266 M *St. James*
This cosy bar/kitchen is set over two floors and has a very relaxing, homely feel about it. Extremely comfortable, with loads of seating, they have a great menu (check out the open plan kitchen) and very reasonable drink prices at all times. It's also a great place to watch sport as they have loads of plasma screens, so you'll miss none of the action.

MADISON'S
Leazes Lane, Newcastle
0191 261 1003 M *St James*
Next door to the Hyena Comedy café bar, this is a great place to go for a drink before or after catching some stand-up.

THE NEWCASTLE ARMS
57 St. Andrew's Street, Newcastle
0191 260 2490 M *St. James*
A smallish, traditional boozer that has long been a favourite for members of the Toon Army since well, United last won anything (yes, that long). It's also handy for a swift one before a gastronomic blowout on Stowell Street - famed for its plethora of Chinese restaurants.

ROSIE'S BAR
2 Stowell Street, Newcastle
0191 232 0339 M *St. James*

A bit of an institution with Newcastle United fans and famed for its welcoming nature. It's also a canny place to watch football, as they have a great big screen. A goodie.

SHEARER'S
St James' Park,
Strawberry Place, Newcastle,
0191 201 8688 M *St. James*
Named after Newcastle United's legendary striker, Shearer's Bar is built into the south-facing stand of the Magpies' stadium. Split over three levels, Shearer's boasts plenty of screens including three of the biggest in the Toon to watch the live sport shown daily. Homemade food is served every day in the heart of the bar and meal deals are available all day. Cocktails are only £2.85 and selected doubles, including draught mixer, only £2.95. Pool is only 50p too... Shearers Bar is the ONLY place to watch every Newcastle United home league game LIVE... Result.

SOHO
Leazes Lane, Newcastle
0191 221 2882 M *St James*
Next to the Hyena Comedy Club, there's some comfy seating and a buzzy little atmosphere at this canny pub. They also have a fab cocktail menu.

THE STRAWBERRY
7/8 Strawberry Place, Newcastle
0191 232 6865 M *St James*
This well loved pub is situated next to St. James' Park, beloved home of Newcastle United's army of ever optimistic worshippers. Inside it's all bare floorboards and big wooden tables etc with loads of NUFC related bumf festooning the walls. As you'd expect, it does a roaring trade on match days, but during the week it gets pretty busy too with a good mix of clientele enjoying a fine selection of ales and the food's worth a go.

Nancy Bordello

The King's Manor

TYNESIDE IRISH CENTRE
43-49 Gallowgate, Newcastle
0191 261 0384 **M** *St James*
It's near the stadium, so if you fancy a pint of Guinness after the match, this is certainly the place to be.

OUT OF TOWN
While Newcastle town centre is packed with pubs and bars to cater for all tastes, it's most definitely worth a short trip out of town for some of the other delights available.

AS YOU LIKE IT
Archbold Terrace, Jesmond
0191 281 2277 **M** *Jesmond*
This is a very laid-back and trendy (without pretension) gastro/lounge, which has three bars and plenty of seating (including an outdoor terrace area). Check out their 'Supper Club' over the weekend where you can enjoy live blues, soul, swing and jazz and scrumptious food.

BAR AT THE BRANDLING
Brandling Village, Jesmond
0191 281 0067 **M** *Jesmond*
Popular with the students, and a mixture of others, it's a good place to include in a bar crawl around Jesmond. There's a nice conservatory

and outside area to enjoy the fresh air too. Or have a tab.

BILLABONG.
Osborne Rd., Jesmond
0191 281 7881 **M** *West Jesmond*
Sizeable inside with a spacious, modern decor at this very popular bar/bistro which has a food menu which is a real cut above. Check out their fabulous quiz nights every Wednesday (with cash prizes) and their open mic and karaoke nights on Thursday. Their cocktail menu is pretty special, too, as are their happy hours. One of the best around.

BAR BERLISE
97-103 Osborne Rd., Jesmond
0191 281 1358 **M** *West Jesmond*
Another of the popular bars on the Jesmond drinking scene with the added attraction of a happy hour machine every night (you could drink free!). Smart and clean.

BAR POLO
1st Floor, 61 Osborne Rd., Jesmond
0191 240 7777 **M** *Jesmond*
Mediterranean feel bar above Scalini's restaurant. Good wine, great atmosphere. Usually quite busy at weekends they're open 7-11pm on Thurdays, and 5-11pm on Fridays and Saturdays.

The Central

Bob Trollops

BL-ANC
38-42 Osborne Rd., Jesmond
0191 281 5126 **M** *West Jesmond*
Linked to an Indian restaurant next door, and they have both an English and Indian menu served from noon-6pm. Modern and stylish this is a dead nice place for a drink or some food.

THE BLUEBELL
Brinkbank Rd., Jesmond
0191 232 1774 **M** *Jesmond*
Totally refurbished this is now a fairly swanky looking bar popular with all types. They've got all the usual plasmas and a canny pool table, but one of the real boons is the beer garden that is a little oasis, which is even bigger now with extra decking added recently.

THE CARRIAGE
Rear of Archbold Terrace, Jesmond
0191 281 2151 **M** *West Jesmond*
Situated just off the Jesmond Metro stop and quite near the universities, this is a welcoming place for a pint. Plush, comfortable seats and loads of fires are ideal for the winter and wooden benches outside for summer make this bar popular with most types.

THE CENTRAL
Half Moon Lane, Gateshead
0191 478 2543 **M** *Gateshead*
Iconic Gateshead pub (which resembles a smaller version of the 'flat iron' building in New York) which has recently been given a massive makeover to restore it to former glories. Now one of the best boozers around with a fabulous range of drinks, great roof terrace and function rooms staging all manner of goodies. Situated near The Sage Gateshead.

THE CHILLINGHAM
89-91 Chillingham Rd, Heaton
0191 265 5915 **M** *Chillingham Rd*
The Chilli is a very pleasant place to down a few pints, which, while roomy (it's split into a bar and lounge area), can still get pretty packed. There's two pool tables and upstairs there's the occasional live band and a comedy club on the first Thursdays of every month.

THE CLUNY
36 Lime St., Ouseburn
0191 230 4474 **M** *Manors / Byker*
Slightly out of town (situated under Byker Bridge), The Cluny continually racks up plaudits by the score in its own field, which just happens to be the world of the bar/cafe/venue. Not many places could pull off a trio of differing disciplines with such dashing aplomb but they manage it admirably here. One of the best.

CLUNY 2

Lime St., Ouseburn
0191 230 4474 **M** *Manors/Byker*

Just over from The Cluny (see above) this is a smashing little venue (with seating for 160) that has a lovely glass-roofed continental-style café-bar, serving the best premium lagers, wines and high quality spirits. Available for private hire at very reasonable rates.

CORNERHOUSE

Heaton Road, 0191 265 9602

Positioned on the corner leading up from Jesmond to Heaton, this place is roomy, has a decent size beer garden and also comes complete with relaxing conservatories. It has an excellent reputation for live music (mainly jazz, both national and international).

THE CUMBERLAND ARMS

Byker Buildings, Byker
0191 265 6151 **M** *Byker*

Situated off Byker Bank The Cumberland Arms boasts a fantastic real ale & cider selection, an exciting & eclectic mix of live music, delicious food & a great outside space with fantastic views of the city. The real ale & cider selection comes from a variety of breweries, many local and are not to be missed - have it served through the pump or in the traditional way straight from the cask. They now also offer a bed & breakfast service.

THE FREE TRADE

St. Lawrence Road, Byker
0191 265 5764 **M** *Byker*

Top notch, no-frills boozer that is perched atop a hill overlooking the river Tyne with marvellous westward views of the broad sweep of the Quayside, which can also be taken in from one of their two beer gardens. Much beloved of musicians and other boho types, the atmosphere is very laid-back as are the ever friendly bar staff. Not many of its type left, so cherish it. They offer specialist cask and craft beers, and definitely have CAMRA's stamp of approval, winning their Cider Pub of The Year 2011.

HYEM

Chillingham Road, Heaton
0191 240 0614 **M** *Chillingham Rd*

Superb freehouse bar that has a great drinks selection. They also do a really canny menu and offer up goodies such as: games room (check out the poker evenings), student club nights with late licence, live bands, (acoustic music on Sundays), and live football. Hyem? It's Geordie for "home" of course (say "Yem").

The Mushroom

Pitcher & Piano

THE KING'S MANOR
132-140 Newbridge St., Newcastle
0191 230 1190 **M** *Manors*
Recently changed hands and now stocking a great range of real ales in the kind of friendly atmosphere which encourages you to discuss the finer points of life while you sup.

THE LONSDALE
Lonsdale Terrace, Jesmond
0191 281 0039 **M** *West Jesmond*
Has long been one of Jesmond's most popular pubs. Big screen TVs cater for the sporting daft and their all-day menu is great value for money and the grub is always top-notch. The real ale could knock a horse out.

MR. LYNCH
Archbold Terrace, Jesmond
0191 281 3010 **M** *Jesmond*
This very popular and rather cool bar is decked out in original, designer furniture from the 60s and 70s. They have background music on each night (live + DJs) with a bit more up-tempo stuff on Friday and Saturday.

NANCY BORDELLO'S
13 Argyle St., Newcastle
0191 260 2929 **M** *Manors*
Another bar from the people behind Mr. Lynch and As You Like It and it's an eccentric little number with nice quirky deco, wholesome

food (served until 9pm), table service, and a sun terrace. It's only a five-minute walk from the Quayside, too.

THE NEW BRIDGE INN
2 Argyle St., Newcastle
0191 232 1020 **M** *Manors*
Nice traditional pub with plenty of seating. Lots of different entertainments like a quiz night. Well worth a visit.

OSBORNE'S
61-69 Osborne Rd., Jesmond
0191 240 7778 **M** *West Jesmond*
Several bars over split levels inside this swanky place and very notable for their huge range of cocktails (including a healthy selection of those infused with champagne - bubblicious). Plenty of seats outside when it's warm and a generally cool vibe mark this place down as a goodie.

RU
44 Osborne Road
0191 281 9111 **M** *Jesmond*
Formerly El Castano, Ru is now a trendy bar offering great pub food including a range of very tasty burgers.

SPY
82-86 Osborne Rd.,
0191 212 5111 **M** *Jesmond*

Annie's Bar

The Cleveland

Another of the popular bars on Osborne Road, a younger crowd enjoy the variety of bottled beers and alcopops. There's plenty of screens (usually showing MTV) and there's a decent, decked sitting area outside. 3D TVs, totally refurbished and contemporary.

STEPNEY'S
3 Bridge View, Stepney Lane, Manors
0191 260 3442 **M** *Manors*
Studenty place, with plenty of seating and a nice airy feel. Monday is their actual student night, with a variety of music and the 'Button Game', where you can get anything from 0%-100% off your drinks. Not too shabby.

THE TANNERS
1 Crawhill Rd., Byker Bridge
0191 222 1817 **M** *Manors*
Only a ten minute walk from the centre of town, this pub attracts everyone from cool kids to crusties to dance music fans to in-the-know grannies... Superb DJs, cool vibes and a retro video-game table. 1-UP! They also have a great pool table, live bands, fab food (their Sunday lunches are possibly the best in Newcastle), and a well tasty stock of ciders. Beyond reproach!

THE TYNE
1 Maling St., Byker
0191 265 2550 **M** *Byker*
First class boozer with a fantastic, laid-back atmosphere, champion beer and superb jukebox. There can be few more agreeable places to quaff frothing ale than the unusual beer garden nestling beneath the Glasshouse Bridge which arcs over the pub (so it doesn't even matter if it's raining!) Also attracts top touring bands as well as those closer to home.

WHITLEY BAY
This coastal town is easy to get to, being on the Metro route, and it has a plethora of pubs worthy of your attention.

THE AVALON HOTEL
26 South Parade, Whitley Bay
0191 251 0080 **M** *Whitley Bay*
This pub is part of the hotel on the popular South Parade and is something of a biker's establishment. And by 'biker' we're not talking pedals, we're talking leather. A real winner.

THE BEDROOM
244 Whitley Road, Whitley Bay
0191 251 3753 **M** *Whitley Bay*
The Bedroom likes to bill itself as stag and hen central and there are a fair few of those

Walkabout

The Hairy Lemon

types that like to get in here over the weekend. By day there's mainly an older clientele and on Sunday the ever-ridiculous karaoke nights holds court.

DEEP CLUB
The Promenade, Whitley Bay
0191 252 3201 **M** *Whitley Bay*
Right on the sea front, Deep is a nightclub that is part of the Rex Hotel and they stage various nights, which are extremely well populated by an always-up-for-it crowd of revellers especially Thursdays, Fridays and Saturdays. They're also open on bank holidays.

EASY STREET
31-33 South Parade, Whitley Bay
0191 252 1236 **M** *Whitley Bay*
This is 'Whitley's Premier Party Bar' according to their blurb above the door and the drinkers who throng this place would surely agree. Drinks promos, DJs and a general sense of being up-for-it are very much the order of the day.

THE FIRE STATION
18 York Road, Whitley Bay
0191 293 9030 **M** *Whitley Bay*
You'll notice this place by the real flames emerging from the two poles outsides... This is part of the J.D. Wetherspoons chain and so you can expect plenty of seating, cheap drinks and OK food.

FITZGERALD'S
2 South Parade, Whitley Bay
0191 251 1255 **M** *Whitley Bay*
This is a traditional pub, all dark woods and little nooks and crannies with plenty of comfortable seating. The ales are of the hand-pulled variety (and are just the job). They serve food Friday, Saturday and Sunday. One to watch out for is definitely their homemade lunch.

42 STREET
1-2 East Parade, Whitley Bay
0191 251 3877 **M** *Whitley Bay*
This good-time joint is part of Whitley Bay's fixtures and fittings. It's canny for a coffee or tea (and meal) during the day and by night it's more of a fun pub. There's also a beer garden overlooking the sea. Champion.

HAVANA
South Parade, Whitley Bay
0191 251 9897 **M** *Whitley Bay*
Plenty of special offers available from this jumping joint, which attracts the younger, up-for-it revellers.

The Zerzura

Spencleys Emporium

PIER 39
60 South Parade, Whitley Bay
0191 251 0868 M *Whitley Bay*
This is a large, fun pub, which is usually running all manner of drinks promos. They have tables outside and inside they promise 'live strippers'. Wonder what 'undead strippers' would be like?

ARUBA BAR
Exchange Square
01642 232 111
This is more of an evening bar, but you can manage to cram a fair few hours of cheese in when the sun goes down. The drinks are cheap and the dancefloor is big. It's a dangerous combination, especially in a place where the Baywatch theme is a floor filler.

BARRACUDA BAR
42 Albert Road
01642 244692
This is a huge South African bar. They're very much into their sports with various sporting memorabilia adorning its walls and a 15ft big screen perfect for watching the match.

THE BLACK BULL
70 High Street, Yarm
01642 793000
This is Yarm's most popular public house, and the public charge towards the Bull regularly. It gets very crowded from Friday night through to Sunday night, but the three bars and the huge beer garden act as a huge magnet, and Teessiders are the iron filings.

THE CAMEL'S HUMP
7-13 Waterloo Road
01642 243 665
The Camel's Hump is popular with students as it is surrounded by the local university campus. The positives of this are its cheap booze, its cheap games of pool and its friendly atmosphere. The negatives are that

you might see students lapping up the lager carefree during the day while you're on your 45-minute dinner break.

CENTRAL
43 Corporation Road
01642 252 804
Central has a really fabulous roster of great nights to tempt you through its doors including Funky Mondays (Monday: cheap drinks + retro/electro/funky house); Central Sessions Live (Thursdays: live bands); El Funk Extreme (Saturdays: great retro night); karaoke (Sunday). They also serve lovely fresh food until 2pm each day.

THE CLEVELAND HOTEL LOUNGE
Linthorpe Road 01642 855131
The Cleveland is quite a way up Linthorpe Road and you would probably need to catch a bus to get there, but it's a big football pub and it serves food on a daily basis.

THE CROWN
143 Linthorpe Rd.
01642 255 311
The Crown is a yellow pub, which means you get £1.50 a pint nights on a Monday; gay night on a Tuesday; rock night on a Thursday; and very drunken people over the weekend. It plays really good sing-a-long music, like James' "Sit Down" and tunes that allow for a dangerous amount of air guitar. It is a harmonious place where students and non-students can strum on their air fenders in peace. It's open during the day and serves good pub food; nothing exotic, but nothing offensive, and great if you're going hair-of-the-dog from the night before. Plus, it's open until 2am every night, so The Crown is always there for you if you don't want to do a Cinderella and go home at Midnight.

DICKENS INN
4 Southfield Road
01642 242 621
This is Southfield Road's pride and joy, as it

leaves the poor Knights of St. Columbus over the road in the darkest of shades. Its décor is light, it has plenty of seating space, it provides all the latest sporting entertainment, it shows live bands and it serves food. Ideal drinking location - done!

DR. BROWNS
135 Corporation Road
01642 213213
Dr. B's is a pub pub: beer, lagers, nuts, big screens and bar stools. It's got a great, friendly atmosphere and is away from the hustle and the bustle of town. It hosts live bands regularly, which makes it welcoming for students, musicians and finger-clicking locals alike. Plus, the cinema is over the road so you can drink before you view or forget a bad film afterwards with plenty of booze.

FLARES
Albert Road
01642 499 201
If you missed the 1970s, Flares is an attempt to take you back to the era of platforms and bell-bottoms. However, I'm a fan of the present, so I tend to avoid Flares: the flashing lights, the garish colours and the loitering "older" men that hide in the crevices of the bar generally give me a headache.

THE GEORGE AND DRAGON
70 High Street , Yarm
01642 780 117
The George and Dragon is a great pub, with a beer garden that stretches down to the river. It is busy most nights, but "grab a granny" Tuesdays tend to be its busiest night. There are singers who perform on Sunday afternoons, so you can sway while you scoff a roast dinner. It's a great venue where even George and his Dragon see eye to eye.

GILZEAN'S SPORTS BAR
Deltic House, 11 Zetland Road
01642 242 450

Gilzean's does exactly what it says on the tin. If you want sport, you've got it!

THE GREEN TREE
24 High Street, Yarm
01642 780 311
This is one of the few real ale pubs in Yarm. It's very long and narrow, which adds to its charm. The beer garden is more like a beer porch in comparison to other places, but the ambience is second to none (as are the Sunday dinners).

H'S BAR
97 Linthorpe Road, M'bro
01642 248 828
Open to everyone Monday-Friday, but Saturdays and Sundays are exclusively gay nights. It's not just the beers and lagers that are on tap here; there are plenty of pool-game opportunities, as well as karaoke.

HARVEY'S
201-203 Linthorpe Rd.
This is the newish kid on the block and it seems to be doing well. The actual location has had more name changes than Prince, but it has been gathering a lot of support from the locals since it opened in August 2007. Let's hope that the champagne and the cocktails keep flowing and it doesn't become the bar formally known as Harvey's.

THE HAIRY LEMON
37-39 Corporation Road
01642 223 045
It's similar to its neighbour, The Central, because it's quite dark, but it always looks busy so it must be doing something right. The people of Middlesbrough must like their lemons hairy. However, I'm more of a satsuma person.

HIDE BAR
32-34 High street, Fairfax Court, Yarm
01642 355 558
Hide Bar is swanky with a capital S,W,A,N,K and Y. It exudes quality, and that's something

you can't hide. Its second floor restaurant serves nothing but the finest foods and its ground floor bar serves nothing but the finest beverages. It is really trendy and you'll struggle to get in there during the weekend without reservations, but it's a treat when your feet finally cross the doorway.

THE ISAAC WILSON
61 Wilson Street
01642 247 708

The Issac Wilson is a J.D.Wetherspoon pub, so it has the same menu as all other Wetherspoons, as you would expect. However, if you want to talk pubs, then this is a great pub on the right nights. It has plenty of seating, the drinks are really cheap, it is happy to shelter anyone, from the drunk and rambling old woman with a moustache to the college student who is in awe of its prices. It's a great meeting place to start the night, and there are plenty of mirrors around the place, so if you have a peanut stuck to your top lip, it won't be there for long.

THE KEYS
208- 210 Linthorpe Road
01642 219 199

Recently opened, this used to be the Blue Lounge. It's the newest sibling of The Keys in Yarm and seems to be following the same

sort of theme. It's open Tuesday, Friday and Saturday. Student night is Tuesday with live bands, DJs and plenty of drinks offers.

THE KEYS
65 High Street, Yarm
01642 782 534

This once traditional pub was renovated a couple of years ago and now it is Yarm's premier evening spot. It has a chic downstairs area with LCD televisions, two large bars and lots of seating. The Keys is the proud owner of a flashing dancefloor, which the locals petitioned should remain in the pub from its pre-renovation days. Anything that makes men feel like John Travolta should be approached with caution in my opinion. I'm sad to say that the menu is more restaurant than pub grub, but so long as people get fed, I'm sure they will be happy.

THE LAUREL
113 Borough Road 01642 245861

The quiz nights, the karaoke and the reggae music are The Laurel's main features but to be honest, it's very much a local pub for local people...

LIBERTYS IN TOWN
266 Linthorpe Road
01642 231387

TS1

The Blue Lounge

The Medicine Bar

Isaac Wilson

You'll always find a friendly mixture of people in here. The music and the ales are good, so it's a no-harm pub to try to begin an evening out.

LINTHORPE HOTEL
The Cresent 01642 819823
The Linthope, or "The Linny" is a Samuel Smith's pub and it has many a picnic bench, lots of greenery for the kids to run around on and cheap booze by the barrel full. It receives a great deal of pre-match attention from the football fans and regular attention from the CCAD and Kirby College students.

LLOYDS NO. 1
Captain Cook Square,
Newport Crescent
01642 260 650
Lloyds is stretched out over two floors and it has a huge projection screen over the main bar. It attracts workers during the week and an older crowd on the weekends.

THE LOBBY
59-61 Albert Road
01642 231 992
The Lobby feeds the office workers of Albert Road during the week with its gorgeous home-made daily specials which are 2 for £5.95. The Lobby pulls out all the stops at the weekend to provide an eclectic musical selection. It has various 2-for-1 offers on

drinks, so it as good a place as any to begin a night out.

THE MEDICINE BAR
72-80 Corporation Road, M'bro
01642 222 250
One of Boro's newest clubs, the Medicine Bar is open on Fridays and Saturdays. Tucked in the cellar of La Pharmacie (formerly the Purple Onion) this is great venue ideal for a night out or private functions.

MOHAN'S
23-29 Bedford Street 01642 249 893
Mohan's is tucked away on Bedford Street; a street which is usually associated with free town parking, one way systems and road rage. However, you can escape all this by stepping into the friendly atmosphere of this Irish-style pub. Grab yourself a paper, a pint of Guinness and you'll forget all about the £4 car-parking fee you have just paid.

THE OAK
23 Newport Road 01642 219 748
The Oak is a loud-and-proud gay bar and is open seven days a week. Its doors are open to everyone, so whether you fancy a spot of lunch while you shop or whether you need a Sunday dinner to digest your hangover away, The Oak will be there.

Dun Cow

Fitzgeralds

THE PRINCESS ALICE
69 Newport Road
01642 232 969
The Princess Alice is opposite the bus station, so whether you've just missed your bus or whether you've had the megabus journey from hell, you don't have to look much further than The Princess Alice for some refreshment. It's light, fresh and breezy inside, much like the Princess herself was...or so I read. I didn't know her personally. The Alice has got its fair share of quiz machines and fruities too, so if the company you keep is dragging you down, you can indulge in some gambling escapism.

THE RUDDS ARMS
Stokesley Road, Marton-in-Cleveland
01642 315 262
The Rudds has just had a major face-lift and is now showing off the results. It offers a music quiz on Wednesday, a general knowledge quiz on a Sunday, a grand sporting atmosphere and drinks promotions every day. The menu, served from 11am –10pm, has everything you would want, from your traditional cuisine to your breakfast menu to (get this) tapas! You wouldn't even need knives and fork, just good ol' fingers-in-mouth goodness.

SPENSLEY'S EMPORIUM
Albert Road
01642 218484
Spensley's Emporium is an ideal post-football match hangout. It plays music such as The Stone Roses, The Charlatans and Oasis i.e. man tunes. However, when Spensley's wants to bring in the nightlife, Spensley's does it with great drink offers, a clubland DJ and brooding lighting. It's a classy joint where trouble is left outside the door.

THE STAR
14 Southfield Road
01642 245 307
Once known as the Star and Garter, The Star, has now realized that there is no need for all that garter nonsense, and it has been twinkling on Southfield Road since it reopened in the summer of last year. It has an autumnal/leather scheme going on and it is at its busiest at the weekend. Though it is sandwiched between Dicken's Inn and The Southfield, it is more tailored to an older market, showing that there's room for everyone on Southfield Road... and don't the taxi drivers know it!

THE SOUTHFIELD
18 Southfield Road
01642 210 414
Ah, The Southfield. It's the sister pub to The

Crown and it shares all its offers and much of its clientele. The student count is as high as a Bob Marley in the 1970s but it tends everyone else in between after the working day is done, or when cheap pitchers of cocktails need to be drunk.

THE TAVERN
228 Linthorpe Road
01642 242 589
The Tavern is quite a friendly, spacious place and it has used this to squeeze in many a pool table. It's an ideal meeting point for friends before the big beers get drank.

TRADER JACKS
19 Corporation Road
01642 249 105
This Jack-of-all-trades pub serves food daily to the town centre of Middlesbrough. Its location is ideal and it always tends to be reasonably full. It is a hit at the weekends because of the cheese that is pumped through its speakers.

WALKABOUT
32 Corporation Road   01642 248 682
You will receive a heart g'day from this pub: Middlesbrough's oldest Australian themed bar. It makes its own hand-made burgers, which is refreshing to hear amidst our fast-food society. Plus, the offers on the drinks vary from day to day, so you won't be stuck buying something from a dodgy crate of imported lager. There's always something on and somebody in the place, so you won't be the only ol' mucker or Sheila there.

TS ONE
200 Linthorpe Road
01642 245 523
I remember that this was one of the first bars to serve Kronenberg Blanc, which shows that it always tries to keep its finger on the alcohol pulse. It has used dark wood to its advantage, creating a wartime hub on the corner of Linthorpe Road. It's comfy through and through,

and tends to be one of the less lairy places to go at the weekend. It is also a corker of a place to read the paper during the day.

YATES WINE LODGE
16-18 Newport Road   01642 243 764
Yates has definitely made itself comfortable in Middlesbrough, but I can't help but feel it has let itself go a little around the love handles. It offers standard pub food during the day and it gets relatively busy, but it doesn't sparkle as it used to. I may be catching it at the wrong times, but I think it needs to step up to the competition of the town's ever-expanding pub scene.

SUNDERLAND

7EVEN
11 Derwent Street M Sunderland
This quirky modern bar is right in the middle of town with an eclectic selection of music to suit everyone's taste. As well as that they have live music every Sunday, Monday and Thursday.

THE BARNES TOBY CARVERY
Durham Road, The Barnes,
M University
0191 528 5644
Huge pub that occupies most of a roundabout island that can certainly pull in the punters. It features a fab carvery restaurant, and a very decent front bar. What a pub should be.

BAR1
1 Tunstall Road   M Sunderland
Opened in 2009, this contemporary bar is committed to providing the cream of local talent with live music as well as DJ sets. Right in the centre of town this bar is in the perfect location for a night out.

BAR JUSTICE
47 West Sunniside
0191 565 2050 M Sunderland
Nestled in the trendy Sunniside, Justice is

The Glass Spider

Greens

a quirky little bar with stylish interior and a rooftop terrace, perfect for smokers. Slightly off the beaten track it's a nice place to relax with friends in a laidback atmosphere that's not quite as frantic as the main part of town.

THE BLACK BULL
309 High St. West, Sunderland
0191 567 5702 **M** *Sunderland*
A pub that bills itself as student friendly means that the drink prices are kept on the manageable side. Inside it's quite barn-like, all wooden floors and plenty of space. However this sizeable pub can seem quite cavernous when empty, which luckily isn't that often. They also have a good big screen.

THE BLANDFORD
Blandford Street, Sunderland
0191 567 3890 **M** *Sunderland*
Pokey and dark this is not particularly inviting despite being on one of Sunderland's main shopping streets. It's bland alright...

THE BLUE BELL
Fulwell Rd., Fulwell, **M** *Seaburn*
0191 549 4020
Strategically placed on a junction of bus routes in the middle of Fulwell. Always pretty busy with a welcoming atmosphere and worth a detour if you're on the north side of the river.

THE BOROUGH
1 Vine Place, **M** *Park Lane*
0191 514 5675
A Sunderland institution with a nice square central bar, good prices and friendly staff. And they stage plenty of gigs in their upstairs room with plenty of metal bands (but look out for others, too) with gigs usually held on Thursday, Friday and Sunday (and there's an open mic night on Tuesday). They often get some of the more obscure (but revered) bands on here and it's well worth checking out.

BROGANS
8/10 Crowtree Rd. **M** *Park Lane*
0191 565 3360
Meal-oriented during the day, we've had many a nice feast here. Situated underneath Privilege, Brogans is another of the Saturday night 'round town' stops. The function rooms have just been done out and they've started putting on match day specials - think big screens and dancers at half time.

THE BURTON HOUSE
Borough Rd., **M** *Sunderland*
A good old fashioned boozer, with loads of old gadgies, a pool table and a promise of 'fine ales and lagers'. It's even got a dartboard for goodness sake.

CHAPLIN'S
Stockton Rd. Park Lane,
0191 565 3964 **M** *Park Lane*
Large bar practically in the middle of the city centre. Tables and stools outside ensure a bustling summer trade and its proximity to the bus depot makes it a popular starting or finishing place for a pub-crawl. There's also a good range of food on offer as well as a kiddies' menu.

CHASE
1/3 Park Lane, **M** *Park Lane*
0191 567 0753
Well known brand Chase's Sunderland branch is a contemporary looking bar which is all low lighting and soft furnishings, which attracts those trendier types. It's a DJ driven experience and they have a very cheaply priced good range of cocktails. They also have a gay night on Tuesdays.

CHESTERS
Chester Rd., **M** *University*
0191 565 9952
The Chesters is slightly outside of the town centre and attracts an older clientele. Two bars, good food, pool tables, quiz night is on a Tuesday from 9pm and a beer garden that comes into its own on balmy summer nights. Top notch pub to start your night out. Sunday dinners are particularly gorgeous.

COLLIERY TAVERN
Southwick Rd., **M** *St. Peter's*
0191 548 7157
A slightly older crowd that suits the classic tunes of the 60s-70s that is played each Saturday. It's also near the Stadium of Light so gets more than its fair share of football fans in.

THE COOPER ROSE
2-4 Albion Place
01915148530 **M** *Park Lane*
Sunderland's latest addition to the Lloyds No.1 chain. The pub has undergone a massive change since it was Blu Bambo with huge intergalactic lighting rig, and of course, cheap beer!

THE CORNER FLAG
278-284 High Street West
0191 447 6608 **M** *Sunderland*
One of the biggest sports bars in the North East, this canny pub is the sister pub to Indigo Rooms. They've got 24 plasmas screens making this an ideal place to chill with a pint on one of their comfy leather sofas and watch the match.

DRAY & HORSES
Hahnemann Court
The perfect combination of restaurant, lounge and bar make this an excellent place for a quality meal or just a decent pint. With gentle background music too, it's ideal for a good old chin-wag.

The Borough

Harleys

ESTABLISHMENT

34 Low Row M *Park Lane*
0191 510 2601
Formerly Baroque, then Aspire, the new Establishment is a well decorated stylish bar, and the makeover will probably attract a younger crowd than its predecessors especially with its very canny list of continental beers and lagers.

FITZGERALD'S

12-14 Green Terrace, M *Park Lane*
0191 567 0852
A splendid relaxing pub with classy decor, good beer and a reasonably priced menu. The beer garden is ideal in the summertime. There's also a back room ('The Chart Room') which has a nautical theme and is the place to catch the footy action.

GATSBY

13-14 Derwent St M *Park Lane*
0191 565 2372
Formerly Oslo Bar and Cafe, this canny place has underwent something of a spruce up and is not a bad place to chill out, although it's doubtful that F. Scott Fitzgerald's most famous creation would see fit to drop in for a cocktail. There's lots of student drinks offers, including cheap bottles from Mondays -Thursdays, too.

GREENS

36 Low Row,
0191 567 2662 M *Sunderland*
Light and airy, this attracts the younger end of the market. They're a good pub to watch the footy in and show most Sunderland matches (both home and away). They have a great selection of cheap food served 11am-6pm, and plenty of drinks offers to keep your wallet happy. They also have a DJ Fridays, Saturdays and Sundays.

HARBOUR VIEW

1 Benedict, Harbour View, Roker
M *St. Peter's* *0191 567 1402*
A surprisingly wide range of beers is the main-selling point of this compact pub, closely followed by the ocean views promised by its name. They also have a carvery on in the restaurant upstairs on a Sunday.

THE GLASS SPIDER

3 Green Terrace, Sunderland
0191 567 7272 M *Park Lane*
This place is arguably the king of the hill in terms of a weekend bender as it's open 'till 5am on a Saturday. The music is pretty much a mixture of dance music and RnB and remains one of the most popular places in town.

The Ivy House

Londonderry

HOLLYMERE
Leechmere Road, Grangetown
0191 521 3809 **M** *Pallion*
Hollycarrside and Leechmere estates, is behind its name. Very accommodating to families, with karaoke on Tuesdays, quiz nights on Wednesdays and Sundays, live bands on Friday. They also do food theme nights with a meal and a drink deal starting £5.99.

HOWARD ARMS
183 Roker Avenue, **M** *St. Peter's*
0191 510 2559
A long time popular with locals and it's easy to see why. For those of you who demand more than drink though. Monday night is darts, and Sunday is dominoes.

INDIGO ROOMS
278-284 High Street West
0191 447 6608 **M** *Sunderland*
Great bar, with nice modern décor. Like the older sibling of Cornerflag, Indigo Rooms is a bit more grown-up. With their low lighting and fantastic home cooked food, they give off a very relaxed restaurant vibe. They hold indie nights on Thursdays and Saturdays. Or if you're feeling a bit posh there's Baby Indy upstairs, a nice little VIP champagne and cocktail bar.

INNFUSION
18 Park Lane, **M** *Park Lane*
0191 564 1746
Playing a mixture of R&B and whatever else is in the charts, Innfusion has a fun, lively atmosphere, and serves up nice cocktails and cheap trebles making it the perfect warm-up for a night out.

THE IVY HOUSE
Worcester Terrace, **M** *Park Lane*
0191 567 3399
Tucked away in a back street but long established as an unmissible port of call on any Sunderland night out. A 'Victorian Ale House', the superb Ivy is a hotbed of soccer passion, and has always attracted a young crowd of locals and students to its many shadowy corners for cheap beer. Quiz night is Wednesday and there's live music on Tuesdays and Thursdays. A quality pub and well known by everyone in Sunderland.

KING'S ARMS
Beach St., Deptford **M** *Millfield*
0191 567 9804
One of the oldest pubs in Sunderland, formerly a 'shipyard' local but now catering to a slightly older blues/jazz/folk crowd. They've won an array of awards for their top-notch beers, including CAMRA's North East Pub of the Year. They offer nine cask ales and also have a pleasant beer-garden ('the Garden of Light' if you will).

LAINGS
26 Olive St. **M** *Park Lane*
A very smart looking place and one that retains its traditional air; with pool, sports on the TV, gaming machines, comfy seating and even WiFi. Noted for its great pub lunches too, it's well worth checking out.

THE LAMBTON WORM
Victoria Bldgs, Low Row
0191 568 9910 **M** *University*
Winner of numerous awards, this pleasant J.D. Wetherspoons pub, is pretty big and very cosy. It's open from 7am every day for breakfasts, perfect for that morning after remedy. Like most of the Wetherspoons family it's cheap and cheerful; it's also perfect for football fans with live Premier League games screened.

LITTLE CUBA
21 Vine Place **M** *Park Lane*
New little trebles bar come café with a South American theme. With a free shot with your first round, what more can you ask for? Situated right next to the likes of Liquid and Diva, it's in a great location to start the night.

LOLA'S

17 Vine Place **M** *Park Lane*
0191 564 1536

One of the newer additions to the Sunderland pub set, Lola's is a trendy boudoir styled pub, think lots of deep colours and red velvet. This a very popular spot with the younger punters.

LONDONDERRY

287 High St. West
Sunderland
0191 567 9251 **M** *Sunderland*

A unique institution in the city. This extremely old, large pub is in the middle of the action that can get unbelievably crowded almost every night of the week. Two separate bars and a back room decked out in Sunderland AFC memorabilia.

LUMA

Derwent St. **M** *Park Lane*
0191 514 5111

A particularly popular bar with a restaurant upstairs, Luma is nothing if not modern. Cheap drinks are on offer Monday to Thursday. The main selling point, however, has to be that you can sort out a taxi at the bar to avoid the miserable queues at the end of the night. How very gentlemanly of them...

THE MARSDEN GROTTO

Coast Rd. South Shields 0191 455 6060

This fabulous bar is actually set inside a cave within the magnesian limestone cliff face at Marsden Bay and is delightful. Food is served daily from 11-8pm, and until 5pm on a Sunday. There is also a function room which is available to hire.

MUSEUM VAULTS

33 Silksworth Row
0191 565 9443 **M** *Millfield*

Unspoilt by progress, the Vaults exist in a kind of miraculous time warp and truly a drinking establishment par excellence. There's nothing immediately striking about the place but the warmth of the welcome is worth it. The regulars are part of the fixtures and fittings; the SAFC crack on matchdays is legendary and the pub just exudes a charisma and charm that is hard to come by.

NEW REGALE TAVERN

4 East Hendon Rd., Hendon
M *Sunderland*
0191 565 8316

A hidden gem and of all the candidates for Sunderland's 'oldest pub', this one is the most plausible. Full of old-town character, this is a must for anyone who's even remotely interested in the history of the East End.

The Black Bull

City Tavern

The Coach and Eight

The Big Jug

ODDIES
58 Hylton Road, Millfield
Ⓜ *Millfield*
One of Millfield's best bets, just a short walk from the city centre, with good value beer and a good old-fashioned atmosphere.

PLUGGED INN
29 Holmeside Ⓜ *Park Lane*
Refurbished, this place has become an eco café, and done out with second hand furniture. With the White Rooms, still above, the bar is still very much about fairly cheap drinks served in a great atmosphere. Opposite Independent, it's the perfect place for a last drink before you head into the club. It's a café, bar and a great venue all rolled into one.

THE POINT
Holmeside, Sunderland 0191 510 8680
Ⓜ *Park Lane*
This former cinema is the Metrocentre of drinking, comprising of four distinct venues (The Union, Purple Bar, Arizona and Velvet). Very popular at weekends and the drinks are reasonably priced once you've paid your way in.

REFLEX 80S BAR
287 High Street West
0191 567 9251 Ⓜ *Sunderland*
Exactly what it says on the tin, 80s themed bar complete with raised stage area, formerly 70s

themed Flares, the bar has got a little more mature, a whole decade in fact.

RIVER BAR
16 Bonemill Lane, Washington
0191 419 0359
Hey! The cocktails here are second to none. And the draught continental lagers are not bad either. A real good 'un with DJs every Friday and Saturday night. Swish times!

THE ROSEDENE
Queen Alexandra Road, Ashbrooke
0191 528 4313
Out of the city centre, this pub targets an older, more affluent clientele in keeping with its leafy, suburban environs. Large carpark services, a huge bar, good restaurant with great food offers and conservatory to watch the world go by. Quiz night is on Monday and there's also the popular 'quiz for people who don't like quizzes' on a Wednesday. This is a great pub for live sport and they also boast they have the best smoking shelter in the north-east (it has its own TV and a heater...).

ROYALTY
88 Chester Rd 0191 565 9930
Ⓜ *University*
An excellent bar, popular with students and locals alike. Live bands most weekends, a popular quiz each Tuesday and drinks

Beamish Mary Inn

The Water House

promotions on Mondays. Gorgeous Sunday dinners as well.

THE SALTGRASS
20 Hannover Place
0191 565 7229 **M** *Millfield*
Very friendly pub with no loud music to stem the flow of conversation. Part of the 'Riverside Route', and for years named as one of the top pubs in the north-east. Two rooms, with low ceilings and nautical paraphernalia that can give the impression of being below decks on an old-style whaling ship... Outstanding beer range (including guest ales), good food (served at lunchtimes and with an a la carte menu in the evening) and worth the trek to the old shipyards area.

SINATRA'S
31 Holmside
0191 565 8186 **M** *Sunderland*
Famed for their prize karaoke on Tuesday, Thursday, Friday and Sunday where they encourage you to 'bring your mam and dad'. Saturdays is DJ night. A café/bar with an older clientele, you'll love it if you like a bit of cheddar.

TTONIC
12-14 Vine Place
0191 565 5755 **M** *Park Lane*
This large disco pub is on two levels and

features a dance area, open main bar and a first floor bar with a laidback, spacious aura. Known by many for its over the top 'Crisco Disco' gay night on a Tuesday.

VARSITY
3 Green Tce. Priestman Building,
0191 565 4783 **M** *Park Lane*
Varsity has a somewhat traditional feel due to its brick walls and stone and wood flooring, but it's a great place for cheap drink and even cheap food during the day. The only thing to note is that the music is sometimes a tad too happy hardcore. Nice burgers, though.

PADDY WACKS IRISH BAR
6/7 Green Terrace. 0191 564 1010
M *Park Lane*
Formerly Vision, Paddy Wacks has a new attitude, a new atmosphere and new clientele. The inside has been done out brilliantly, the main bar is downstairs with a roomy sofa area and reasonably sized outside balcony area. The drinks aren't a rip-off which is always a bonus.

VODKA REVOLUTION
Victoria Buildings 1-6 Low Row
M *Park Lane*
The Revolution finally came to Sunderland about a year ago and is a firm favourite with anyone in town. Offering mouth-watering cocktails and more vodka than any liver could

ever cope with, as well as serving up food. The décor is nice and classy and there's a large outside terrace perfect for summer drinkers and smokers.

THE WHEATSHEAF
Moor St., Monkwearmouth
0191 565 7401   **M** *St. Peter's*
An authentic Sunderland landmark - giving its name to the nearby bus terminus - and perpetually voted the best pre-match pub by the SAFC faithful. Big, old style horseshoe bar and dozens of classic pub-architectural touches, from the windows to the carved stone sign at the front.

THE WILLIAM JAMESON
30-32 Fawcett St.
0191 514 5016   **M** *Sunderland*
For a place for tranquillity this traditional, comfy bar has no music, no pool table and reasonable prices - heaven. Food is served from 8-10pm and you can get anything from a nachos grande to a minted lamb burger. Part of the J.D. Wetherspoons chain.

THE WILLOW POND
Hylton Road
0191 567 6742   **M** *Millfield*
The Willow Pond is a traditional, white-washed pub a few minutes walk from the city centre. Lots of football on the telly, a pool table and

jukebox make this popular with the matchday crowd, though all kinds are tempted by the cheap drinks and Wednesday night quiz.

YATES'S WINE LODGE
3/4 Burdon House, Burdon Rd.
0191 567 1649   **M** *Sunderland*
You know what you're going to get if you visit one of the many Yates's around the country - a traditional bar with good food and beer (cheaper than most). They had a refurb last year, so now the purple has been replaced with a nice modern looking interior.

DURHAM

THE ANGEL INN
53 Crossgate 0191 386 5561
Don't be put off by Crossgate's steep hill - this pub is worth the effort. The rock-oriented jukebox lends credence to its reputation as the definitive hard rock pub in Durham and it also has a pool table.

THE BEAMISH MARY INN
No Place, Stanley 0191 370 0237
Built in 1897, the Beamish Mary Inn is a family-run traditional 'local' public house in the former mining village of No Place. With open fires, a large collection of memorabilia from the '20s and '30s, the pub evokes a unique

Boathouse

The Swan and Three Cygnets

and special atmosphere. A unique pub with lots of character and indeed characters too.

THE BIG JUG
83 Claypath 0191 384 8354
Not the biggest of places and unfortunately expensive but very friendly and serves regular guest real ales. Also hosts a regular poker night.

THE BISHOP'S MILL
Unit 1 and 2, Watergate Leisure Complex 0191 370 8510
This is a large and relatively new Lloyd's No. 1 Bar, so plenty of cheap drinks and loads of seating. Also serves the usual plethora of food. Typical Lloyds bar by day but transforms into a popular nightclub later on. There's an outside terrace too... if you like looking at concrete.

THE BRIDGE
40 North Road 0191 386 8090
Yet another little bijou place, situated beneath the railway viaduct (replete with bare floorboards) serving some canny cask ales. Well popular with locals and students alike, there's also a challenging quiz each Tuesday and Sunday and they serve up a cracking Sunday roast to boot.

CHASE
The Boathouse, Elvet Riverside 0191 386 6210
Set right down on the riverside, this bar is split over two floors and aims at the trendier end of the market. Stupendous views of the river, as you'd imagine, with plenty of plush seating inside. A comprehensive food menu is available during the day with prices starting at around four or five quid and some good two-for-one offers.

THE CITY HOTEL
84 New Elvet 0191 386 9936
Noted for the quality of its fine real ales and speciality bottled beers, you can also get a

decent roast dinner here. Big screen action for you footie fans, too.

THE COACH AND EIGHT
Bridge House, Framwellgate Bridge 0191 386 3284
All things to all people, this pub has an extensive food menu, a beer garden, live music, DJs most nights, party nights, a pool table and video games. Oh and it's ludicrously cheap, too.

THE COLPITTS
Hawthorn Terrace 0191 386 9913
The decor here is decidedly '1930s pit village', it's up a huge hill and you'll generally just find a load of old blokes having a good old chin-wag within. We like it actually; don't ask us why, it's just got a certain charm.

THE COURT INN
Court Lane 0191 384 7350
Nattering away on a mobile phone will get you several withering looks in this traditional-looking pub situated next to – surprise, surprise – a court. It's very popular with all walks of life due to the reasonably-priced food served between 11am and 10.30pm, 7 days a week. Also has a good selection of wines as well as an extensive cocktail list, not to mention frequent drinks deals.

THE DUN COW INN
37 Old Elvet 0191 386 9219
This is one of Durham's many quaintly-designed pubs, consisting of two separate rooms linked by a rather seedy passage around the back and a bar to the front. The front room is smaller than most living rooms and generally consists of blokes playing dominoes. If you ask nicely, the landlord will probably give you a game...

THE DURHAM LIGHT INFANTRYMAN
110 Gilesgate 0191 386 5522
About as "real" a pub as you're ever likely to find in the city, The Durham Light Infantryman is almost as tough as the former army regiment

from which it takes its name. Look beyond the occasionally gritty clientele though and this place is very accommodating, with friendly staff, good bar banter and a pool table too. Also occasionally screens football matches.

EBONY
Walkergate 0191 375 7121
Built as part of the new Walkergate bar and restaurant complex, inside this venue oozes class thanks to decadent décor and equally decadent prices. Its relatively small size lends the bar an intimate atmosphere.

THE FIGHTING COCKS
4 South Street 0191 383 6970
Avoid this one. There's simply no reason to be here and if you walk past on a Friday or Saturday night you'll see for yourself why you should heed the advice.

THE GARDEN HOUSE
North Road 0191 384 3460
For those who prefer the more sedate pace of life, this public house offers a quiet ambience with very friendly service and excellent food. It's a bit out of town – through the park behind the railway station - but well worth the hike if you fancy a nice, juicy steak or a quality pint. Also screens plenty of live sport and hosts a regular pool tournament.

THE HALF MOON INN
New Elvet 0191 383 6981
One of many 'Ye Olde Durham' styled pubs, with plenty of black-and-white pictures of old Durham on the wall. The bar is a little spit-and-sawdust, and the beer garden is not the best but we reckon this is a very decent boozer all the same.

THE HEAD OF STEAM
3 Reform Place, North Road
0191 3832173
Situated just off the North Road up a "ginnel" this two floor modern bar has an unrivalled

selection of ales, world and Euro beers, wines, spirits and cocktails. All of the food is home cooked (including fabulous Sunday lunches) and for sun lovers the first floor balcony terrace is a must! The regular live music and function room hire make this a not to be missed venue.

MARKET TAVERN
Market Place 0191 386 2069
In 1853 the council committee of Durham declared the water in the market place unfit for human consumption, so customers could only quench their thirst from the excellent ales served in this public house. Steeped in history (the Durham Miners Association was also originally formed here), this is a busy little pub, situated as it is bang in the centre of Durham. Great cask ales and a lively atmosphere make this one of the best all-rounders in the city. Pretty expensive, mind.

MARKET VAULTS
Back Silver Street 0191 386 7700
Formerly known as Warehouse, the Market Vaults represents one of Durham's more high-end drinking establishments. Spread across two floors and replete with stone walls and a plush interior, the bar boasts a truly impressive range of cocktails and a laid-back, cosy atmosphere.

THE NEW INN
29 Church Street 0191 374 6901
Cocktails, beers, a huge menu, endless sports coverage, outside seating and cheap prices to boot. This place tends to get busy, so be prepared to fight your way to the bar. A beehive of student activity during term time and only a little less chaotic at other times.

POPOLO CAFÉ & BAR
81 New Elvet
The latest edition to Durham's drinking scene and what a real looker. Swish without being pretentious, you'll find some quality imported lagers here along with good food.

THE QUEENS HEAD

2 Sherburn Road 0191 386 5649

In similar vain to the Durham Light Infantryman opposite and The Woodman down the hill, this place is frequented both by locals and students. Like The Woodman, the beer range here is mediocre but is compensated for by a cosy feel on winter evenings, plenty of televised sport and some decent pub grub. Also hosts its own weekly quiz.

THE SHAKESPEARE TAVERN

63 Saddler Street 0191 384 3261

The most notable feature of this popular bar is its curious layout. There's the bar and snug as you enter and then a wander through labyrinthine passages brings you to another room only slightly bigger. The little snug is the darkest little room we've ever been in, making your average black hole look positively bright. It's also reputedly one of the most haunted pubs in Britain, if you happen to believe in such rubbish.

THE SHOES

16 Sunderland Road 0191 384 4099

Easily the most peculiarly-named of Durham's watering holes, The Shoes is a family-run affair that caters primarily to locals and offers a solid lunchtime food menu. Also functions

as a bed-and-breakfast, so you can stay the night if you're enjoying yourself.

THE SLUG AND LETTUCE

Unit 7, Walkergate 0191 384 3564

Large, smart bar split over two levels but not too barn-like thanks to some nice booths and plenty of comfortable seating. Extensive food menu, too, with delights such as salmon and spinach risotto and minted lamb shank on offer for around eight or nine quid, while the wine list is one of the best in Durham.

VARSITY

46 Saddler St. 0191 384 6704

A spacious, modern-looking chain place (nice cream and deep red colour scheme) split into several areas, including a second bar and projection television downstairs and a beer terrace. Serves food better than most other pubs too (the Thai chicken is divine) and with two meals yours for around £6 you really can't go wrong. Very popular with students.

THE SWAN AND THREE CYGNETS

Old Elvet Bridge 0191 384 0242

A very decent pub with a back room reminiscent of a gentleman's club. Bertie Wooster would be at home here. Good quality ales too and has seating outside for when you want to feel

The Half Moon Inn

Head of Steam

the sun (or more likely the rain) on your back. Interestingly, doesn't serve major brands of beers or soft drinks.

THE VICTORIA HOTEL
Hallgarth Street 0191 386 5269
As featured in many a good pub guide, this is perfect for the whisky connoisseur as it offers over 50 varieties among the usual wet delights. Ideal for a pre-dinner drink and perfect to huddle up to one of its magnificent coal fires on a cold, rainy day.

THE WATERHOUSE
65 North Road 0191 370 6540
Part of the Wetherspoons chain so predictably the drinks are pretty cheap. Quite dark inside too, lending it an unlikely cosy feel. Aubergine-coloured walls, exposed brick work and dark wood add to the effect. Split over two levels. Worth visiting for Tuesday's Grill Night alone, where an 8oz rump steak, chips and a drink can be yours for less than £6.

THE WOODMAN
23 Gilesgate 0191 386 7500
A real local pub with a healthy dose of student patronage, The Woodman has the usual range of drinks but is set apart by its sports coverage, quiz nights and of course its gigantic annual summer barbeque.

YATES'S WINE LODGE
80-83 North Road 0191 384 1775
Only included here to facilitate this warning: don't go. Ever. Especially not on a Friday or Saturday night. It's as simple as that. Along with the Fighting Cocks this is easily a candidate for the worst pub in Durham.

YE OLDE ELM TREE
12 Crossgate
0191 386 4621
This place is possibly the best watering hole in the city. A real ale pub very popular with students and locals alike. It's all very traditional with friendly staff, fine banter and no blaring music to disturb the perfect equilibrium that exists within its walls. Accommodation is also available if you can't bring yourself to up and leave. Perfect.

The Shakespeare

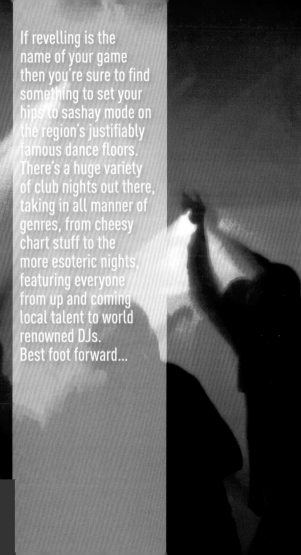

If revelling is the name of your game then you're sure to find something to set your hips to sashay mode on the region's justifiably famous dance floors. There's a huge variety of club nights out there, taking in all manner of genres, from cheesy chart stuff to the more esoteric nights, featuring everyone from up and coming local talent to world renowned DJs. Best foot forward...

ATTIC

25-27 Mosley Street, Newcastle
0191 233 1396 **M** *Central Station*

A multi-floored bar/club which has plenty of top tunes with great sound and light system. The music policy is drawn from the slinkier end of r'n'b and house and the club's guestlist in the past has included everyone from Wayne Rooney to Prince William. Look out for Havana (the student night on Saturday) and Sugar (r'n'b on Sunday) as well as some canny nights during the week.

BAMBU

Bigg Market, Newcastle,
0191 261 5811 **M** *Monument*

This is a loud and up for it club with a great range of club nights. They offer a wide range of music, from party to r'n'b and dance. Smart dress (or barely any dress if you're a female judging by the lasses we see shivering, queuing outside waiting to get in...). Mainstream and for the young.

COSMIC BALLROOM

Stowell St., Newcastle
M *St. James*

The longest running nightclub venue in the city (used to be The Stage Door) and it still can get really busy. It has had a long and distinguished history in Newcastle has really been put back on the map again after a grand refit. A variety of nights are held here including Soul Connection on Saturdays: a night of soul, funk and disco.

THE CUT

7 St Nicholas Street
0191 261 8579 **M** *Central Station*

One of the newer clubs in town, this little gem is above Tup Tup. The deconstructed urban loft décor of the club has won its designer an award. Imagine the aftermath of a good house party: holes in the walls, exposed bricks and pipes and that's what we mean. Already

a popular venue, there are some great nights to watch out for. Check out their indie night Connection on a Monday and Dragnet on a Saturday which offers a brilliant range of electro, pop and funk. The popular dubstep night Rub a Dub is also now hosted here.

DIGITAL

Times Square, Newcastle
0191 261 9755 **M** *Central Station*

One of the biggest clubs in town and what a stunner! Two rooms, a 1,400 capacity and one of the best sound systems you'll ever encounter, namely the Funktion One Dance Stack (there's only a handful in the whole world and they've got four of them). Check out: Born In The 80s (cheapo dance night (cheap entry and cheap drinks) with music from the 80s to the present day); Stone Love (Thursday - an indie night institution and we're using indie in a very broad sense. You can hear anything and everything here from the last 40 years with the one criteria being it has to rock or groove or funk); a variety of nights on alternating Fridays; and their latest extravaganza Love (Saturday – three rooms of great music (room 1: upfront dancefloor destroyers; room 2: FOX RnB from Play & Devon; room 3: soul, funk, disco in the terrace bar). A stormer.

LIQUID & ENVY

49 Newbridge St., Newcastle
0191 261 2526 **M** *Monument*

The biggest club in Newcastle with a capacity of 2336 who do their "stuff" across three rooms, fuelled by one of the six bars. They have a state-of-the-art sound system and lighting, plush seating and booths plus a VIP area. Comedy club, Jongleurs also hold nights here featuring some of the UK's best comedians. These are usually held each Friday and Saturday and tickets will allow entry into the club nights afterwards.

GREY'S CLUB
Grey's Court, Newcastle 0191 261 4066
 *Monument*
For the more mature club goer, Grey's Club is open to over 25s but mainly appeals to people a tad older. None too threatening party music over the weekend is the soundtrack to desperate blokes trying to hook up with anyone with a perm.

FLORITA'S & MADAME KOO
Collingwood Street, Newcastle
0191 261 8271  *Central Station*
Floritas and Koo's used to host the extremely popular Koosday, but since it moved to Tiger Tiger, they're going for something a bit more tropical with their new night Waikiki on a Tuesday. Downstairs is Koo's, one of the slinkiest clubs/bars around with its bare-brick, red upholstery and lanterns. Upstairs you'll find more contemporary décor for the Miami themed Florita's.

LEGENDS
Grey St., Newcastle
0191 232 0430  *Monument*
 basement club that proves a perennial draw for the region's rock lovers and beyond. They're one of the main driving forces for the rock and alternative scenes in the north-east. Their big nights are Suspiria Saturdays (all your metal and unadulterated rock needs – Saturday); Riot Rock N Roll (rock classics alongside pop cheese and guilty pleasures – Monday); and Deluge (student night – Wednesday).

THE LOUNGE
8 Neville St., Newcastle
0191 261 2211  *Central Station*
Usually popular over the weekend, The Lounge has a canny bar upstairs while the downstairs area is the place to cut a rug to all manner of sounds. And recently they've been branching out with some independent promoters putting some really corking nights on.

NEWCASTLE UNIVERSITY
Kings Walk, Newcastle 0191 239 3926
Ⓜ *Haymarket*
Many a top night has been had at this university that has a very good room which is just the ticket for a variety of club nights. It's just been refurbished so we're looking forward to a range of great nights being put on this year.

NORTHUMBRIA UNIVERSITY
Sandyford Rd., Newcastle,
0191 232 6002 Ⓜ *Haymarket*
There's a variety of fabulous club nights at this university including the brilliant Get y'Skates On which is one of the longest running alternative nights in the north east. They play an up front and elated mix of punk, ska and hip-hop and lately they've not been adverse to seeking out the finest in dubstep and drum and bass.

THE OTHER ROOMS
Times Square, Newcastle
0191 261 9755 Ⓜ *Central Station*
The sister bar/club to mega club Digital (see above) and one of the best live and club venues around. Well worth a particular gander is Jukebox every Friday which is all underground indie and electro barnstormers (and live bands). A real goodie and if you're a fan of indie, rock and roll, punk, garage, rockabilly, electro, new wave, post punk, new rave, glam rock, art rock, Two Tone, Trojan, surf, psych, Northern soul, hip-hop and drum and bass – check it out. Phew.

PERDU
20 Collingwood Street
0191 260 3040 Ⓜ *Central Station*
Trendy club/bar which is a particular favourite with a younger crowd who flock to their night Social Butterfly on a Monday.

POWERHOUSE
7-19 Westmorland Road, Newcastle
0191 261 6824 Ⓜ *Central Station*
The north-east's only exclusively gay club (see Queer section for more details).

RIVERSIDE
Quayside, Newcastle
0191 230 5893 Ⓜ *Central Station*
Superb new(ish) venue down by the banks of the river Tyne and their tip-top club nights include Vice City (two rooms, no cheese and crowd pleasers all night long plus great drink promos – Friday) and The Voodoo Project (Room 1: face-melting elctro, house, anthems, mash-ups, bootlegs, dubstep and d'n'b; Room 2: RnB, hip-hop and everything in between including old skool, new school, commercial and underground) – Saturday).

Cosmic Ballroom

Perdu

Madame Koo

World Headquarters

TIGER TIGER
The Gate, Newgate St., Newcastle
0191 235 7065 **M** *Monument*
A variety of environments, spread over several floors, the individually designed rooms include the laid-back Lounge Bar, funky Kaz Bar, sophisticated restaurant and up-beat club area - perfect for a lunch, dinner with friends, a relaxed drink or a night out until late. They now host the extremely popular Koosday on Tuesdays.

TUP TUP PALACE
7 ST. Nicholas St,
0191 261 8579 **M** *Central Station*
This boutique nightclub is right near central station. This is a popular venue with anyone looking for good R&B music in a trendy setting. They offer some great nights including Kinky Disko on a Saturday playing a range of funky house, R&B, and dirty pop.

THE VENUE
Market Street, Newcastle
0191 232 1111 **M** *Monument*
This decent sized venue has a variety of regular nights vying for your attention including: SalSeduce (Tuesday – salsa) and the popular Krash (Saturday – ska/rock/punk/alternative – they also have live bands on).

WORLD HEADQUARTERS
Curtis Mayfield House, Carliol Sq.,
Newcastle 0191 281 3445
M *Monument*
Truly fabulous club that's something of a legend in the region and with good reason. During the week they have an ever changing line-up of some of the best independent clubs in Newcastle where you can literally hear anything and everything, and come Friday and Saturday they host their storming weekend sessions where you'll encounter the best in uplifting block party action. They reckon "cool people who really dig music come here" and it's true. A Newcastle institution and rightly so.

TEES VALLEY

THE ARENA
204 Newport Road, Middlesbrough,
01642 358 928
The recently rejuvenated Arena is, and always has been, a club where music rules the roost. "SKINT" on a Thursday is one not to miss- with extremely cheap drinks - 99p shots and cocktails, accompanied by pop, house and R&B music.

CHICAGO ROCK CAFE AND LOVE TO LOVE
Wilson Street, Middlesbrough,
01642 230 400

On the cheesy scale, this club is stilton. It prides itself on its hen night packages and its ability to make you want to dance as though no-one is watching...which they probably will be. Bear that in mind. If you book a booth, you receive complimentary cocktails, which will help you on your way to dancing to those chart hits of the 90s! The club nights run on Fridays, Saturdays and Sundays, and it is available to hire throughout the week, so if the telly is getting you down, check 'em out.

CLUB BONGO
11-12 Bridge Street West, Middles-
brough, 01642 246 697

This is one of the oldest clubs in Britain having been open for a mammoth 46 years and it devotes itself to reggae music. It serves Jamaican lagers and it adopts the friendly and relaxed approach of the Caribbean. It's reaching out to the student market more recently and rightly so, because who wouldn't want an authentic 'Boro experience to a reggae rhythm? It's open Wednesdays-Saturdays, which gives you plenty of time to pay it a visit. It made it onto Middlesbrough's edition of Monopoly, so pass go, collect £200 and go to Club Bongo.

THE CORNERHOUSE
8-8a Exchange Place, Middlesbrough
01642 890588 or 253053

This is a literal and metaphorical cornerstone to Middlesbrough's clubbing scene. The Cornerhouse attracts a wide range of up for it punters who love good music. Take caution: dress cool in every sense of the word because it can get very hot in here! It is an intimate club of nooks and crannies, but be careful not to become too engrossed in them because it doesn't make for a pretty sight when the lights come on!

THE EMPIRE
Corporation Road, Middlesbrough,
01642 253553

Much like a cream egg, The Empire is as good as it is on the outside as it is on the inside. This three-floored art deco Victorian Theatre has been a unique clubbing venue for 18 years now and its easy to see why. With regular club nights, Fridays are with Sumo the best rock, mosh and indie night around with regular live acts. Saturday nights are with Metropolis offering five rooms from indie, electro, pop and RnB. To top it off they offer great gigs from some of the world's top bands on tour. The admission price varies depending on whose playing but you always get your dollars worth!

ESCAPADE
67-69 Gladstone Street, Darlington.
01325 460 057

You should be one of the 1,500 who will be raving in Escapade every night from Thursday-Sunday. Why? It has three rooms of pick-and-mix music all guaranteed to get your hips shaking. Thursdays host a £1 Party where every beverage is a cool £1, and Fridays are for frolicking to the tunes of the 70s, 80s, 90s and now. It is bound to keep you on your toes with its drinks offers and its guest appearances.

KU-BAR
Prince Regent Street,
Stockton-on-Tees,
01642 860068

The Ku-Bar doubles up as a club and a music venue most Fridays. You can drench yourself in cheap drinks and lose yourself in the live music. The venue puts on some corking bands and admission is free until 10pm. You'll probably see some great bands, but at the price of the drinks in this place, you'll probably think they are the best thing since the first beef joint was roasted.

Powerhouse

Attic

THE MEDICINE BAR
72-80 Corporation Road, Middlesbrough
01642 222 250
Formerly the brilliant Purple Onion and now the brilliant Medicine Bar. Plenty of great nights to be had here including the fabulous Revival every Friday playing the best in indie classics from days of yore. A real goodie.

ONYX ROOMS
2-6 Albert Road, Middlesbrough,
01642 213 658
The Onyx Rooms is the latest reinvention of the Albert Road corner building, and it seems to be giving the punters what they want. "Feel Good" Saturday's are a hit with all drinks £1.50. The lavish décor make the Onyx Rooms like a boudoir from home only better, and they even make your tea and toast to thank you for your company. Now that's utterly butterly.

ZANZIBAR
89-91 High Street, Stockton-on-Tees,
01642 671 671
Here's the run-down on Zanzibar: every Friday it's "Double Your Money", where you can exchange cash for drinks vouchers twice the value before midnight. Then there's free entry and £1.50 drinks on a Saturday before 11pm. Always a popular place to party.

CAMPUS
St Peter's, 0191 515 2000
Ⓜ *St. Peter's*
Sunderland's first frat house bar located at St Peters University Campus. Campus offers great theme parties, celebrity appearances such as Coolio and Radio One's Scott Mills. Their American style food is tasty and cheap, especially if you get your hands on a voucher that benefits your table, not just you. Campus brings a whole new experience to student life

INDEPENDENT
36 Holmeside, 0191 568 9770
Ⓜ *Park Lane*
Great venue that pulls in the majority of the big names into Sunderland. Past gigs include: Reverend and the Makers, The Klaxons, The Zutons and Robots in Disguise. Music is a mix of indie and anything alternative. Cheap drinks and good atmosphere.

LIQUID/DIVA
Galen Building, Green Terrace
0191 567 0760 Ⓜ *Park Lane*
The venue is split into two distinct areas Liquid and Diva. The décor and vibe in Liquid is modern

and stylish and caters for more of dance/hip-hop audience. Diva offers a more eclectic/alternative variation of music but once you pay in one of the clubs you can drift between the two as you see fit and get a 2-4-1 experience.

PASSION
Holmeside 0191 5166898
M *Park Lane*
Some will remember this venue fondly as Pzazz, now Passion has a great range of nights and is drawing in plenty of punters. Studisex on every Monday, is a cheap night for students with Thursday nights being predominantly rock music. Entry is £2 with student ID and drinks start from 50p.

UNION
The Point, Holmeside,
0191 510 8680
M *Park Lane*
One part of three part complex, The Point has anything you want when it comes to mainstream music, everything from dance to pop to RnB. Definitely worth checking out if you like a boogie and drinks are cheap once you've paid in.

DURHAM UNIVERSITY
Students' Union Dunelm House,
New Elvet 0191 334 1777
Nightspot of choice for the area's student population by virtue of the fact that it's both the biggest and cheapest in the city. The Union runs a variety of nights which are a cut above and cater for all tastes. Often packed to the rafters, it's advisable to phone ahead to check on entry requirements; depending on the event an NUS card might be required.

FISHTANK
Neville Street,
just off North Road
If good things really do come in small packages, Fishtank ought to be one of the best nightclubs on the planet. Only slightly larger than your average garage, the venue nevertheless hosts a truly eclectic selection of DJ nights and live showcases with an independent edge. Also plays host to comedy offerings and frequent open mic nights.

The Empire

Riverside - Newcastle

KLUTE
Elvet Bridge 0191 386 9859

Whether or not you buy into the hype hailing Klute as "the worst nightclub in Europe," a night spent on its infamously sticky tiles is sure to be an "experience," though whether this is good or bad will depend on your perspective. Famed for cheesy music and a perpetually sloshed middle-class student clientele, you'll either love this or loathe it. Open to students (and the odd VIP) only.

THE LOFT
15-17 North Road 0191 384 3900

Not the most eye-catching of places on the outside, The Loft has nevertheless managed to keep going for a number of years under various guises by dishing out "quality" cheese, up-tempo house and indie music for those who crave it. A couple of years ago attempted to gain permission for lap dancing only to be thwarted by locals' protests. Avoid at weekends at all costs.

LOVESHACK
Walkergate Complex 0191 384 5757

A veritable behemoth amongst Durham's otherwise diminutive nightspots, the multi-million-pound Loveshack has everything you might look for in a nightclub. Everything, that is, apart from class. With invariably cheesy music and cheap drinks, the club will likely appeal strongly to some quarters while leaving others wanting more. Avoid this one at weekends as well.

MARKET VAULTS
Back Silver Street 0191 386 7700

Essentially a continuation of the old Warehouse from a couple of years ago, the Market Vaults builds on that venue's legacy, offering a more laid-back, classier (and pricier) club experience. Various DJ nights keep things relatively esoteric, while the broad range of cocktails won't fail to impress the ladies.

STUDIO
15-17 North Road 0191 384 3900

Studio stretches across two floors and plays host to diverse club nights and live bands along with its infamous 50p Tuesday nights. Fridays, for example, bring Skool of Rock; a rock extravaganza over both floors with punk, indie and even electro alongside the usual rock fare plus live touring bands. New nights regularly start during university term time, though campus/NUS cards may be required.

Studio

Independent, Sunderland

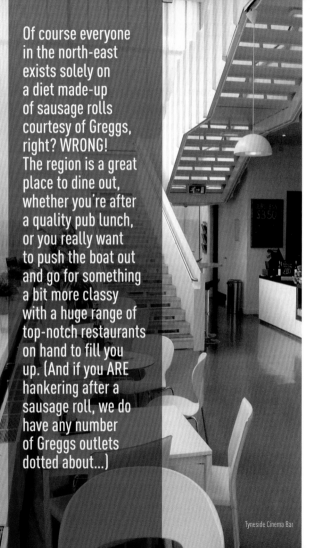

Of course everyone in the north-east exists solely on a diet made-up of sausage rolls courtesy of Greggs, right? WRONG! The region is a great place to dine out, whether you're after a quality pub lunch, or you really want to push the boat out and go for something a bit more classy with a huge range of top-notch restaurants on hand to fill you up. (And if you ARE hankering after a sausage roll, we do have any number of Greggs outlets dotted about...)

Tyneside Cinema Bar

ARABIC

AL BASHA
7-9 Bigg Market, Newcastle
0191 222 1303 M *Central Station*
Whether it's something from the grill or even a sandwich, this place has a great range. And with a variety of rice and other sides to choose from you're certain to get your money's worth. One thing to remember is they don't serve alcohol, so don't ask to see their wine list.

EUROPEAN / MODERN

BLACKFRIARS RESTAURANT AND MEETING ROOMS
Friar Street, Newcastle
0191 261 5945 M *Central Station*
Located in a 13th century refectory, this is the oldest purpose-built restaurant in the country. The quite unique setting (beautiful courtyard, quadrangle and stone buildings) is matched by the food which is excellent: British cooking at its best.

BUEE AT THE SIDE CAFÉ & BISTRO
1-3 The Side, Newcastle
0191 231 4080 M *Central Station*
Superb French establishment that is a delightful café by day and bistro by night. The café serves up lovely soups, sandwiches, omelettes and at night tuck into the likes of French black pudding & pork tenderloin, coq au vin and seared fish of the day. And the sweets? Formidable! It's not been unknown for them to stage live music events, too. Highly recommended.

BRASSERIE AT THE SAGE GATESHEAD
The Sage Gateshead, Gateshead Quays
0191 443 4654 M *Central Station*
Open daily from 12-3.30pm and 5-10pm, the Brasserie at The Sage is the ideal place to

grab a bite to eat before or after a gig and you can even save your dessert for the interval!

CAFÉ 21
Trinity Gardens, Newcastle
0191 222 0755 M *Central Station*
This smart place (whites, greys, chocolates) has won a raft of awards and they maintain a high standard. A good choice of dishes (particularly fish) it usually attracts the business or older end of the market who can't get enough of these simple yet imaginative dishes with real respect given over to the ingredients.

CAFÉ 21 AT FENWICK
First floor, Fenwick,
Northumberland St., Newcastle
0191 260 3373 M *Monument*
Found inside one of Newcastle's most cherished department stores (if any department store can be cherished, it's this one) you'll find breakfast pancakes to afternoon tea to knickbocker glories! More than enough to refuel your shopping urges.

CAFÉ ROYAL
8 Nelson Street, Newcastle
0191 231 3000 M *Monument*
The downstairs area here is very popular during the day with both a breakfast menu and a stunning all-day menu providing such delights as mussels steamed with cider or a classic Waldorf steak.

THE CANTEEN & BAR
32 Clayton Street West, Newcastle
0191 261 6295 M *Central Station*
A great range of full meals and yummy smaller plates. Cool, airy and even the Sunshine Underground have eaten here. Why not give it a try?

THE CHERRY TREE
9 Osborne Road, Jesmond 0191 239 9924 M *Jesmond*
For classic British fare and an extensive wine

list, this is somewhere to try. From pan fried sea bass to twice baked cheddar cheese and spinach soufflé, there's sure to be something to get your mouth watering.

DAVID KENNEDY'S FOOD SOCIAL
The Biscuit Factory, 16 Stoddart St., Newcastle 0191 260 5411 **M** *Manors*
Formerly The Black Door Brasserie, this little gem is situated right next to the Biscuit Factory. The new restaurant of former North-East Chef of the Year, David Kennedy, and is less formal than Black Door. His mantra is to keep things simple with locally sourced, beautifully dishes.

INDIGO
The Gate, Newcastle 0191 243 5558
M *Monument*
Café, restaurant and bar, whatever you fancy, Indigo's got it. And as it's situated in the Gate, why don't you catch a film after?

JACK SPRATS VEGAN AND VEGETARIAN CAFÉ & RESTAURANT
413 Chillingham Road, Heaton
0191 265 7708 **M** *Chillingham Road*
With a menu made up of home-cooked food from fresh ingredients, this place, which has recently had an extensive refurbishment, is a constant marvel. It's open from 10am-9pm and during the day it's a lovely laid-back café, while the back room is a restaurant at night serving up an exciting, seasonal menu. Prices are pitched just right and you'll save more money by bringing your own booze. They also have a great take-out menu (pizzas, cakes, falafels etc), free wi-fi and students get 10% discount. Hooray!

JESMOND DENE HOUSE
Jesmond Dene Road, Newcastle
0191 212 3000 **M** *Jesmond*
The emphasis here is on creating fine, flavoursome food where there's both respect and passion for the ingredients. The cooking

Jack Sprats
free wi fi

10% Student Discount

Vegetarian ❋ Vegan
Wheat/Gluten free
Cafe & Restaurant

413 chillingham rd, Heaton
tel: (0191) 265 7708 f

jackspratscafe.co.uk

is skilful, generous and heartfelt with dishes inspired by the rhythm of the seasons - asparagus and tender lamb in spring, for example, wild mushrooms and game in autumn. Although the cooking style has an assured, classic foundation, it takes a fresh and spirited approach with each dish created as a response to the day's market produce. With a brand new look from this summer the dining experience is sure to be matched by the fresh décor.

THE LIVING ROOM
12 Grey Street, Newcastle 0191 255 4450 **M** *Monument*
Both a restaurant and a bar, you can't expect anything less than a wide variety of food and beverages from this venue. Whether you choose from their "home comforts" section of the menu or treat yourself to a wrap at lunchtime, you'll no doubt be tempted by their 20 page drinks menu.

MALMAISON BRASSERIE
104 Quayside, Newcastle 0191 245 5000 **M** *Manors*
One of the plushest, most popular hotels in town with a good restaurant focusing on continental cuisine, particularly the finest our French chums have to offer, but with locally sourced ingredients. There's usually a nice buzzy atmosphere, too.

NOOSH
Amen Corner, The Side, Newcastle 0191 232 4663 **M** *Central Station*
Experiencing and sharing unique dishes and drinks from four corners of the world, Noosh is a restaurant-cafe bar offering high quality international cuisine; open all day all year for lunch, dinner or just a glass of wine or a coffee. Many UK dishes but also Asian, Middle Eastern, and grills. Tasty? You bet.

NO. 28
27-29 Nelson Street, Newcastle

0788 612 6409 **M** *Monument*
Tucked away down one of the alleys that leads to the Grainger Market (and then up some stairs) this is a very funky new addition to Newcastle's laid-back quota. Well worth hunting out as they do delicious comfort food using local ingredients where possible. Whether you fancy a pub classic, nibbles with your drink or something a little more adventurous, give them a whirl. (You don't have to be eating to call in, however)

O DE V
Pipewellgate House, Gateshead Quayside 0191 341 0031 **M** *Gateshead*
If you're a steak lover then this should be on your "must visit" list. It's a deluxe brasserie, fusion steak house and margarita bar and pretty chilled out. Our favourites? Rib eye done Caribbean style (or maybe sirloin Morocan).

THE OAK
Milburn House, Dean Street, Newcastle 0191 232 3200 **M** *Monument*
A new restaurant/deli/lounge and something of a looker and well worth giving the once over. They serve classic and modern dishes and also have an extensive drinks menu and music from a variety of top local DJs and musicians. From gourmet breakfasts to late night dancing, they've got it all covered.

PAN HAGGERTY
21 Queen Street, Newcastle 0191 221 0904 **M** *Central Station*
Pan Haggerty has swiftly established itself as a favourite of those who appreciate traditional British food that is cooked in an imaginative way. Good 'early bird' deals and scrummy puddings.

POPOLO BAR & KITCHEN
82-84 Pilgrim Street, Newcastle 0191 232 8923 **M** *Monument*
Vast variety here, with burgers, mussels, pizzas and loads more. Leather booths, red

mood lighting and decent prices mean that this is a tasty place for a meal.

RU BAR: LOUNGE: KITCHEN
44 Osborne Road, Jesmond
0191 281 9111 **M** *Jesmond*
Situated in a bustling area, RU is a brilliant place to eat, drink and relax in Jesmond. They have a great menu offering a range of pub-friendly food including paninis, grilled dishes and a range of posh burgers (all sourced locally).

SCRUMPY WILLOW AND THE SINGING KETTLE
89 Clayton Street, Newcastle
0191 221 2323 **M** *Central Station*
Organic food in a relaxing environment for those who fancy guilt free eating.

SIX
BALTIC Centre for Contemporary Art, Gateshead Quays
0191 440 4948 **M** *Central Station*
Housed on the top floor of the fantastic BALTIC art gallery, this restaurant affords fantastic views across the river Tyne and the city. The food is bang on the money too, with fish from North Shields, Northumbrian duck and Blagdon chicken just some of the dishes you're liable to encounter on a menu which uses the best of local produce. A winner.

SKY APPLE CAFÉ
182 Heaton Road, Heaton
0191 209 2571 **M** *Chillingham Rd*
A superb vegetarian eatery serving up all manner of delights. The menu changes every month or so, and the top chefs here always keep the dishes on the right side of imaginative. Even if you're not a veggie, we'd whole-heartedly recommend this rare gem.

GREEK

CAFE NEON
8 Bigg Market, Newcastle
0191 260 2577 **M** *Monument*
A sparky Bigg Market establishment that gets busy during the day, mainly with office workers and people taking a break from shopping. There's a range of dishes to choose from, with Greek inspired hummus and tzaziki to chicken and feta fajitas. Whether it's a light bite or something a bit more substantial, you can sit at tables outside when the sun deigns to shine or inside where there's a light, Mediterranean feel.

SIMPLY GREEK
Bigg Market, Newcastle
0191 222 0035 **M** *Monument*

dabbawal

Zonzo

A relaxed, friendly and at times, boisterous atmosphere in this Greek restaurant and, as it's situated slap bang in the middle of one of Newcastle's drinking hot-spots, it's a great place for a party with a menu bursting with a mouth-watering selection of Greek goodies.

INDIAN

AKBAR'S
Unit 1 City Quadrant, Newcastle
0191 232 3234 **M** *Monument*
High quality Indian cuisine coupled with a vibrant atmosphere and fantastic service. Akbar's offers modern South Asian cooking in a modern and chic restaurant. Be sure to check out the fancy Versace carpets.

DABBAWAL
69-75 High Bridge, Newcastle
0191 232 5133 **M** *Monument*
Taking its name from the lunchbox delivery men, Dabbawal offers diners a new take on traditional Indian cooking. They offer a range of tapas-style dishes inspired by Indian street food, freshly prepared and made to order. One of the newest restaurants to hit Newcastle and they already have a loyal following.

KOH-I-NOOR
26 Cloth Market, Newcastle
0191 232 5379 **M** *Monument*
A traditional Indian in the middle of loads of boisterous pubs. Established back in 1982 it still pulls 'em in despite the uninviting facade. With late night opening times and happy hour special offers between 6-9pm, it's no wonder. The four course meal is particularly good value.

THE GOLDEN BENGAL
39 Groat Market, Newcastle
0191 232 0471 **M** *Central Station*
Tasty Indian restaurant right next to the Bigg Market, and with a late opening. Damn handy.

LATIF RESTAURANT
1a Clayton Street West, Newcastle
0191 230 3780 **M** *Central Station*
Just up from Central Station, The Latif is a large capacity Indian restaurant with plenty of relaxing seats. Good food at very reasonable prices means it has a loyal customer base.

RAJ TANDOORI
31 Pudding Chare, Newcastle
0191 232 1450 **M** *Central Station*
Cheap and decidedly cheerful restaurant featuring typical Indian fare with plenty of happy hours to be enjoyed.

RANI
2 Queen Street, Quayside, Newcastle
0191 231 2202 **M** *Central Station*
Great location near the river, great variety of dishes (you can even get a whole roasted leg of lamb!) and great atmosphere. Plus you can make reservations online so you're sure to get a table.

RASA
27 Queen Street, Newcastle
0191 232 7799 **M** *Central Station*
A real good quality restaurant, near the River Tyne, which specialises in South Indian cuisine. More than one critic has described the food as being nothing short of celestial and we're not arguing.

RUPALI
6 Bigg Market, Newcastle
0191 232 8629 **M** *Monument*
One of the oldest Indian restaurants in town and full of character with plenty of special offers. It bills itself as "Newcastle's most famous Indian restaurant" and this is due to its countless appearances in Viz comic. Their pride and joy is "Curry Hell"; a challenge to eat the world's hottest curry. If you do, you get it free and get a certificate. Worth a try? Maybe just stick to a good old korma...

SACHINS
Forth Banks, Newcastle
0191 261 9035 or 0191 232 4660
Ⓜ *Central Station*
Punjabi cuisine of the highest order at this fine restaurant which has been doing the biz for over 25 years now. They're renowned for their use of really fresh ingredients and subtle use of herbs and spices. Make sure that you don't miss this one. They've recently started a partnership with Fenwick's, so their dishes are now available on the shelves for you to cook at home. Handy.

SAFFRON
27 Sandhill, Quayside, Newcastle
0191 230 5786 Ⓜ *Central Station*
Contemporary Indian cuisine in this quirky restaurant which is at the heart of the hub-bub that is the Quayside. Huge range of dishes on offer and has an invariably bustling atmosphere. Great value and they do a buy one get one free offer on takeaway curries.

SIMLA
39 The Side, Newcastle
0191 232 1070 Ⓜ *Central Station*
Good food at reasonable prices. Attracts a lot of late-night revellers piling out of the pub which makes it sound for a party curry. Open late.

SPICE CUBE
The Gate, Newgate St., Newcastle
0191 222 1181 Ⓜ *Monument*
Taking Indian dining to a new dimension at The Gate, this trend-setting restaurant/café/bar offers mouth-watering, traditional and modern tandoori cuisine with imaginative variations, including a light and fresh lunch menu.

TANDOORI NIGHTS
17 Grey Street, Newcastle
0191 221 0312 Ⓜ *Monument*
Massive menu with all your favourites; balti dishes and thali too! The service is great and it's in a brill location, whether you're heading on to a bar, the theatre or the Quayside.

THALI
44 Dean St., Newcastle
0191 230 2244 **M** *Monument*
Indian restaurant where it's great to try little bits of everything from their Thali dishes. Has steadily built up a good reputation and has had the distinction of being included in the Cobra Good Curry Guide.

VUJON
29 Queen Street, Newcastle
0191 221 0601 **M** *Monument*
Superb original Indian cuisine set in a rich, opulent room with heavily draped windows and crisp linen tablecloths etc. Formal atmosphere and a bit pricey but if Indian food is your forte you should check it out as they offer a wide range of dishes from many Indian regions. Was recommended in the 2009 Michelin Guide.

ITALIAN

ASK
The Gate, Newgate St., Newcastle
0191 230 4530 **M** *Monument*
Fresh and contemporary Italian cuisine at The Gate. Delicious pasta and handmade pizzas are cooked in a traditional oven and open kitchen. Informal wooden tables and chunky leather chairs create a friendly and airy atmosphere, making it a great place to dine day or night.

AVANTI
52-54 Brentwood Avenue, Jesmond
0191 281 4240 **M** *Jesmond*
A family run business with a mouth-watering array of desserts (you've got to try their own take on the Eton Mess – the Heaton Mess), and a great happy hour offer from 12-2 or Monday-Thursday 5pm-7:30pm, Friday & Saturday 5:30-6:30pm and Sunday 5pm-9pm.

AZZURI
Forster Street, Quayside, Newcastle
0191 222 1110 **M** *Central Station*
The bar has a smart casual dress code so you can probably guess the prices, but if it's a special occasion and you're after a nice range of Italian cuisine, this might just be the place. To catch the same sort of atmosphere on a bit of a budget, try out their Credit Crunch lunch menu, 12-2pm Mon-Sat.

BABUCHO
26 The Side, bottom of Dean Street, Newcastle
0191 231 2840 **M** *Central Station*
This is a New York style Italian brasserie and bar with a menu full of fantastic home-style Italian dished, fused with some splendid local favourites. A bustling café during the day and a hip restaurant and lounge by night, this is well worth checking out.

BARKOLLO
22 Leazes Park Road, Newcastle
0191 232 5871 **M** *St. James*
This is a pretty new addition to the scene and is something of musical restaurant with regular gigs and loads of other interesting events. Food wise, they're spot on, too, with some authentic Italian cooking always going down very well. Great to pop in just for a drink, too, so do check it out.

BAR ROCCO TRATTORIA
22 Leazes Park Road, Newcastle
0191 232 5871 **M** *St. James'*
Previously La Toscana. A wayward punt away from St. James' Park this fab place is the real deal with the owner, Salvatore, and his family running this place for over 30 years, and despite the change of name they seem to be offering the same great experience. Superb menu and an atmosphere that is second to none keep diners coming back for more.

CAFFÉ VIVO
Live Theatre, 29 Broad Chare, Quayside, Newcastle
0191 232 1331 **M** *Manors*
Situated within the brilliant Live Theatre

complex this is a fabulous café by day and fabulous restaurant by night, capturing everything that is gorgeous, crazy and fun about Italy. No frills, no fuss, just very friendly service, a great buzz and superb food.

CAFFÉ Z
2 Goldspink Lane, Sandyford
0191 230 4981 **M** *Jesmond*
Slightly out of the city centre, this is a glorious little restaurant which has captured the imagination of the local - as well as national - press. The regional Italian dishes and deli-bar snacks are a constant delight as are their quality wines and cocktails. The nice laid back, unhurried air only adds to its attraction. Make a date.

CAFFE VIVO
29 Broad Chare
0191 232 1331 **M** *Manors*
This former warehouse is now a bright and airy Italian style restaurant and bar. Whether you're looking for a place with a friendly atmosphere or somewhere to sit and have a proper meal, this place is just the ticket.

DON VITO'S
86 Pilgrim Street, Newcastle
0191 230 0444 **M** *Monument*
Great that this lovely Italian is up and running

again as they do the kind of authentic cuisine that we love at very decent prices (pizzas around seven quid). If you're strapped for cash they do a three course meal (Monday-Saturday, 12pm-6pm) for £5.95 which is great value.

FRANKIE & BENNY'S
The Gate, Newgate St., Newcastle
0191 230 4077 **M** *Monument*
A fusion of New York City and Italian cuisine comes to The Gate. Aromas from the char-grilled burgers fill the air of this traditionally designed restaurant. Relax and watch experienced chefs create a delicious meal of your choice in the open kitchen.

THE GODFATHER
3 Market Street, Newcastle
0191 232 6171 **M** *Monument*
Near the Theatre Royal, The Godfather has an ok a la carte menu and a typical main course will probably set you back around seven or eight quid. The Godfather's not only authentic but semi-famous in Newcastle due to the celebs who've dined here with everyone from Gazza to Charlton Heston nipping in for a bite to eat.

GUSTO
Quayside, Newcastle
0191 260 2291 **M** *Central Station*
By trying to ensure all their ingredients are

Baltic

Simply Greek

supplied from traditional and sustainable sources Gusto offers up a tasty selection of dishes; some classics and some more original. With a terrace and a massive cocktail menu, they've covered all the bases.

THE ITALIAN GRILL
32 Pudding Chare, Newcastle
0191 230 1037 **M** *Central Station*
There is a wide selection of fine cuisine here and the menu is kept on the interesting side if you fancy a break from the more usual pizza/pasta dishes. It's also in a prime spot (overlooking the river) and the patio is the place to be when the sun shines. Plus they offer alfresco drinks before and after your meal, so dining can be a whole evening experience.

MAMMA MIA'S
46 Pudding Chare,
Bigg Market, Newcastle
0191 232 7193 **M** *Central Station*
You've seen the film, and the stage play, now experience the food...! This place has been up and running for 30 years now and punters are attracted by the filling food and cheap prices.

MARCO POLO
33 Dean Street, Newcastle
0191 232 5533 **M** *Monument*
This is one of the oldest and liveliest pizzerias in town and has been owned by the same Italian family since 1976. Ideal for celebrations and private functions.

MARIO'S
23 Pudding Chare, Newcastle
0191 261 9955 **M** *Central Station*
Italian known for its lively atmosphere, with happy hours running from 5.30pm-7pm with pizza/pasta coming in at around four quid.

NINO'S
The Gate, Newgate St, Newcastle
0191 261 5799 **M** *Monument*
Old school Italian at The Gate. This new restaurant, conveniently located on the first floor, offers a vibrant and funky dining experience. With a great menu at affordable prices Nino's offer tastes that take you to Italy.

PANI'S CAFÉ
61-65 Highbridge St., Newcastle
0191 232 4366 **M** *Monument*
Stylish cafe/bar run by an Italian family who are so hot on service it's scary. If you peer in and it looks full, don't be put off - there's another room at the back. Unusual sarnies and pasta dishes and fantastic cakes are a must during the day, while on an evening they offer a good range of traditional Italian dishes. A cracker. Plus they offer Italian classes on a Monday.

PARADISO
1 Market Lane, Newcastle
0191 221 1240 **M** *Monument*
Tucked away upstairs, this stylish, happening place is very popular and rightly so. An imaginative menu keeps customers more than happy, with dining also available al fresco style out on the balcony or in a private dining room for the more intimate occasions or celebrations. An ideal place to relax.

PINOCCHIO IL RISTORANTE
61 Westgate Rd., Newcastle
0191 232 0708 **M** *Central Station*
If your palate demands Italian this is above average and consequently can get pretty full. Their wine list also offers a huge range of different varieties which is always a bit of a boon.

PIZZA HUT
The Gate, Newgate St., Newcastle
0191 261 8261 **M** *Monument*
Great deals at this popular chain including the weekday lunchtime buffet – pizza only £4.99; pasta, salad only £5.99. Students get 20% discount off full price menu items – Sunday to Thursday (excluding buffet and meal deals). Mosey on down for their new happy hour offer

3-6pm with £4 for a pizza, a side and a drink.

PIZZERIA FRANCESCA
Manor House Road, Jesmond
0191 281 6586 M *West Jesmond*
Muted lighting and music in this rustic looking Italian which is always a veritable hub-bub due to its loyal customers who return again and again to pack the place out creating one of the best atmospheres around. You can't book in advance but there's a cosy bar area in which you can wait for a table to come free - which to us is part of the fun. The menu consists of the usual pizza, pasta and chicken dishes although they're straight out of the top drawer. Always an experience.

PORTOFINO
12a Mosley Street, Newcastle
0191 261 5512 M *Monument*
Lovely restaurant with high ceilings that add to the ambience. They bring you delightful Italian dishes, whether it's seafood, steaks, pasta or pizza.

PRIMA
40-46 The Side, Quayside, Newcastle
0191 233 1011 M *Central Station*
Very popular Italian, which is stone clad of wall but warm of heart. They mainly serve up pizzas (which you can watch being made!) but there are plenty of pasta dishes, too.

PUCCINI
29 Pudding Chare, Newcastle
0191 232 1961 M *Central Station*
This family-run restaurant has long been a feature on the Newcastle scene and you're guaranteed a warm welcome and friendly service. Always competitively priced this is unpretentious and filling Italian food.

ROBERTO LA DOLCE VITA
59 Westgate Road, Newcastle
0191 232 6178 M *Central Station*
Good, classic Italian food and a range of meat dishes as well. And if you're having difficulty choosing you can always opt for the half pizza/half pasta option.

ROSCO'S
Tyne House, Dean Street, Newcastle
0191 231 2840 M *Central Station*
In a prominent location near the Quayside, you can enjoy Rosco's during the day as a café-bar, or during the night where their extensive cocktail menu comes alight. As well as gorgeous pizzas and pasta dishes they also serve a wider range of dishes including Tuscan lamb stew and veal Milanese.

RUMPOLI'S ITALIAN KITCHEN
17 Sandhill, Quayside, Newcastle
0191 232 6969 M *Central Station*
A family run Italian with an ever changing specials board and a huge choice on the menu.

SABATINI
25 King St., Newcastle
0191 261 4415/ 0191 261 6830
M *Central Station*
Another of the Quayside's bustling restaurants. A wide ranging menu (more than one type of garlic bread on offer - gosh!) - plenty of chicken, fish, veal and beef dishes (with an array of sauces) as well as a vegetarian menu.

SCALINI'S
61 Osborne Road, Jesmond
0191 240 7777 M *Jesmond*
Of course a great range of pizza and pasta, but also steaks, seafood and starters. And if there is a bit of sunshine there's a heated patio area for that genuine Mediterranean experience.

STRADA
Old Eldon Square, Newcastle
0191 261 6070 M *Monument*
Split over two floor with stunning views overlooking the war memorial at Old Eldon Square. Strada is a very stylish contemporary

Jack Sprats Vegan & Vegetarian Restaurant

Barn Asia

Italian serving up great quality dishes that are freshly prepared and don't cost a fortune. A goodie and very friendly, too.

TICINOS
39a Bigg Market, Newcastle
0191 233 0088 **M** *Central Station*
Cheap and very cheerful, authentic Italian food at this restaurant which is situated in the heart of Newcastle's boisterous Bigg Market. Great for a party night out. Oh, and their Sunday dinners (English) are good, too.

UNO'S TRATTORIA
18 Sandhill, Quayside, Newcastle
0191 261 5264 **M** *Central Station*
The reputation of its Italian food regularly sees Uno's packed out and you'll often have to wait in the bar area for a table even if you've booked, although it's always well worth it as the atmosphere here is second to none - every night's a party! What makes it such an attraction is that while the food is fab their prices are within the reaches of most pockets.

ZIZZI
42-50 Grey Street, Newcastle
0191 261 8360 **M** *Monument*
Like most Italians, Zizzi serve up an array of pizza and pasta dishes, but unlike most Italians, these particular dishes are their own speciality (and just about the only main

courses they provide). Mouth-wateringly good and the open plan split level design creates a buzzy atmosphere.

MEXICAN / SPANISH / LATIN AMERICAN

EL COTO
21 Leazes Park Rd., Newcastle
0191 261 0555 **M** *St. James*
A fantastic tapas restaurant, which has a cool, Spanish feel and a lovely secluded little courtyard for al fresco dining. One of the best of its type.

EL TORERO
Milburn House, The Side, Newcastle
0191 233 1122 **M** *Central Station*
Clock the decidedly un-PC bull-fighting posters on the walls and you'll almost immediately recognise this establishment as a Spanish restaurant, serving up tapas and paellas by the score. OK.

LA TASCA
106 The Quayside, Newcastle
42-50 Grey Street, Newcastle
0191 230 4006/ 0191 260 3533
M *Central Station*
Large tapas restaurant (part of a national chain) with a typically Spanish feel - orange washed walls, picture tiles, huge windows etc.

and good atmosphere. Tapas are reasonable in price but not particularly inspiring.

SALSA
89 Westgate Rd., Newcastle
0191 221 1022 M *Central Station*
"Enticing flavours and chilled out style" is the promise of this little gem and it certainly delivers. Weathered timbers, beaten-up tables, mismatched chairs, comfy sofas and smooth tunes all combine nicely for some social grazing. Superb tapas, sandwiches etc and don't miss their English Big Breakfast on Sunday afternoon. Still refered to as "a little place I know" and still got its groove.

PERSIAN

REZA
87 Westgate Road, Newcastle,
0191 221 2500 M *Central Station*
Bringing a Persian flavour to Westgate road. Stuffed vine leaves, stews and skewers of meats; there's a great choice of some delicious dishes.

PORTUGUESE

NANDO'S
Eldon Square, Newcastle
The Gate, Newgate St., Newcastle
0191 233 1535 / 0191 261 0131
M *Monument*
All chicken is marinated in the famous Portuguese Peri Peri sauce for a full 24 hours before being flame-grilled to perfection at this relaxing restaurant which is a great addition to The Gate's line-up of quality eateries. And they do a mean veggie burger too. Yum.

ORIENTAL

BANGKOK CAFÉ
Low Friar Street, Newcastle
0191 260 2323 M *Central Station*
Specialising in Thai food, here they provide us with traditional and trendy food with an atmosphere to match. All their food is cooked to get the authentic Thai flavours, with various rice, soup and noodle dishes all being offered at a pretty reasonable price.

BARN ASIA
Waterloo Square,
St James Boulevard, Newcastle
0191 221 1000 M *Central Station*
Definitely one of the best places to eat around. Combining the best in Vietnamese, Cambodian and Thai cuisine - served up tapas style - in one of the coolest looking joints around, this is a must-visit.

FUJIYAMA
35-39 Bath Lane, Newcastle
0191 233 0189 M *St. James*
This teppan-yaki restaurant is resplendent in Japanese-style decor and consists of long tables suitable for big parties with exciting culinary shows from the chef. There is a fantastic range of steak and chicken dishes, as well as raw fish including red tuna, cuttle fish and octopus.

HANAHANA
45 Bath Lane, Newcastle
0191 222 0282 M *St. James*
There's very much a party atmosphere generated at Hanahana. There is a variety of set lunches, and especially recommended is the Hanahana special, which is a selection of meats and seafood hand-picked by their head chef.

HEI HEI
46 Dean St., Newcastle
0191 222 1882 M *Central Station*
Small but perfectly formed Chinese restaurant which is modern looking and with a nice bubbly atmosphere. Great menu of the usuals as well as more authentic Chinese cuisine, a fabulous happy hour and top-notch staff. What's not to love?

KING NEPTUNE
34-36 Stowell Street, Newcastle
0191 261 6657 **M** *St. James*
A sumptuous Chinese restaurant that has received numerous awards from Egon Ronay's Guide. Works well for parties.

KUBLAI KHAN
23-29 Proctor House, The Side,
Quayside, Newcastle
0191 221 2203 **M** *Central Station*
This little gem has both a Chinese and a Mongolian buffet. But the twist is that for the Mongolian buffet you choose your ingredients, mix up your own sauce and then hand it in to the kitchen for them to cook it up for you. Perfect for those who want a bit of individuality.

LAU'S 202 BUFFET HOUSE
92-98 Newgate Street, Newcastle
0844 980 2020 **M** *Central Station*
Recently opened this is a buffet which offers not just a wide range of choice but an exquisite experience to go with it. Their centre piece is "the island"; a sushi bar with chefs on-site to prepare your food in front of you. Swish!

LAU'S BUFFET KING
44-50 Stowell St., Newcastle
0191 231 4466 **M** *St. James*
They have over 90 varieties of different dishes daily in their popular Chinese buffet, eat all you can. Comfortable, modern surroundings and seating for over 300. Good stuff if you're a fan of this style of restaurant. Plus there's a happy hour from 4.30pm-7pm (as long as you've paid by 7 on the dot.)

LITTLE ASIA
16 Stowell Street, Newcastle
0191 261 7960 **M** *St. James*
Chinese restaurant with a good reputation and wide variety of dishes.

LITTLE SAIGON
6 Bigg Market, Newcastle
0191 233 0766 **M** *Central Station*
This is a right little cracker. Nicely done out (check out the hand-painted murals) and the food – asparagus & crabmeat soup, caramel pork, Saigon chicken claypot rice etc – is flavoursome to its core.

LOVE'S
32 Mosley Street, Newcastle
0191 233 2828 **M** *Central Station*
Lovely new Thai restaurant this isn't too big, but is very tasteful of décor and tastier of menu. They do everything from delicious soups to salads (you can't beat Thai salads) to curries and more. And it's not expensive either with mains coming in at around £8-£10. Give this one a go.

THE MANDARIN
14-18 Stowell Street, Newcastle
0191 261 7960 **M** *St. James*
With a range of banquet meals on offer, there'll be something to suit most groups in want of a pleasing Chinese meal. And there's a nice wide range of wines to match.

MANGOS
43 Stowell Street, Newcastle
0191 232 6522 **M** *St. James*
A more modern take on the usual kind of establishments you'll find in Newcastle's Chinatown area. Really good quality food and they have the widest range of dim sum in town. Thumbs aloft!

NUDO
54-56 Low Friar Street
0191 233 1133 **M** *Central Station*
If you're after comfort food then you'll not go far wrong at this lovely noodle house. All the food is freshly prepared and just the job. We like to start with a few sides, and some sushi, and we suggest that you do too.

THE WATERSIDE PALACE
Forth Banks, Quayside, Newcastle
0191 232 6090 M *Central Station*
Both Peking and Cantonese style dishes are available at this striking restaurant. And there's some stuff for the veggies too.

WAGAMAMA
6 Eldon Square, Newcastle
0191 233 0663 M *Monument*
A welcome addition to Newcastle, Wagamama slots in nicely to Old Eldon Square where a bewildering, yet truly scrumptious, array of meals await you. It's all communal and it's all good.

POLISH

GOSPODA
Upper Level, Princess Sq., Newcastle
0191 261 0197 M *Monument*
This little haven has a wonderfully intimate vibe and serves up a fabulous selection of traditional Polish specialities. Great drinks menu with 11 different types of vodka available.

SEAFOOD

BIG MUSSEL
15 The Side, Quayside, Newcastle
0191 232 1057 M *Central Station*
As the name suggests they're very big on mussels and seafood in general at this restaurant, which is famed for its great atmosphere and delicious Belgian food. If you're not a seafood fan, don't fret, they have a corking range of meat dishes and deserts too. They also have live bands from 7pm every night (apart from Saturdays) to give you an all round dining experience.

FISHERMAN'S LODGE
Jesmond Dene 0844 809 0992
Beautifully situated in the woodland of Jesmond Dene and once the town residence of Lord Armstrong this is an upmarket eatery

with good food (and also worth popping in for afternoon tea).

TURKISH

RED MEZZE
34-36 Leazes Park Road, Newcastle
0191 261 9646 M *St. James*
With traditional Turkish dishes and techniques this could be perfect if you fancy venturing out of the same old food routine. Quite a decent veggie range and "mezze" ("tasty snack") are perfect for sharing.

SEVEN HILLS
Sandhill, Quayside, Newcastle
0191 232 2122 M *Central Station*
Delectable restaurant serving up great Turkish cuisine. Everything on the menu is freshly made and prepared in the traditional manner. A clay dome oven has been specially made for the restaurant and wood-fired bread baking adds immeasurably to the wonderful assault on the senses.

UNITED STATES

STATESIDE DINER
37 Pink Lane, Newcastle
0191 261 7370 M *Central Station*
This smart little diner is a great place to grab a burger, some ribs, a juicy steak - or whatever - and wash it all down with a frothy milkshake. It's done out in authentic US style (complete with 50s jukebox) and has the added attraction of being fully licensed.

T.G.I FRIDAY'S
The Gate, Newcastle
0191 261 8676 M *Monument*
Grills, seafood, burgers and more. This chain has a great range of food and an upbeat atmosphere.

CAFES

BALTIC
Gateshead Quays
0191 440 4948 **M** *Manors/Gateshead*
BALTIC's (the huge contemporary art gallery) café/bar serves up a lovely array of hot and cold snacks, soft and alcoholic drinks plus light bites and sweet treats. A nice piece of cake and a cup of tea somehow makes the vaguer end of conceptualism much easier to digest.

BLAKE'S COFFEE HOUSE
53 Grey St., Newcastle
0191 261 5463 **M** *Monument*
They don't half pack 'em in here. The tables are rammed together making for a very lively atmosphere. Hot and cold dishes are available (chilli, lasagne etc.) as well as a huge variety of sandwiches with extravagant fillings. A good 'un.

BUTTERFLY CABINET
178 Heaton Road, Newcastle
0191 265 9920 **M** *Chillingham Road*
One of the best little joints in Heaton serving up very filling soups, door-stopper sandwiches, hearty breakfasts (from fry-ups, to eggs Benedict to apple and cinnamon pancakes) and a load of cultural chatter.

COFFEE BEANS CAFÉ
3 Old Eldon Square, Newcastle
0191 222 0213 **M** *Monument*
Situated in the hustle and bustle of Old Eldon Square, take a break with a coffee and watch the world go by.

GALLERY CAFÉ
67 Westgate Road, Newcastle
0191 261 5999 **M** *Central Station*
In the heart of Newcastle Arts Centre the café offers a free fairtrade filter coffee or tea with every purchase in details art shop. Run by Arts Centre staff in their own creative

way, you can sample homemade treats, from quiches and cakes to panini, spuds, salads and soups. On warm days you can chill in their sunny courtyard.

HEATON PERK
103-105 Heaton Park Road, Newcastle
0191 276 2000
Where do you start with a café that's got everything? Superb range of coffees, paninis, toasties, breakfasts, cakes and more. Super friendly staff, homely décor and they've even got plenty of board games if you fancy a blast of Buckaroo. Gold medal stuff.

HIPPO HOUSE
27 Collingwood St., Newcastle
0191 222 1007 **M** *Central Station*
Open from 8am-3pm, Monday-Friday, this super little café serves their sandwiches with 'proper' bread (oh yes), offer up generous portions, and their coffee is some of the best around. Hooray.

LA BOCA
6 Upper Princess Square, Newcastle
M *Monument*
This lovely little café (just up from the central library) hasn't been long opened but is a real winner if you're after a sandwich, pasta dish, a delectable pudding or a coffee (or all of the above).

LA FIESTA
150 Heaton Park Road, Heaton,
0191 265 5558
Quite a recent addition to Newcastle's café scene, but this little deli is a real hit. Whether it's a delicious slice of cake, a hot burrito or a healthy portion of paella, you can find a variety of scrummy dishes in this cosy place.

MARK TONEY'S
Percy Street, Newcastle
Grainger Street, Newcastle
Grainger Arcade, Newcastle

0191 232 1021 **M** *Monument*
The best bit about these cafes is of course the ice cream! Mark Toney's is first and foremost an ice cream maker and you can taste it. But they also do some yummy cakes, sandwiches and the like.

SAPORI CAFÉ
21-25 Starbeck Avenue, Sandyford
0191 230 3190
This friendly little Italian café is one of Sandyford's hidden gems. Offering an array of mouth-watering pastas, Sapori offers the comfort of a home-cooked lunch in a relaxed atmosphere.

THE SETTLE DOWN CAFE
61-62 Thornton Street
0191 222 0187 **M** *Central Station*
The Settle Down Cafe is a small independent cafe in the heart of Newcastle, serving toasted ciabatta sandwiches, soups, salads, hot and cold savouries, cute homemade cakes and some of the best coffee around. The vibe is very relaxed and very cool with a mix of old chairs, leather sofas in a snug back-room, and comfy armchairs in the window.

TEA SUTRA TEAHOUSE
2 Leazes Park Road
0191 447 3731 **M** *Haymarket*
A chilled-out world of exotic teas, cakes, snacks, wraps, chai of the day and multiple lounging opportunities. A brilliant place to while away some hours in relaxed conversation. Complementary therapies are also available in the associated therapy rooms. You don't get that in Greggs.

THE URBAN COFFEE HOUSE
6 Brentwood Avenue,
M *West Jesmond*   *0191 281 9000*
In the heart of Jesmond, this locally owned coffee house offers a warm and friendly atmosphere to relax with friends.

TYNESIDE COFFEE ROOMS
10 Pilgrim St., Newcastle
0191 227 5520 **M** *Monument*
Situated within the Tyneside Cinema complex, the Tyneside Coffee Rooms has one of the most relaxing vibes around. It's been on the second floor of the cinema for 70 years now and its mix of comfort food and genuinely warm-hearted service has made it a favourite of Newcastle café life for many a year and for all ages. You don't have to be seeing a film to pay it a visit either.

URBAN CAFÉ
Dance City, Temple Street, Newcastle
0191 269 5590 **M** *Central Station*
Located inside the Dance City building this is a lovely café which serves up an enticing menu of sandwiches, salads and soups as well as breakfast, desserts and a range of hot and cold drinks (including smoothies). Everything is made from fresh ingredients, too.

TEES VALLEY

EUROPEAN / MODERN

THE BRASSERIE
19 High St. Yarm *01642 890 020*
The Brasserie prides itself on its traditional and its modern dishes. It cooks whatever is in season, and if you crave something out of season, you'll just have to wait, impatient Annie! Its wine list boasts an impressive 40 wines, so you'll soon forget about the out-of-season vegetables you craved. Plus, you can make your troubles melt away with music on a Monday, as anything that is considered "easy listening" is played live for all to hear. What a treat for the senses.

CAFFÉTESSEN AT ARC
ARC, Dovecot Street,
Stockton on Tees 01642 525195
Whether you pop in for breakfast or a light lunch, something more substantial or a pre-

show meal, Caffétessen at ARC is the perfect venue. Gold & Brown is a company founded on ethical business practices and as a result they are committed to Fairtrade, protecting the environment, recycling and sustainability which is why all their fresh supplies come from local independent butchers, bakers and fruit & vegetable suppliers. A goodie.

CENTRAL PARK
337 Linthorpe Rd., M'bro 01642 820 586
Having opened Central Cafe next door, it seems the Central Park empire is growing and growing. It can get very busy in here around dinner time and in the evening, so be prepared to wait at the bar until a table becomes available. The food is reasonably cheap and the service is quick, and it can provide for many a palette, from pasta to parmos.

EVERLY'S
104b High St., Yarm 01642 788 558
Everly's is a newish Continental Café open from 10am right through until 12 at night and its evening menu starts from 6pm serving a wide range of continental dishes all made with local fresh ingredients. It also does Sunday lunches.

CIARA'S
58 HighSt, Yarm 01642 788944
Ciara's is quality restaurant-ified. The steak melts in your mouth quicker than you can realise it's probably the best steak you've tasted. It specialises in chicken and fish of the a la carte variety. The prices are quite steep in comparison to other places, but you get what you pay for. They do offer a tea-time special, which does not hit the funds as hard, and you still get all of that a la carte goodness.

EUROPA
10 Borough Rd., M'bro 01642 247 925
This is small restaurant where meat dishes are its speciality... but what it does, it does well! It's open until 4am, so for those who can still walk and have still got more than taxi fare in their pocket, this is the place to head. Rumour has it that Europa was the first restaurant to coin the "parmo". For that, we must salute this quaint checked-table cloth eaterie.

FRANKIE AND BENNY'S
Teesside Leisure Park, Thornaby, Stockton-on-Tees, 01642 673 972
Frankie and Benny are all about 1950s Italian/American chic. It serves mainly pizza and pasta in a place that looks like the set from "Guys and Dolls" and that's not a bad thing. It can get quite busy in here though, so if you wanted some alone time with your guy or doll, you'll probably have to share it with a stranger behind you.

THE KANSAS BAR AND GRILL
Teesside Leisure Park, Thornaby, Stockton-on-Tees 01642 607 000
The Kansas is an American themed restaurant, where racks of ribs, southern fried chicken and any meat that can be grilled is bound to be on the menu. It gets good reviews because of its large portions and quick service. The interior is quite 1940s - a bit Pearl Harbour (the film, not the actual attack), which will invite questions from the kids, but just fill their mouths with more meat and the questions should cease.

GENGIS RESTAURANT
Thistle Hotel, Fry St., M'bro 01642 232 000
Gengis is a Bistro restaurant. It always has a welcoming atmosphere, as expected with a hotel like the Thistle, and is the perfect occasion for you to say, "Hey baby, put on your gladrags. I'm taking you out somewhere fancy."

KELZ
427 Linthorpe Rd., M'bro 01642 825 644
Kelz is the best of British: fish and chips, and Yorkshire puds etc. However, they always do so with a flare and with amazing prices on the

Central Park

East Ocean

courses. It's a little set back from the buzz of town, so you won't usually have to worry about booking tables. All there is to worry about is which county will inspire your cuisine. They do special offers of two meals for £12 and children under 10 eat free.

LEWIS'S
146 Linthorpe Rd., M'bro
01642 243 319
The setting alone is good enough to eat in this place. It's full of antiques, art work and exposed brick work. Plus, it is very humble, which always makes something more inviting. Its continental menu has an undeniable air of the Italian as it has many a pizza/pasta to serve. However, it deals with chicken, steaks and the vegetarian with equal flare, so you'll be spoilt for choice.

MCCOY'S AT TONTINE
The Cleveland, Tontine,
Staddle Bridge
01609 882671
I'm not going to mince my words; you will have to book a table before coming here. It's the perfect setting for a romantic evening. There's no chance for elbow-banging or manoeuvring yourself around a family to get to the toilets. This is a place where understated elegance is as important as the food. It IS expensive, but when have you known of a place with a chandelier that isn't? The food is more like

an elegant soiree in your mouth rather than a party, but that's McCoy's bistro to a T.

MCQUAYS OF YARM
85 High St., Yarm   01642 785 808
The quality speaks for itself at McQuays and the setting compliments this with its simple decor and uncomplicated arrangement. It offers everything from homemade scones in the morn, to an extensive a la carte menu after 6pm. It's not too expensive in comparison to other places, but its atmosphere is priceless.

LA PHARMACIE
80 Corporation Rd., M'bro
01642 222 250
Having not long opened La Pharmacie has become a favourite already. With its chic décor, you could almost be fooled into thinking you're visiting a Parisian brasserie and the delicious food served is a combination of British and French classics. And don't forget about the Medicine bar: a great venue in the cellar of La Pharamcie.

TGI FRIDAYS
Teesside Retail Park, M'bro Road
01642 613135
Ok, so the staff appear so enthusiastic you swear they have been drinking artificial colouring in the cloakroom, but at least you know what you're getting with TGI Fridays. It was established in New York in 1965, hence the blatant Americana theme.

Prego

Their attention to detail continues from the walls and into the food. They fry, grill and smother every meat going, and do so with many delicious side orders. One thing that must be said is that their Jack Daniels sauce is to die/dip for!

JAPANESE

LIN PALACE TEPPANYAKI AND SUSHI
186 Linthorpe Road, M'bro
01642 213 551
This is one of the few authentic Japanese restaurants in the area. It turns up the heat on excitement with its TeppanYaki hot plate, and its interior is authentically decked with lanterns and simplistic furniture...so say konnichiwa to my new favourite restaurant!

ETSUKO
2a Marton Rd, Middlesbrough,
01642 225888
Etsuko is a great way to experience the taste of Japan if you're a novice. The quality of the food is excellent and the prices are too. They offer a fantastic lunch menu Mondays-Fridays up until 4pm where you can get a soup and a main dish for £2.99!

CHINESE

BANANA LEAF
124-130 Linthorpe Rd., 01642 247 100
Banana Leaf is a Chinese buffet restaurant with

prices from £5.90-£6.30 for various menus. It can get very hectic and busy, so you could say it's the authentic atmosphere of China.

CHINA BUFFET KING
477 Linthorpe Rd., M'bro
01642 820 808
This is an all-you-can-eat buffet, hence why it believes itself to be the king. It's always very busy because Teessiders are always hungry. There should be a warning taped to the door that clothing, especially around the waistband area, may no longer fit once you have finished your meal. It has a wide selection of products, so you find yourself spoilt for choice.

ORIENTAL PEARL

96 NEWPORT ROAD
01642 220 292
Recently took over and renamed (previously called the Dragon's Pearl) the Oriental Pearl is a high class restaurant serving quality Chinese food - the owner has recently returned from London to his home town to run the restaurant.

EAST OCEAN CANTONESE RESTAURANT
34-36 Borough Road, M'bro
01642 218 655
The East Ocean's forte is traditional Cantonese seafood. I've yet to read a bad word about it, and

that's the way it's going to stay, especially as I have a lot of love for ocean cuisine.

GOOD LUCK CHINESE RESTAURANT
64 Yarm Lane, Stockton 01642 606695
How could you NOT want to go somewhere named "Good Luck"? It serves Hong Kong-inspired dishes and is Stockton's top choice of Chinese restaurant.

MANDERIN
236 Linthorpe Rd., M'bro
01642 222 191
Mandarin is a new Chinese restaurant with a modern feel yet still retaining Chinese elements. The restaurant also does a takeaway menu as well.

SOHO
156 Northgate, Darlington
01325 486 896
This is Darlington's premier Chinese buffet restaurant. It follows the same formula as most other buffet restaurants, but it would be able to cope with larger parties. Open 7 days a week.

INDIAN

AKBARS
192-194 Linthorpe Road, M'bro
01642 244566
Opening in 2009, this is the latest in the chain of Akbars. Each of the restaurants has a different theme but the food is consistently good throughout the chain. Be sure to try the naan breads, huge and delicious and well worth the money.

BALTI RAJ
294-296 Linthorpe Road, M'bro
01642 232 357
This is the town's first contemporary Indian restaurant and it is right on Middlesbrough's main road. About time.

JAMAL'S
92 Corporation Rd, M'bro 01642 645255
Jamal's is Middlesbrough's worst kept secret. It's tucked away in the corner of Corporation Road, yet it still manages to be packed to the rafters at weekends. It makes some of THE best curries in Teesside and everything is cooked to order. This can mean that you will have to wait a while before you get stuck into your grub, but you can always ply yourself with some of Jamal's delicious garlic naan bread to silence the stomach grumbles.

KHAN TANDOORI
42 Borough Rd., 417 Linthorpe Rd,
349 Linthorpe, M'bro 01642 813 559
Khan's is cranking up the life span, as it has been open since 1976. It offers great deals on two and three course meals, and it has a fantastic buffet menu. It has everything a foodie could want under one roof, and it does takeaway. Ding dong!

MASSALA
118 Borough Rd., M'bro 01642 250 145
Massala is Middlesbrough's most loved Indian restaurant. Its trusted reputation means that any of its more outlandish dishes are always as well received as the traditional dishes it has perfected so well.

ITALIAN

AL FORNO
2 Southfield Road, M'bro 01642 242 191
Al Forno is the fresh meat of Italian restaurants for the Teesside area. The restaurant promises to deliver flavours from Old Italy in a contemporary setting, so if you like juxtapositions, cop a load of Al. Happy hour is 12pm-6.30pm with 2 courses from £7.95. Plus students get 20% off orders on a la carte menu.

ELIANO'S
20-22 Fairbridge Street, M'bro
01642 868 566

Eliano's is Italian food at its best. It's tucked away down a side street, just like the ones which you struggle to find in Italy. The offers are plentiful at Eliano's too, two course for £6.95 between 12-2 and two courses for £8.95 between 5.30-6.30 Wednesdays-Saturdays, and you can get a three course dinner Wednesdays and Thursday for £14.95...and that includes a free glass of wine! Hey Presto!

FELLINI'S
325 Linthorpe Rd., M'bro   01642 814597
Fellini's has enjoyed success since it opened a few years ago, but I can't help but feel that it struggles in Central Park's limelight. The tables are very close together, even on a quiet evening, and this can make for a difficult job for the waiters. The Italian food is very tasty, but Fellini's is best visited when you have plenty of time and patience.

JOE RIGATONIS
212-216 Linthorpe Rd., M'bro
01642 244 777
Joe Riga's is quickly becoming a north-east chain of Italian restaurants. It has always been renowned for its happy hour pizza and pasta promotions, and its warm and inviting atmosphere. The prices are very reasonable, so this also attracts a lot of attention. A day will hardly go by when Joe Rigatoni's isn't filled with happy customers.

SANTORO
56 High Street, Yarm, 01642 781305
Santoro has been giving Yarm a taste of Italy with the help of father and sons, Vince, Ricci, Ross and Gianni. They're extremely welcoming and I for one love a healthy family business, so why not sample some of their family values. After all, they are open Monday-Saturday for lunch and dinner.

SASSARI
193-195 Linthorpe Rd., M'bro
01642 218 600

Sassari was Middlesbrough's first modern Italian restaurant when it opened over five years ago, and it's breezy lunchtime menu and cool atmosphere have prolonged its reign. The restaurant is guided into the evening with its soft lighting and charming waiters and waitresses. It is not pretentious in any way, shape or form, so you can always feel comfortable to dine.

THE TAVISTOCK
Marton Road, M'bro,   01642 817 638
The Tavistock is a recent renovation of an old hotel. It serves pizza and pasta on a happy hour Monday-Saturdays from 12noon-2.30pm and Monday to Sunday 5pm-6.45pm. The menu offers a great range of seafood, chicken and vegetarian dishes and is tavi-stocked with great desserts.

CAFES

CAFE PREGO
Onelife Building, Linthorpe Rd, M'bro,
01642 228744
Why not begin your cafe tour of Middlesbrough here? It is at the top end of Linthorpe Road, so you can grab a mocha and chill in its burgundy splendour and then head down towards the busy bustle of 'Boro.

CAFE PRONTO
65 Albert Rd. M'bro, 01642 230077
Cafe Pronto encourages locals to write while they slurp on their herbal tea. It has various cork boards dotted around so you can pin up any illustrations or poetry that you may feel compelled to create. A degree of balance is necessary because this place is a huge fan of barstools, but as long as you don't go there drunk, you'll be right as rain...but if you did go in drunk, just imagine the poetry!

THE OLDE YOUNG TEA HOUSE
84 Grange Road, M'bro
A haven for tea lovers everywhere, this newly

McQuays

Frontline

opened tea house wants to be something a little different than your average café. It was inspired by the fashionable tea houses of London and is striving to bring back high tea. Offering an array of over 60 world teas they have plenty for you to choose from. There's also a great selection of little cakes and sweet treats, including cupcakes from the fabulous Mama Dot's Bakery.

OODLES
136 Linthorpe Rd., M'bro
01642 243 809
Oodles is a New York-style noodle bar and whether you choose to eat in or take out, it's a prime eatery for the dinner hours of any young professional. Just make sure you don't spill any of the sauce on the cream walls.

UPPERCRUST
2a Dunkerque Mall, Hill Street Shopping Centre, M'bro 01642 211 538
Uppercrust is a legendary cafe where the question, "Can I have eggs on a raft?" is still probably used. It's your no frills cafe; you get a tray, you pick what you want, it gets placed on said tray and you try to grab a seat under one of the ceiling fans. I'll still be going to this place until I can no longer walk up its stairs, and even then, I might fund a stair-lift installation.

EUROPEAN / MODERN

THE BARNES TOBY CARVERY
Durham Road 0191 528 5644
M *University*
A popular carvery serving traditional English food at reasonable prices. Meat eaters swear by it, with their roasts coming up trumps. There's also a function room available for hire for any occasion.

TOBY CARVERY
Front Street, Cleadon 0191 536 4198
Traditional British meals including your good old bangers and mash with a twist. Great for families and for those of you who want nothing too fancy, just big helpings of fish and chips, steaks, scampi, chicken etc. Nice carvery.

D'ACQUA
Basement / 26-28 John Street
0191 565 1988 **M** *Sunderland*
This fantastic restaurant, venture of local lad James Shadworth, is a modern contemporary restaurant in the heart of sunderland. D'acqua prides itself on using locally sourced quality produce to create an eclectic mix of Italian, French and English cuisine. Don't pass up the chance to sample their signature meatballs dish.

ROSEDENE
Queen Alexandra Road 0191 528 4313
Excellent food in attractive surroundings, which attracts a mixed clientele. They also have a function room to cater for occasions such as weddings or christenings. They also do daily specials and Sunday lunches if you don't feel like cooking.

RUMBLING TUMS
154 Chester Road   0191 565 5247
Nice little café perfect for a quick bite, they sell sandwiches and all the usual wares, they also offer a catering service for buffets. A good place to visit! It's one of the best breakfasts in town, you get plenty for your money and they're a snip at £4.20.

SIGNATURES
34 West Sunniside
0191 567 4041 **M** *Sunderland*
A new addition to Sunderland, this restaurant and café bar specialises in fine dining. They offer a mouth-watering array of dishes like fillet of beef with king prawns in lime and mango sauce, that are guaranteed to impress.

THROWING STONES
National Glass Centre, Liberty Way
0191 5653939 **M** *St. Peter's*
Sited in the stunning steel and glass architecture of the National Glass Museum at the mouth of the river Wear, this is a fab restaurant with a European feel, and has to be recommended for the view alone. The traditional food has a contemporary twist and it is the ideal place for a full-blown meal or just a cappuccino. Open Monday-Sunday during 10am-4.30pm.

ITALIAN

AMIRO'S
55 New Road
0191 419 5161
Formerly the George pub, this Italian offers a range of classic dishes from pizzas and pastas to a la carte, all at reasonable prices. They also have seating outside so you can enjoy drinks in the sunshine if the weather's nice.

AMORE
11 Tavistock Place 0191 565 0077
M *Sunderland*
This stylish award-winning restaurant is a delight. The leather couches and décor give a NY loft style vibe. Amore specialise in Italian fusion cuisine and is run by excellent hosts. Happy hours run between 5pm-6pm.

ANGELOS
48 West Sunniside 0191 565 4888
M *Sunderland*
The younger sibling of Luciano's, this is a very smart restaurant and very popular. Their happy hour menu (12pm-2pm and 5pm-6.30pm) is grand, with meat dishes always hitting the spot. The canny wine list doesn't go amiss either. Mark it down as a goodie!

DUE'S TRATTORIA
3rd Floor, Marine Activities Centre, North Dock, 0191 510 0600
M *St. Peter's*
Great views over the harbour marina, this restaurant is from the same people behind Newcastle's Uno's Trattoria and consequently is something of a winner. They provide top-notch Italian cuisine with a laid-back, friendly service. Happy hours for pizza/pasta run from 12pm-2.30pm and 5.30pm-7pm.

FRANKIE & BENNY'S
2 Lambton St. Sunderland 0191 514 7369 **M** *Sunderland*
Everything you'd expect from the increasingly popular restaurant chain: a large, reasonably priced menu, friendly service and – of course – a selection of classic Italian-American warblers in the background.

GUSTO VERO
18a John Street 0191 567 0000
'Gusto Vero' is Italian for 'Real Taste' and that's exactly what you'll find here. They offer a great range of pizzas and pastas in a nice contemporary setting.

LA TOSCANINA
25 Derwent Street
0191 564 0246 Ⓜ *Park Lane*
A place with a good and growing reputation. A family restaurant with a nice soupy warm atmosphere and great staff. Their a la carte menu is well worth your attention and there's the usual array of happy hours (which is 12pm - 1.45pm or before 7.45pm) for all you pizza/pasta junkies. Tell them it's your birthday and you might even see the tambourine come out...

LUCIANO RISTORANTE
278 High St. West
0191 564 0200 Ⓜ *Sunderland*
An Italian retreat with a wide and varied menu, from the usual Italian staples to Gamberoni Alla' Luciano (king prawns pan-friend in olive oil with smoked salmon, spring onions, basil, brandy and cream with a hint of fresh orange juice) The New Zealand green tipped mussels and pan-fried Monkfish are lovely too. Happy hour is 5.30-7pm during the week and 5.30-6.30pm on Saturday.

MARCELLOS
4-5 Albion Place
0191 567 1032 Ⓜ *Park Lane*
Right in the heart of town, traditional and continental Italian cooking can be found in this small, cosy restaurant. There's a great roof top terrace which opens in summer, allowing you to dine outside or just have a few drinks al fresco. Or if you're feeling lazy you can even get it delivered with their new "Marcellos express" service which launched in March this year.

RISTORANTE FIUME
16 Bonemill Lane, Washington
0191 415 0007
Great restaurant which has built up a truly enviable reputation over the last 15 years or so. Why? Mouth watering, homemade Italian food and some of the very best around. They offer a great two course special that's available noon-7pm Sunday to Thursday, and noon-5pm Friday and Saturday.

ROMA
13 Mary Street
0191 565 8569 Ⓜ *Sunderland*
Brilliant Italian offering classic pizzas and pastas served at prices that won't break the bank. Plus they offer a happy hour 5-7pm seven days a week.

VILLA DEL PORTO
Low Street 0191 567 4119
Ⓜ *Sunderland*
New on the Sunderland dining scene and what a stunning addition. It's an Italian with French influences and has superb views over the River Wear. And given its location there's no surprise that they specialise in seafood. They also do excellent pasta and pizza dishes which have a slight twist to reflect the head chef's home in Puglia. A must visit. They also offer a delivery service if you're feeling lazy.

INDIAN

CAFÉ BLUE COBRA
15-16 Green Tce.
0191 567 2022 Ⓜ *Park Lane*
Ooh... the duck with tamarind and honey will make you go weak at the knees here. Indian food of a consistently high standard and staff that are attentive without ever being intrusive. The décor has recently been updated and modernised this year. A friendly and welcoming atmosphere is guaranteed in this contemporary restaurant which has quickly gathered a loyal customer base.

CAFÉ SPICE2000
6-7 Douro
0191 510 2002 **M** *Park Lane*
This elegantly presented restaurant, with its white linen table clothes and napkins and smartly dressed waiters offer an element of class to your evening. Enjoy their set lunch menu Mon-Sat from 12pm-2pm and their extended mouth-watering evening menu 6pm-Midnight every day, and a three-course special on a Sunday for £8.95. You're seriously spoilt for choice when dining out here.

MOTIRAJ
6 Church Lane
0191 565 6916 **M** *Sunderland*
One of Sunderland's best curry houses, Motiraj Tandoori is a stone's throw from the Empire Theatre. Ideal for that pre or post-theatre visit to sort your curry carvings. They do a great special on a Thursday and Sunday: starter, curry and rice, then ice cream or coffee all for £8.50.

SPICE EMPIRE
3 Church Lane
0191 565 7750 **M** *Sunderland*
Formerly Amalfi, Spice Empire is one of the newest additions to Sunderland's restaurants. Situated below the very popular Moti Raj, they also offer a similar special on a Thursday and Sunday, serving up five courses for £8.95.

MIDDLE EASTERN

ALI BABA
3 Olive Street **M** *Park Lane*
Normally kebabs are the sort of thing you find yourself tucking into drunk on your way home, not the sort of thing you'd expect tuck into in a restaurant. However Ali Baba offers Middle Eastern cuisine kept nice and simple, without the grease and with plenty of spice.

ORIENTAL

ASIANA FUSION
Echo 24 Building 0191 510 0099
M *Sunderland*
Delicious fusions of Asian food and panoramic views of the River Wear, make this stylish restaurant perfect for a lovely meal.

BORNEO BISTRO
Hylton Road 0191 565 9505
Brilliant all-you-can-eat Asian buffet. The décor is basic but there's such a fantastic variety of food you're probably only paying attention to what's on your plate.

DENG'S EASTERN GARDEN
24 Hylton Road
0191 564 1084 **M** *Millfield*
Chinese, with intimate surroundings, this is

often the ideal haunt for business folk and couples. They do evening set meals and an excellent three-course lunch for great prices.

MING DYNASTY II
7 High St. West
0191 510 9904 **M** *Sunderland*
Not particularly inviting from the outside but it's certainly warm and pleasant enough inside. The food is good too with a classic combination of traditional and innovative oriental cuisine. They also have good lunchtime and early bird specials.

THAI MANOR
5 Foyle Street 0191 567 6297
M *Sunderland*
Opening just after Sunniside was developed Thai Manor has come on strides since then, earning a name for itself as the place to get good Thai. The dishes are always freshly prepared to the highest standard and their different menus include the Hot and Spicy Set and the sumptuous Seafood set.

CAFES

BIZ R
99-101 High Street West
0191 514 2828 **M** *Sunderland*
One of the city's best coffee shops, the 50s style décor and original art work and great music make it a perfect setting for a relaxing coffee or lunch with friends. They offer good coffee (their own blend of Arabica beans) and a great selection of paninis and sandwiches freshly prepared on the morning, sometimes to order. Not to mention the selection of freshly handmade cakes and danish pastries.

COFFEE CABAN
22 Blandford Square
0191 567 7030 **M** *Sunderland*
A huge range of coffees are available from this very relaxing joint which also serves up a good range of hot and cold food from breakfasts to

jacket potatoes to sandwiches.

ESQUIRES COFFEE HOUSES
Unit 66 The Bridges
0191 510 0979 **M** *Sunderland*
This new franchise has everything: stylish desserts, gorgeous toasties, great selection of hot and cold drinks. Even better it's all Fair Trade at a standard price, so help yourself while helping others.

EXPRESSO'S COFFEE SHOP
79b Ewesley Rd., High Barnes
0191 522 0258
A cool little place for coffee and sandwiches. They have tables outside if you fancy doing it al fresco stylee.

THE GALLEY
33-42 Fawcett St.
0191 565 0007 **M** *Sunderland*
A family restaurant and coffee shop above Wilkinsons on Fawcett St. No frills but tasty and friendly nonetheless.

HAVERSHAMS
27 Fawcett St. 0191 565 0807
M *Sunderland*
A classic café in the Mark Toney's mould, offering everything from full roasts and fish 'n' chips to mouth watering homemade pastries and those huge jars of traditional sweeties. Easy on the wallet, even easier on the taste buds.

LICKETY SPLIT CREAMERY
13 North Terrace, Seaham
0800 917 5531
Fabulous 50s style ice cream parlour by the sea, offering a mouth-watering array of sundaes. Decorated like a traditional American diner, even the staff are committed to the theme with 50s uniforms. There's even a jukebox. Go visit for an indulgent ice cream experience but set some time aside as it's almost always packed!

Thai Manor

The Place

LOUIS'
12-14 Park Lane
0191 514 2053 **M** *Park Lane*
Sunderland has unaccountable cafes and fast food outlets with too many mediocre ones to list, however, take time out for Louis' - a huge cafe with a fish restaurant upstairs. Louis' is nowt fancy but makes a mean cup of coffee.

THE OLIVE CAFÉ
18 Olive Street
0191 514 4588 **M** *Park Lane*
Formerly an old record store that was visited by The Beatles, now it's a bright and modern café that's all wooden furniture and lime coloured cushions. They offer a brilliant range of home made Italian snacks from paninis to salads at good prices available from 10-3.30pm Monday to Saturday. They also have a sister, The Olive Express which is situated in Park Lane Interchange, offering a range of hot and cold food from 7-4pm Monday to Saturday.

PAPRIKA CAFÉ
46 Frederick St. 0191 564 0606
M *Sunderland*
Lovely laid-back, quality dining at this chilled joint. Call in for breakfast, lunch (wraps, paninis, salads) or for an evening meal (Thurs-Sat, 4pm-7pm). They now offer a full evening menu, with two courses setting you back £15.95 and three courses £18.50. The

nice and creative menu is a boon and they hold a gourmet night on the last Friday of each month. Call for more details on this.

THE PLACE CAFÉ
Anthenaeum Street
0191 5106171 **M** *Sunderland*
Modern and stylish café situated in Sunniside. This is a great place to sit and relax with a coffee, or if you fancy a bite they have a great menu offering sandwiches, wraps and all-day breakfasts. Not to mention a whole range of scrummy cakes.

DURHAM

CONTEMPORARY EUROPEAN

BISTRO 21
Aykley Heads 0191 384 4354
Neighbouring the University Hospital a few minutes outside of Durham City Centre, this French eatery is well worth seeking out as it provides one of the best dining experiences around. Definite bistro feel with some top-notch continental food in addition to British fare. Excellent lunches too and booking in advance is advised.

CAFÉ ROUGE
20-21 Silver Street 0191 384 3429
Another French restaurant, this chain venue

serves reasonable quality cuisine, albeit at a price that's perhaps a little ambitious for Durham. Predictably, the atmosphere is more that of a café than full-blown restaurant, which lends itself well to the lunch deals on offer that are arguably superior to their evening counterparts.

HIDE CAFÉ BAR AND GRILL
39 Saddler Street 0191 384 1999
This little café/restaurant is one of our favourite restaurants in Durham, due in no small part to its informal air and relaxing, modern interior. Stop in for a coffee, a quick spot of breakfast, or indulge in some of the incredible evening meals. Not the cheapest, but worth every penny.

KINGSLODGE HOTEL
Waddington Street 0191 370 9977
This hotel has a very well-regarded restaurant with an emphasis on relaxation. Gentle lighting and pleasant décor combine for the perfect dining ambience. The food slants towards imaginative British-themed dishes such as black pudding with smoked trout and bread and butter pudding with honey ice-cream.

OLDFIELDS
18 Claypath 0191 370 9595
A very stylish, traditional British dining experience; all oak-panels, stained glass windows and high ceilings spread across two floors. As well as the aforementioned chocolate pudding, they do gorgeous steak, lamb and other sumptuous dishes, all made with locally-sourced produce.

MARRIOTT HOTEL DURHAM
Old Elvet 0191 386 6821
One of Durham's top hotels is the location for two decadent dining rooms. The Cruise Brassiere has a relaxed, contemporary atmosphere and The County Restaurant carries an imaginative, more British-based menu.

Excellent service and one of the best wine lists around only add to the sense of occasion.

CHINESE

DYNASTY BUFFET
51 North Road 0191 370 9180
Perhaps tellingly, precious few people of Chinese origin actually frequent this place but it pulls in local punters all the same with its reasonably-priced buffet deals.

INSHANGHAI
Unit 30B, Lambton Walk 0191 375 7333
This cosy lounge-bar and restaurant is all dark woods and comfy booths and has a very popular all-you-can-eat buffet. Alternatively, simply order something off the menu.

NEW KWAI LAM
32A Saddler Street 0191 386 4726
Its food described "as uneven as the floor" by the city's own Durham Times last year, New Kwai Lam is for tea-total diners commanding a seriously limited budget and perhaps equally-limited palette. With no alcohol license and decidedly mediocre service, there aren't many reasons to visit this Chinese eatery.

JAPANESE AND OTHER ASIAN

FAT BUDDHA ASIAN KITCHEN
Units 6B-6C, Walkergate 0191 383 1390
Self-described as Asian Fusion in character, Fat Buddha Asian Kitchen is a superb restaurant, with a vast range of first-rate dishes to choose from. Well-lit and perfectly styled, the only fly in the ointment is the price range – it isn't cheap. There's also a classy bar below (not Loveshack, which is - bizarrely - owned by the same company).

NUMJAI THAI RESTAURANT
19 Milburngate Shopping Centre
0191 386 2020
In a prime location overlooking the river with

unrivalled views of the magnificent Durham Cathedral, Numjai Thai Restaurant brings the finest selection of Thai and Japanese cuisine to Durham City. Definitely give this one a try if you're adventurous.

SAKURA TEPPANYAKI RESTAURANT
69-70 Crossgate 0191 383 2323
If you've ever ventured to Fujiyama in Newcastle, you'll already know what to expect from Sakura Teppanyaki Restaurant. Fresh Japanese food is cooked to perfection before your very eyes at your own table, which incidentally you may find yourself sharing with others. Fun, tasty but also a little on the pricey side.

ZEN
Court Lane 0191 384 9588
Another Asian Fusion affair, Zen also certainly isn't the cheapest restaurant in Durham but it could well lay claim to being the best. Offering up everything from Asian-style tapas to sirloin steaks, the restaurant boasts an impressive range of food and equally impressive décor. The drinks selection is more than respectable, too.

INDIAN

CINNAMON
3 North Road 0191 374 0750
With its simplified take on a traditional Indian menu, one of Durham's relatively new restaurants happily marries the old with the new. You'll find it up tucked away up a flight of stairs.

THE CAPITAL
Claypath 0191 386 8803
Perhaps Durham's most-well regarded Indian, this classy restaurant is hidden away further up the hill from Rajpooth (see below). Serves all the usual dishes and is usefully positioned near The Big Jug and Woodman for a few pints afterwards.

RAJPOOTH
80 Claypath 0191 386 1496
Offering a menu full of a bewildering array of Tandoori dishes to choose from, this restaurant is certainly a popular one. The award-winning Indian also has a loyalty scheme, so the more you feast the more you save. Avoid the house white wine, though.

SHAHEEN'S INDIAN BISTRO
48 North Bailey 0191 386 0960
Cheap and with a really relaxed feel about the place with the emphasis on comfort food. Serves up a combination of Anglo-Indian bites along with an excellent selection of vegetarian dishes. Make sure you check out the demon hot chilli sauce, but be warned - only the hardened curry connoisseur will be able to handle it.

SPICE LOUNGE
St. Nicholas Cottage, Market Place 0191 383 0927
Classical yet modern, exquisite and exotic, there's much to recommend about this cosy restaurant which is not too pricey. Take-away service, too.

ITALIAN

ASK
Unit 4, Walkergate 0191 383 2567
Part of the popular chain of Italian restaurants, this is pretty standard stuff and at a price that's ever so slightly steep in these recession-dominated times.

BELLA ITALIA
Silver Street 0191 386 1060
This delightful restaurant, part of the Bella Italia chain, is located down the steps just next to Topshop on Silver Street and has some great panoramic views over the river thanks to its conservatory-style dining area. It's open for breakfast, lunch and dinner and students get 20% off between Monday and Wednesday inclusive.

BISTRO ITALIANO
70 Claypath 0191 383 0374
Plenty of good-natured hustle and bustle at this lively Italian specialising in fish and shellfish. Their home-made sweets are divine and they have the usual array of happy hours, too; a good combination by any account.

CHE VITA RISTORANTE ITALIANO
Station Lane 0191 384 1010
Perhaps the most memorable aspect of this place is it occasionally dispenses vouchers throughout the city that entitle diners to buy two main courses for the price of one. Freebies aside, Che Vita Ristorante Italiano is a huge if relatively mundane chain restaurant, dispensing the usual pizzas and pastas at a reasonable price.

EMILIO'S
96 Elvet Bridge 0191 384 0096
A thoroughly pretty little Italian restaurant (set in historic chapel dating back to 11th century), with a dark interior offset by lovely crisp white linen tablecloths. Does a mean risotto (i.e. it's gorgeous, not stingy) and its fillet steaks are some of the best around. Astonishingly cheap during its frequent happy hours, too.

LA SPAGHETTATA
66 Saddler Street 0191 383 9290
A student favourite but equally accommodating of locals and visitors, La Spaghetta - affectionately known as 'La Spag' - serves up an adequate range of Italian favourites. If the food is a little bland, the décor, low-level lighting and cheap prices make this one worth a visit. Note that the restaurant is hidden up a long staircase.

MICHELANGELO'S
Neville's Cross Complex 0191 370 9922
Held in high esteem by Italian cuisine aficionados, Michelangelo's is a few minutes outside of Durham City Centre but well worth the jaunt. Classic dishes combine with traditional décor to create an authentic Italian dining experience at a reasonable price. Don't forget happy hour, either, between 5-6.30pm on Thursdays and Fridays.

PIZZA EXPRESS
64 Saddler Street 0191 383 2661
Established and somewhat well-regarded chain serving pizzas, believe it or not. This particular branch has bagged itself a fine location on Saddler Street, with decor verging on the minimal. Very good quality which is unfortunately reflected in the prices - slightly more than your average - but worth it all the same.

RISTORANTE DE MEDICI
21 Elvet Bridge 0191 386 1310
A very small, very busy Italian restaurant which is purportedly the oldest in Durham. Booking a table is recommended, especially if you want the Romeo and Juliet type window seat for that romantic meal with someone special.

MEXICAN, PORTUGUESE AND SPANISH

CHIQUITO
6A Walkergate 0191 370 6470
The popular Mexican chain has a venue in Durham for all your nacho needs. There are doubtless cheaper and more authentic Mexican restaurants out there but for parties in particular Chiquito serves up a winner, with a fun selection of foods and an interesting range of cocktails.

EL COTO
17 Hallgarth Street 0191 384 4007
A third outlet of the north-east mini-chain that just opened a few of years ago, El Coto serves up an exciting range of value-for-money Spanish tapas with style. Easily has the edge over the more well-known La Tasca (see below). Booking is certainly advised.

Bella Italia

Vennels

LA TASCA
58 Saddler Street 0845 126 2958
La Tasca probably falls short of serving the best tapas in the city owing to the brilliance of the aforementioned El Coto, but it is well worth a visit all the same. The splendidly cosy decor and friendly staff contribute to a warm and inviting atmosphere, while the food – if a little pricey – is authentic enough, though dishes vary in quality.

NANDO'S
Unit 5, Walkergate 0871 960 6153
A Portuguese-themed chain restaurant perfectly suited to parties but perhaps a little loud for more relaxed diners. Prices are reasonable if not fantastic, and the Portuguese twist makes things slightly more interesting.

TIA'S
84 Claypath 0191 383 9001
Ugly on the outside, ugly on the inside, Tia's certainly isn't the prettiest of Tex-Mex restaurants. But if you can stomach the decor, you'll love the food. Formerly Rock'n'Amigos for over 10 years, the family-friendly venue rustles up a range of interesting Mexican dishes as well as a host of pastas, pizzas and steaks. Come during happy hour for a cheap and fun meal out with a difference.

CAFÉS

9 ALTARS CAFÉ
Rear 19a, Silver Street 0191 374 1120
Serving hot and cold food - made-to-order from fresh ingredients - alongside an extensive range of hot, chilled and alcoholic drinks, 9 Altars Café is situated on the banks of the River Wear yet still close enough to the centre of town not to inconvenience anyone. Well worth a visit by any weary shopper or sight-seer.

THE ALMSHOUSES
Café-restaurant, Palace Green
0191 386 1054
Situated at the heart of a UNISCO World Heritage Site, The Almshouses Café-restaurant could hardly boast a better locale. All the same, its reputation for an exceptional range of cakes and puddings has been what's really enchanted locals and tourists alike for 25 years.

CAFÉ CONTINENTAL
87 Elvet Bridge 0191 387 0000
Once situated on Milburngate Bridge, this little place was much-missed when it closed its doors the first time around only to be replaced by a chain operation. However, Café Continental is back in business on Elvet Bridge and doing what it does best – serving up scrumptious cakes, delicious deserts and

other tasty morsels along with a range of hot and cold drinks.

CAFFÉ NERO
34 Silver Street 0191 384 9444
A very tidy – albeit wholly ubiquitously branded - little café that serves up tremendous toasted Italian baguettes alongside a range of pastries, cakes, muffins and coffee. Promising as it does to serve up 'the best espresso this side of Milan', why don't you be the judge and give it a go?

COSTA COFFEE
Prince Bishops Centre, High Street
0191 383 0082
With so many altogether more interesting cafés on offer in Durham the only reason one might visit the rather mundane Costa Coffee is for one of its bucket-sized coffees. Mind, they are rather good.

ESQUIRES
22 Silver Street 0191 375 7578
Just off Framwellgate Bridge, this reasonably-priced café harbours a fine selection of sweet treats, meat feasts and veggie bites for morning, noon or night. Given its central location, Esquires makes for a good stop to rest in the midst of a day out shopping. Also boasts a small outside terrace overlooking the river for in the event that the weather's decent.

THE GEORGIAN TOWNHOUSE
11 Crossgate 0191 386 8070
Where to begin?! Forming part of a cosy bed-and-breakfast and situated inside a Grade II-listed building, this family-run pancake café is something special. A warm, welcoming feel will greet anyone lucky enough to sit down and slurp or chomp on the range of homemade soups and sweet or savoury pancakes on offer. Opening times may vary.

RUMBLETUMS OLD
English Tea Rooms
32 Silver Street 07929963614
About as quaint as it gets, this is a proper set of English tea rooms serving home-baked snacks and light meals in addition to the quintessential tea. Perhaps slightly overpriced but a worthwhile experience.

SADDLERS BISTRO
36 Saddler Street 0191 370 9470
A superb café-cum-restaurant spread across two floors and several rooms and situated on Saddler Street, a stone's throw from both the historic Bailey and Palace Green. Serving up everything from bacon sandwiches and steaks through to homemade cakes and milkshakes at reasonable prices, Saddlers Bistro probably has something for you. The service can be pretty erratic, mind.

THE UNDERCROFT RESTAURANT
Durham Cathedral 0191 386 3721
Enjoy friendly service and home-cooked food in the former monks' wine cellar beneath the ancient Cathedral on Palace Green. A vow of silence is optional.

VENNELS
71 Saddler's Yard 0191 375 0571
This well-respected café is always packed and when you see the size of their flapjacks it's no wonder. Perfect for those post-book-browsing afternoons at Waterstones next door, Vennels is light, airy and has a wonderful courtyard that predictably gets crammed in the summer. Everything sold is baked on the premises (their Bannoffee Pie is trés bien) and they also serve speciality sandwiches, pâtés and even have a vegan bar.

From the very old (the Castle Keep which gave Newcastle its name) to the relatively modern (Gateshead's magnificent The Angel of the North) the north-east is resplendent with iconic buildings and structures. Add in the likes of Middesbrough's magnificent Transporter Bride, Tynemouth's ancient Castle and Priory and Durham Cathedral (voted the nation's favourite building by Radio 4 listeners) and you'll get an inkling of just what's out there.

Bottle of Notes, Middlesbrough

Chinatown

Grey's Monument

NEWCASTLE & GATESHEAD

ALDERMAN FENWICK'S HOUSE
98 Pilgrim Street, Newcastle
M *Monument*
This house is one of the most important mercantile town houses in any city in the north of England. With medieval origins, it occupies two burgage plots on the main route to the North and seems to have been substantially built in the mid-17th century. The oak stair, rising into the lantern tower to give access to the roof - a close relative of the famous 'black staircase' in Durham Castle - and the ceiling of the 'Great Room' are of this period.

ANGEL OF THE NORTH
A1, Gateshead
One of the most stunning pieces of sculpture in the country, the fantastic 'Angel' created by Anthony Gormley OBE, and built from 200 tonnes of steel, stands 20m high and is seen by 33 million people per year.

BESSIE SURTEES HOUSE
41-44 Sandhill, Quayside, Newcastle
0191 269 1220 **M** *Central Station*
Mon-Fri 10am-4pm
The 18th century home of Bessie Surtees, who caused much local uproar when she eloped (by ladder out of the window) with the

future Lord Chancellor of all England in 1772. A rare example of well preserved domestic architecture from the Jacobean period. Also plays home to the regional office of English Heritage.

BLACKFRIARS
Monk Street, Newcastle
0191 232 9279 **M** *Central Station*
This former monastery, dating from the 13th century and later used as a meeting place for the city's craft guilds, has now been renovated as shops, restaurant and outdoor meeting place.

THE BLACK GATE
Castle Arch, St. Nicholas Street, Newcastle
M *Central Station*
A medieval gatehouse to the Castle Keep surmounted by a 17th century house.

CASTLE KEEP
Castle Garth, St. Nicholas Street, Newcastle
0191 232 7938 **M** *Central Station*
10am-5pm Mon-Sat (12pm-5pm Sunday). £4 adults, £2.50 concs. Newcastle got its name from the 'new' castle founded in 1080 by a son of William the Conqueror and the Castle Keep followed in 1168-1178. The Keep survives and is an outstanding example of Norman architecture, and is worth a visit even if only

for the tremendous views of the city it affords from its battlements. Limited disabled access.

THE CATHEDRAL CHURCH
of St. Nicholas
Mosley St., Newcastle
0191 232 1939 **M** *Central Station*
Mon-Fri 7am-6pm; Sat 8am-4pm; Sun 7am-12noon & 4pm-7pm. Dating mainly from the 13th and 14th centuries this is a magnificent building with its most distinguished feature being the Lantern Tower (1448), a prominent landmark for over five hundred years.

CHINATOWN
Stowell Street, Newcastle
M *St. James*
As well as an array of top quality Asian restaurants (see restaurant section), the Chinatown district is also noted for its specialist supermarkets, craft shops and vibrant New Year celebrations.

CITY LIBRARY
Charles Avison Building, 33 New Bridge Street West, Newcastle
0191 277 4100 **M** *Monument*
Opened in June 2009, Newcastle's fantastic new state of the art library is a fabulous glass construction with six floors. Inside you'll find a fabulous café, express email facilities, a performance space that can seat up 185 people, music scores, DVDs, CDs, PCs, local collections and oh, loads of books.

DUNSTON STAITHES
Dunston Riverside, **M** *Gateshead*
A Grade II listed structure, which consists of 1,700ft of braced timber. Built in 1890 to move coal from local pits on to the colliers berthed directly below on the River Tyne. Best seen from the Newcastle banks of the Tyne.

THE GATESHEAD MILLENNIUM BRIDGE

Quayside **M** *Manors / Gateshead*

The stunning bridge takes walkers and cyclists over the river into the heart of the Gateshead Quays and on to BALTIC Square and to BALTIC The Centre for Contemporary Art. The bridge opens and closes like a gigantic eyelid to let shipping pass; the technology is a world first and at night the coloured lighting is spectacular.

GATESHEAD HERITAGE @ ST MARY'S

St Mary's Church, Oakwellgate, Gateshead
0191 4336965

In addition to the heritage information on display, this beautiful building hosts a varied programme of lunchtime concerts, craft workshops, evening performances, music and reading group meetings and magical installations.

GRAINGER TOWN

Grey Street, Newcastle
M *Monument*

Described as the 'city of palaces' when completed in 1842, Grainger Town is an historic area right in the heart of Newcastle. Recently regenerated, the elegant stylish Victorian and classical Georgian architecture can now be enjoyed to the full. The area takes in Grey Street, probably the most magnificent classical Georgian street in England, Grey's Monument and the Edwardian Central Arcade.

GREY'S MONUMENT

Grey Street, Newcastle
M *Monument*

The central feature of central Newcastle commemorates Earl Grey, promoter of the Reform Bills. The monument now lends its name to the adjacent Mall and Metro station. The sculptor Edward Hodges Baily was also responsible for the figure of Lord Nelson on Nelson's Column in Trafalgar Square, London.

KEELMAN'S HOSPITAL

City Road, Newcastle

The Keelmen were the men who transported coal on the River Tyne and they built the Almshouses in 1701 to house the aged and sick Keelman and their dependants.

THE LITERARY AND PHILOSOPHICAL SOCIETY

23 Westgate Road, Newcastle
0191 232 0192 **M** *Central Station*

The Literary & Philosophical Society (Lit & Phil) is the largest independent library outside London, housing over 160,000 books. A wide selection of current fiction and non-fiction can be found alongside historical collections covering every field of interest. The building

Bessie Surtees House

The Literary and Philosophical Society

Seven Stories,
the Centre for Children's Books

Ouseburn Valley, Newcastle

Seven Stories celebrates the wonderful world
of children's books. Our events and exhibition
programme is bound to excite book lovers
of all ages.

Mon-Sat 10am-5pm
Sun 10am-4pm

For more info visit:
Www.sevenstories.org.uk
Tel: 0845 271 0777

Supported by Arts Council and Newcastle City
Council. Registered charity number 1056812.

seven
stories

the centre for children's books

West Walls

Newcastle City Library

is one of the most intriguing and beautiful in Newcastle.

PATH HEAD WATER MILL

Summerhill, Blaydon 0191 414 6288
1 April-30 Sept 10am-5pm, 1 October-March 31 11am-3pm. Adult £3.50/Concs £2
A restored 18th century watermill complete with working waterwheel and machinery. Grounds with exhibits, picnic area and local wooded walks & renewable energy exhibits (wind and water power).

NEWCASTLE QUAYSIDE & GATESHEAD QUAYS

M *Central Station / Gateshead*
A riverside walkway takes you past fine buildings and public art. The many waterfront restaurants and bars make this famous area of the city a magnet for pleasure-seekers.

TYNEMOUTH CASTLE & PRIORY

end of Front St., Tynemouth
0191 257 1090   **M** *Tynemouth*
April – Sept 10am –5pm daily. Oct –Dec 10am-4pm Thurs – Mon. Jan- March 10am-4pm Thurs – Mon.
Adult £4.50, Conc. £4.10, Child £2.70, family £11.70.
The priory is situated on a rocky outcrop at the mouth of the river Tyne. Originally an Anglican

monastery (destroyed in the 9th century) it was re-founded a religious house in 1085 with a colony of Benedictine monks. Building on the great Norman church began in 1090 and the whole monastery was substantially completed by the end of the 13th century. Today, much of the priory church remains standing to a good height.

WEST WALLS

Bath Lane, Newcastle   **M** *St. James*
Best remaining stretch of the city walls, Newcastle's main Medieval defensive fortifications. Also seen at Forth Street/Hanover Street and Broad Chare/City Road. Several wall towers remain, including Durham, Heber and Plummer, with Morden now used for poetry readings.

WINLATON COTTAGE FORGE

Winlaton, Gateshead. For access contact Winlaton Library: 0191 4336418
The last remaining link with the Crowley family that once ran iron manufacturing trade in the north-east. The forge dates from the 1690s.

TEES VALLEY

BOTTLE OF NOTES

The Boulevard, Central Gardens, Middlesbrough
The Bottle of Notes was welcomed into

Tynemouth Priory

Temenos

Middlesbrough in 1993 and it is a steel sculpture comprised of quotes from Captain Cook's journals. It's the work of work renowned artist Claes Oldenburg and remains one of the key pieces of Central Gardens.

GUISBOROUGH PRIORY
Church Street, Guisborough TS14 6HG
01287 633801
Opening times- 1 April -30 Sept 9am-5pm Tue, Wed, Thur, Fri, Sat, Sun. 1 Oct – 23 Dec 9am-5pm Wed, Thur, Fri, Sat and Sun. Closed 24 Dec- 1 Jan.
Price- Adult £1.80, Children 90p, Concession 90p, English Heritage Members free.
The skeletal ruins of this 12th Century-monastery are given life through its rich history. Despite being almost completely destroyed by Henry VIII, the east end ruins of the original building have survived to pierce the skyline of Guisborough to this day. Forget Albert Square, because this an east end worth seeing.

NEWPORT BRIDGE
Newport Approach Road, Middlesbrough. Free Entry
Newport Bridge was the first large vertical lift bridge in Britain and is Middlesbrough's very own Sydney Harbour Bridge. Like two hands outstretched, it joins Middlesbrough to its neighbour, Stockton, as well as being a symbol of Tees Valley's Industrial success.

ORMESBY HALL
Church Lane, Ormesby, Middlesbrough
01642 324118
Admission: adult £5.50, child £3.50, entry to tea-room and gardens is free. The 300yr old Hall is a spot of rural splendour amidst Teesside's urban chaos (you know it has to be good when the National Trust puts its name on it!) The decor of the home is a testament to the 18th Century and the grounds make the average garden look like a humble plant pot in comparison.

PIERCEBRIDGE ROMAN FORT
Piercebridge Village, Darlington,
01325 460532.
Free entry, open any reasonable time. The Piercebridge Roman Fort was built around 260- 270 AD on the banks of the River Tees and was used regularly by the Romans up until the 5th Century. It's a great way to go back in time without trying to build a dangerous contraption.

RABY CASTLE
Staindrop, Darlington, Co. Durham,
01833 660202.
May, June and September: Sunday to Wednesday. (Guided tours only Monday to Wednesday). July and August: Daily except Saturdays. Park

and Gardens: 11am to 5.30pm. Castle: 1pm to 4.30pm. Castle, park and Gardens: Adult £9.50, Child £4, Over 60s and Student £8.50, Family Ticket £25. Park and Gardens: Adult £6, Child £2.50, Over 60 and Student £5. A visit to Raby Castle will put all property programmes to shame because this Medieval fortress has being showing the north-east how to live in style for nearly 1,000 years. It has a traditional 18th Century garden and a deer garden. You move through the ages as you move through the interior; from the medieval kitchen to the Gothic vaulting in the hall ways- a great day out for all the family.

ST. HILDA'S
Church Walk, Headland , Hartlepool
01429 267030. Free Entry
The original Anglo-Saxon monastery was founded in 640 AD by St. Aiden on the site of St. Hilda's, but it was destroyed by the Danes in the 9th Century. The church that we all know and visit tells the story of the original monastery and life at St. Hilda after the Danes; of how the church was initially built as a burial place for the DeBrus family and how it has now reverted back to its medieval purpose by serving the entire community. Tours are available, but if you want to guide yourself freestyle, there are display panels, sound wands and interactive

screens to aid you. So shake your buttresses and go to see its buttresses.

TEMENOS
Middlehaven Dock, Middlesbrough
This incredible piece of public art by internationally acclaimed sculptor Anish Kapoor, and leading structural designer Cecil Balmond, stands almost 50 metres high and is 120 metres long, and stands shoulder-to-shoulder with the Transporter Bridge as one of THE icons of the town. It looks like a huge, suspended net.

TRANSPORTER BRIDGE
01642 247563
This is Teesside's pride and joy, as it one of the few transporter bridges in the world that is still functional. It was erected in 1911 and has since been an industrial giant watching over Middlesbrough like a big, blue security guard. It is open Monday- Friday 7am-9pm, Saturdays 11am-5.30pm and 2.00pm- 5.30pm on Sundays, so there's plenty of time to see the old girl in action. If you're on foot, it's 50p per person to cross the river but if you're in a car, it'll cost £1.00 per bay. It's only fair that you pay because the bridge has certainly paid its dues to the north-east over the years.

Ormesby Hall

Transporter Bridge

Penshaw Monument

Fulwell Windmill

SUNDERLAND

FULWELL WINDMILL
Newcastle Road, Fulwell
0191 516 9790
Open: 12pm-4pm everyday.
Sat – May-Sept, Sun – all year.
The Fulwell Windmill opened in 1808 and recently restored. It now boasts a new visitor's centre, a guided tour and various special events throughout the year.

HYLTON CASTLE
Hylton Dene 0191 548 0152
Heritage open days:
 Feb-Nov 10am-5.30pm daily, free admission. Set within 200 wonderful acres the Dene provides country walks, fab kids' play park, a fishing lake and even a haunted castle dating from the 15th century.

PENSHAW MONUMENT
Penshaw Hill
The monument dominates the skyline on Penshaw Hill, overlooking the river Wear. This Sunderland landmark was built in 1844. It is dedicated to John George Lambton, first Earl of Durham and the first Governor of Canada.

ST. ANDREW'S
Talbot Rd, Roker 0191 516 0135
Usually Open: Mon-Fri 9am-1pm or by arrangement.
Often called the Cathedral of the Arts and Crafts movement, this fine church contains work by Pre-Raphaelite's Eric Gill, Burne-Jones, Gimson and William Morris.

ST. PETER'S CHURCH OF MONKWEARMOUTH
St. Peter's Way 0191 567 3726
Call Parish office for opening times.
One of Britain's most important early Christian buildings, St. Peter's was built in 674 AD. It was also the home of the Venerable Bede, the first English historian.

DURHAM

BARNARD CASTLE
County Durham, off the A67
01833 638 212
Open: April-Sept. 10am-6pm (daily) / Oct.-March 10am-4pm (weekends only)
Adults £4.30 / Concessions £3.90 / Kids £2.60
A picturesque ruined castle overlooking the Tees and reputed to have inspired Sir Walter Scott to paint; worth taking a look at, especially if you're visiting either the Bowes Museum a

Palace Green Durham

Durham

mere 15 minutes' walk away or the surrounding market town.

BROWN'S ROWING BOATS / PRINCE BISHOP RIVER CRUISER
Elvet Bridge
0191 386 9525
Rowing boats: Adults £3.50 / Children £2.50
What better way to take in Durham's beauty than by rowing boat? Get your friend to row, drape your hand in the water and admire the view. Alternatively, if you'd both rather relax then hop on board the Prince Bishop River Cruiser for a boat cruise around the city.

CATHEDRAL CLOSE
Off South Bailey
Situated behind Durham Cathedral, this is the location of the Chorister's School and the Dean and Chapter Office, as well as beautiful Georgian houses surrounded by lawns and trees and is widely considered one of the prettiest places in Durham.

DURHAM CASTLE
Palace Green
0191 334 3800
Open: Easter - 30 September: guided tours daily / At other times: Monday, Wednesday, and Saturday (afternoons only) However, closed June 26-October 3 due to major refurbishment. Contact the Castle for details.
Adults £5 / Concessions £3.50 / Family £12
Durham Castle dates from 1072 and was the seat of the Prince Bishops of Durham until 1832. It is one of the largest Norman castles and Romanesque palaces to survive in England and as such is a UNISCO World Heritage Site. Oh and it's also the oldest inhabited university accommodation in the world.

DURHAM CATHEDRAL
Palace Green
0191 386 4266
Open: Worship and prayer between 7:30am and 9:30am Monday to Saturday, 7:45am and 12:30pm on Sunday / Tower: Oct.-March 10am–3pm (excluding Sundays) / April-Sept. 10am-4pm
Free but donations appreciated. Tower: Adults £5 / Children £2.50
Rightly considered to be one of the most important church buildings in Britain, the Cathedral is arguably the finest example of

Durham Cathedral

Durham Castle

Norman architecture in the world and houses the tombs of St. Cuthbert and Bede.

DURHAM WORLD HERITAGE SITE VISITOR CENTRE
7 Owengate   0191 334 3805
Provides an overview of what a World Heritage Site is, what makes Durham important enough to be a World Heritage Site, and what there is to see and do. Features displays and interactives for adults and children. Also hosts temporary exhibitions and cultural events. A good place for information about events in Durham, and to book tours.

FINCHALE PRIORY
North-east of Durham, Off A167
0191 386 3828
This comparatively small priory is situated in a scenic spot on the banks of the River Wear, about 4 miles from Durham. From its lowly beginning as a hermitage for St. Godric, Finchale became a Benedictine priory, dependent on Durham Cathedral, towards the end of the 12th century.

PALACE GREEN
Durham City Centre
Forming part of a UNISCO World Heritage Site, with the Castle on one side and the Cathedral on the other, Palace Green lies at the centre of a truly spectacular scene. Framed by the University of Durham Music Department, Palace Green Library and the Union Society Debating Chambers. Easily accessible from Durham train station by the regular Durham Cathedral Bus.

PREBENDS BRIDGE
Durham City Centre, southern peninsula of river
Dating from 1777, this bridge has one of the best river views in the city. The Cathedral spirals up above, whilst trees and foliage adorn the riverbank.

When the movers and shakers behind the Turner Prize decided to hold the competition outside of a Tate gallery for the first time they chose well when they brought it to BALTIC at Gateshead, one of the biggest and best spaces for modern art in Europe. Of course, this is just one of the region's arty jewels; we have everything, from small pop-up galleries to a huge variety of museums. So whatever your tastes, you're sure to find something that'll help you sort out your art from your elbow.

Durham Light Infantry Museum & Durham Art Gallery

36 LIME STREET
36 Lime Street, Ouseburn
0191 261 5666 **M** *Manors*
36 Lime Street Ltd's guiding principle is to provide secure, affordable studio spaces for rent for creative artists, and in doing so to contribute towards the regeneration of the building and the area.

BALTIC CENTRE FOR CONTEMPORARY ART
South Shore Road, Gateshead Quays
0191 478 1810 **M** *Manors / Gateshead*
Mon-Sun 10am-6pm (Tues 10.30am-6pm). Free
BALTIC is a major international centre for contemporary visual art, situated on the Gateshead side of the river Tyne. The landmark building (formerly the Baltic Flour Mills, a disused 1950s grain warehouse) has been transformed into a leading contemporary visual art gallery; one of the biggest temporary art spaces in Europe. It's also a place to socialise, relax and revel in the artistic atmosphere within, with great areas where you can have food, get a drink or browse around the excellent shop.

THE BISCUIT FACTORY
16 Stoddart Street, Newcastle
0191 261 1103 **M** *Manors*
Sun/Mon 11am-5pm; Tues-Sat 10am-6pm. Free
The Biscuit Factory is Britain's biggest commercial gallery and quite the beauty with 35,000 square feet consisting of two floors of exhibition spaces and two floors of artists' studios. Selling paintings and prints, ceramics, glass, and sculpture from local, national and international artists they also have an excellent café and restaurant ran by award-winning chef David Kennedy. A must visit.

BOWES RAILWAY
Springwell Village, Gateshead
0191 416 1847
Mon-Sat 10am-3pm. Free (charges apply on special days). This railway is the only preserved standard gauge rope haulage railway in the world. The oldest part of the line dates from 1826, designed by George Stephenson. Visitors can see the historic workshops and visit the permanent exhibition.

THE CUSTOMS HOUSE
Mill Dam, South Shields
0191 454 1234 **M** *South Shields*
Daily 10am-8.30pm (open 11am Sunday and Bank Holidays). Sandford Goudie Gallery at The Customs House showcases the very best of national, international and regional contemporary arts practice. With a changing programme of nine exhibitions a year, it is the only contemporary gallery space in South Tyneside, enabling the broadest spectrum of audiences and communities to participate and engage with contemporary art.

DISCOVERY MUSEUM
Blandford Square, Newcastle
0191 232 6789 **M** *Central Station*
Mon-Sat 10am-5pm, Sun 2-5pm. Free
Discovery Museum is a veritable treasure trove of exhibitions (both permanent and temporary), regarding life on Tyneside. From the area's renowned maritime history to world-changing science and technology it has something for everyone. One of the prized exhibits is the record-breaking vessel, Turbinia. Built in 1894 it became the fastest ship in the world at the time.

GALLERY NORTH
Sandyford Road, Northumbria University
0191 227 3105 **M** *Haymarket*
Mon-Thurs 10-5pm; Fri 10-4.30pm. Free
Gallery North is a contemporary exhibition space (found on the ground floor) with artists' studios upstairs (Graduate Studio Northumbria). They offer a combined unique exhibition and enterprise area supporting contemporary arts in the north-east with fantastic opportunities for enterprise, innovation, networking and exhibition practices. Gallery North hosts an

exhibition programme each year providing the sense of energy, expertise and intellectual and imaginative adventure that a university teaching and learning environment can bring.

THE GALLERY
AT GATESHEAD LIBRARY
Prince Consort Road, Gateshead
0191 433 8420
A new gallery space reopened in January 2011 with a programme of temporary exhibitions across two floors of Gateshead Central Library. The Gallery mainly showcases professional regional artists with some national touring shows. Work is often for sale and The Gallery has supporting workshops and talks for all ages.

THE GREAT NORTH
MUSEUM: HANCOCK
Barras Bridge, Newcastle
0191 222 6765 **M** *Haymarket*
Mon-Sat 10am-5pm; Sun 2pm-5pm. Free
The Great North Museum: Hancock is an exciting and innovative world-class visitor attraction which had a grand reopening in 2009. Highlights of the new £26 million museum include a large-scale, interactive model of Hadrian's Wall and major new displays showing the wonder and diversity of the animal kingdom, life and death in Ancient Egypt, and spectacular objects from the Ancient Greeks. There is also a planetarium, a life-size T-Rex dinosaur skeleton and much more...

THE HATTON GALLERY
The Quadrangle, Newcastle University,
M *Haymarket 0191 222 6059*
Mon-Sat 10am-5pm, Sun 2-5pm Free
The Hatton boasts the internationally renowned Schwitters' Merzbarn, which was described by art critic Andrew Graham-Dixon (in a History of British Art, Channel 4) as 'the seminal piece of 20th century British art'. It also houses a permanent African collection, as well as temporary exhibitions.

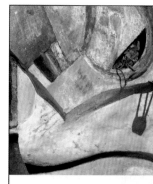

LAING ART GALLERY
New Bridge St., Newcastle
0191 232 7734 **M** *Monument*
Mon-Sat 10am-5pm; Sun 2-5pm. Free
The Laing is the major public art venue in Newcastle. There's a comprehensive permanent collection, including some impressive Pre-Raephelite works, as well as pieces by John Martin and Henry Moore. There's also a continuing programme of temporary exhibitions. Thankfully the Laing isn't afraid to embrace new ventures and happily includes the work of artists who explore new avenues in art as well as showcasing work by Britain's hip young art warriors.

LAZARIDES 77 QUAYSIDE
77 Quayside, Newcastle
0191 221 2560
M *Central Station*
Tues-Sat 12pm-6pm. Free
A gallery on the banks of the river Tyne showing contemporary paintings, prints, sculptures etc from the hipper end of the market. And if you see anything you like, chances are they'll let you have it (if you give them some money).

LIFE
Times Square, Scotswood Road,
Newcastle 0191 243 8210
M *Central Station*
Mon-Sat 10am-6pm; Sunday 11am-6pm; tickets start from £6.25
An award-winning attraction that is full of hands-on exhibitions and activities. Watch out for their friendly 'science explainers' who really add to the experience. Home to the North's biggest planetarium and outdoor skating in Times Square from November-February. Whee!

LOCUS+
Rm 17, 3rd floor, Wards Building, 31-39 High Bridge, Newcastle 0191 233 1450
An arts commissioning agency that presents new projects by visual artists outside of the traditional gallery space.

NEWBRIDGE SPACE
18 New Bridge Street West
M *Monument*
NewBridge Space is an artist led exhibition and project space that shows the work of emerging artists in Newcastle city centre.

THE NEWCASTLE ARTS CENTRE
67 Westgate Road, Newcastle
0191 261 5999
M *Central Station*
Mon-Fri, 9am-5.30pm; Sat, 9am-5pm. Free
This fantastic exhibition space is home to both touring and one-off exhibitions with some challenging pieces being shown alongside more traditional works. The ideal place to catch some up and coming, as well as more established, artists.

NEWCASTLE UNITED STADIUM TOUR
St. James Park, Newcastle
0844 372 1892
M *St. James*
Taking you on an amazing journey through the history of Newcastle United. The knowledgeable guides will show you areas that fans wouldn't usually see as well as some very famous ones! £10 adults/£7 Concessions.

NORTHERN PRINT
Stepney Bank, Newcastle
0191 261 7000
M *Manors*
Wed-Sat 12pm-4pm. Free
Northern Print is the centre for contemporary printmaking in the north-east and they have a beautiful and welcoming space devoted to showing the very best in printmaking.

OPUS ART GALLERY
Milburn House, Dean Street, Newcastle
0191 232 7389 **M** *Central Station*
Mon-Sat 10am-5pm. Free
Browse and buy original art, prints and photography from some of the world's best modern artists. Visits to the gallery are by appointment only.

SEGEDUNUM ROMAN FORT,
Baths & Museum
Buddle Street, Wallsend
0191 236 9347 **M** *Wallsend*
1 Apr-31 Oct Mon-Sun 10am-5pm; 1 Nov-31 Mar Mon-Sun 10am-3pm. Adults £4.50 / children free / concs £2.70.
Discover what life was like at the last outpost of the Roman Empire. Displays chronicle the changes at Wallsend from Roman times to present day. Segedunum features the only reconstructed bath-house in the country, and also provides a chance to see the original remains of Hadrian's Wall.

SEVEN STORIES, THE CENTRE FOR CHILDREN'S BOOKS
30 Lime St., Ouseburn Valley
0845 271 0777 **M** *Manors / Byker*
Mon-Sat 10am-5pm; Sun 10am-4pm. Adults £6.50, child £5.50, family ticket £19
Seven Stories is Britain's first gallery and archive dedicated to children's books, situated in an imaginatively converted Victorian mill. Discover exhibitions, events and activities inspired by children's books and the centre's growing collection of original manuscripts and illustrations. A thoroughly entertaining experience. Includes a great bookshop and café.

SHIPLEY ART GALLERY
Prince Consort Rd, Gateshead
0191 477 1495 **M** *Gateshead*
Mon-Sat 10am-5pm; Sun 2pm-5pm. Free
The Shipley is the north-east's leading gallery of design and contemporary craft. The stunning Designs for Life gallery showcases over 300 objects from the collections. The Shipley also houses an outstanding painting collection including William Irving's The Blaydon Races. A varied programme of temporary exhibitions are held each year including many partner exhibitions with large National Museums and Galleries such as the V&A in London.

SIDE GALLERY
9 Side, Quayside, Newcastle
0191 232 2208
M *Central Station*
Tue-Sat 11am-5pm. Free
Since opening in 1977, Side Gallery has achieved a legendary reputation in documentary photography. Alongside the exhibition of international work by many of the world's leading photographers, the gallery continues to commission an unparalleled documentation of northern lives and landscapes. Exhibitions are often accompanied by talks and events.

THE UNIVERSITY GALLERY
Uni. of Northumbria,
Sandyford Rd., Newcastle
0191 227 4424 **M** *Haymarket*
Mon-Thurs 10am-5pm,
Fri/Sat 10am-4pm. Free
Presents a programme of temporary and touring exhibitions by artists of national and international reputation as well as exhibitions by lesser known, but promising, artists.

VANE
1st Floor, Commercial Union House,
39 Pilgrim Street, Newcastle
Newcastle 0191 261 8281
M *Monument*
Wed-Sat 12noon-5pm (during exhibitions). Free
Having staged exhibitions around Newcastle since 1997 Vane has just moved to new, larger premises. They present around six exhibitions a year of work by emerging and established contemporary artists from the region, UK and internationally. They also hold talks and other events.

WORKPLACE GALLERY

The Old Post Office, 19/21 West St.
M *Gateshead*
Tuesday-Sat 11am-5pm (when exhibiting). Free
Workplace Gallery is a contemporary art gallery
run by artists. Based in Gateshead it represents
a portfolio of emerging and established artists
through the gallery programme, curatorial
projects and international art fairs.

TEES VALLEY

ARC

Arc, Dovecot Street, Stockton on Tees,
01642 525 199.
Ground floor gallery and ARTSPACE. Open all
day. Free admission. ARC displays ever-changing
exhibitions aiming to display high quality and
unique art. ARC exhibits work from the best
local artists found across Tees Valley. Original
artwork is displayed on all floors, so your eye
can wander with your legs.

BUTTERFLY WORLD

Preston Park, Yarm Road, Stockton,
01642 791 414.
Open March until the end of October, daily from
10.00am - 4.30pm (last entry 4pm). Adult: £3.75,
Child/ Concessions: £3.25, Family ticket £13 - 2
Adults and up to 3 Children.
Butterfly World is full of creepy crawlies. If
you can catch a spider and not wince at the
thought of it wriggling around in your clasped
hands, then you will enjoy this tropical and
unusual experience with its many endangered
species of insects.

CAPTAIN COOK'S
BIRTHPLACE MUSEUM

Stewart Park, Middlesbrough,
01642 311 211.
Open March-October Tues-Sun 10am-5.30pm,
November-February Tues-Sun 9am-4pm. Closed
Mondays. This is a fantastic and interactive
museum for children and adults alike. It focuses

Vane - 'Yummikraut' installation view, January 2011

on the life of Captain James Cook and delves into the world of one of the greatest navigators through permanent and temporary exhibitions. It goes on to explore into the life of a seaman in general and the difficulties that were attached; the truth behind the wooden legs and bottles of rum, if you will... and all for free.

CLEVELAND IRONSTONE MINING MUSEUM
Deepdale, Skinningrove, Saltburn, 01287 642 877.
1st April - 31st October, Mon - Fri, 10.30am - last tour 3.30pm. Sat open 1.00pm, last tour 3.30pm. Open Sundays in school holidays. Adult £5, concessions £4.50 Children- £2.50, Family- £12. The mining museum is a tribute to one of the aspects of industry that Teesside is renowned for. It is based on the site of a Loftus Mine, but you won't hear of any dwarves singing as they were digging for diamonds. It informs you of the skills and the customs of mining Victorian and Edwardian England. You can also dare to submerge yourself into the depths of Loftus in an authentic underground mining experience.

DARLINGTON ARTS CENTRE
Vane Terrace, Darlington, 01325 489094.
Open Monday - Saturday 9am- 8pm.
The centre features local arts in "The Lounge Gallery" and touring exhibitions in the "Myles Meehan Gallery". It also offers adult courses, holiday workshops and arts management apprenticeships, all the while hoping to get children involved with the new ArtsSpark programme. There's something for everyone.

DORMAN MUSEUM
Linthorpe Road, Middlesbrough, 01642 813 781.
Open Tues-Sun 9.30am-5pm, last entry is 4.45pm. Closed Mondays.
The Dorman Museum was opened in 1904 and began life as a natural history museum. However, it is now much more diverse as it uncovers different cultures, items of local interest, the fields of archaeology and of geology. This is all within its eight themed galleries, its varied programme of changing exhibitions and its family friendly workshop. The educational experience of the Dorman Museum is the proof in the pudding that you can teach old dogs new tricks. Free admission.

GUISBOROUGH MUSEUM
Sunnyfield House, Westgate, Guisborough, 01287 203 617.
Open April – October every Thursday and Saturday 10am - 4pm. Free Admission. Guisborough Musuem relies solely on voluntary workers, and it is built within an old stable block. It was

established in 1989 to preserve Guisborough's heritage and to inform the locals of how the town developed, with over 1,000 objects displayed that best symbolise the town's past to the people of its future.

THE MUSEUM OF HARTLEPOOL
Jackson's Dock Maritime Avenue, Hartlepool, 01429 860 077
Open daily from 10.00am to 5.00pm (including Bank Holidays). Do you think that sea monsters and lighthouses are a combination for Disney only? Think again! Hartlepool's awarding winning museum has a fishing coble, a Celtic round-house building and the fully restored paddle steamer, the "PPS Wingfield Castle." However, don't forget to take your sea legs with you!

HARTLEPOOL'S MARITIME EXPERIENCE
Jackson Dock, Hartlepool 01429 860 077
April - October: 10.00am - 5pm, November - March: 10.30am - 4pm daily (except Christmas Day, Boxing Day and New Year's Day).
Adults £7.95, Children (over 5, under 5s go free), Unwaged, students: £4.95, Over 60s: £5.95, Family ticket (2 adults and up to 3 children): £21, Travel Trade Groups: £3.95, School Groups: £3.40, Other Groups (Adults): £7.20, Other Groups (Child): £4.20, Other Groups (Over 60's) £5.20. If you like the sound of the Museum of Hartlepool, then feed your seafaring interests by taking the Maritime Experience. A full day's admission will pay for you to discover Hartlepool's Historic Quay, to discover the HMS Trincomalee aka Britain's oldest warship still afloat! Canons at the ready, quayside steady, fire!

"HEAD OF STEAM" DARLINGTON RAILWAY MUSEUM
North Road Station, Darlington, 01325 460 532.
Open April – Sept Tues-Sun 10am- 4pm, Oct – March 11am – 3.30pm. Adult - £4.95 per visit, Over 60s - £3.75 per visit, 6 - 16 years - £3.00

per visit, under 5 years– free. Family Pass, 2 Adults and up to 3 children per visit - £10.00. £1.7 million has been invested into this museum and it was re-launched April 2008, but it promises to keep developing significantly within the next 12 months. The traditional locomotives continue to be the backbone of the museum but the flesh and organs that complete the body are the new and interactive displays. If you feel yourself losing your "steam" (pun intended), you can refuel in the new and improved cafe.

HM BARK ENDEAVOUR
Moat Street, Stockton-on-Tees, 01642 608 109.
Booked guided tours by appointment only. Prices vary. Take a walk on the Cook side of life by booking a guided tour on a full-size replica of his ship, "The HM Bark Endeavour".

KIRKLEATHAM MUSEUM
Kirkleatham, Redcar, 01642 479 500.
Open Tuesday - Sunday 10am-5pm in summer and Tuesday - Sunday 10am- 4pm in winter. Closed Mondays except Bank Holidays. Free Admission. This is a favourite museum for many Teessiders, as it details the history of Redcar and Cleveland and the people who lived there. It provides activities for the kiddy-winks during the school holidays. Plus, there is a drop-in crafts workshop between 10am-12pm and 1pm-4pm during summer holidays.

MIMA
Centre Square, Middlesbrough, TS1 2AZ 01642 726720
Open Tues, Wed, Fri & Sat 10.00am–4.30pm, Thurs 10.00am–7.00pm, Sun 12noon–4.00pm. Closed Mon & Bank hols. Free Admission mima is a stunning art gallery in the heart of Middlesbrough town centre, presenting temporary exhibitions of modern and contemporary art and craft. Featuring work by artists of international repute, mima brings some of the most celebrated art in the world to Middlesbrough.

ORMESBY HALL
Church Lane, Ormesby, Middlesbrough, 01642 324 188.

Admission: National Trust members free, Adult £5.50, child £3.50, under 5s free, family £14.50. Entry to tea-rooms and garden free. 13 Mar – 31 Oct 1.30pm-5pm Sat/Sun. A stunning National Trust park with guided tours around the rural mansion and its interior, as well as its surrounding Georgian stable blocks and gardens.

POP UP GALLERY & ARTIST STUDIO
148 Linthorpe Rd & Broadcasting House, Middlesbrough

High street spaces that stage some of the most imaginative and vibrant happenings from secret cinemas to live performance. Also meet the artists at Broadcasting House the north-east's newest and most exciting artist studios and exhibition space. Always worth investigating.

PRESTON HALL MUSEUM
Yarm Road, Eaglescliffe, Stockton-on-Tees, 01642 527 375.

Open Tues to Sun 10.00am - 4.00pm. Last Admission 4.00pm. Free Admission. The Preston Hall Museum displays art, armour and social history within 100 acres of surrounding park land. The hall was built in 1825 and it is truly beautiful. There is a replica 1890s high street for visitors to walk down and to see if the "old days" were truly better than the present.

PYTHON GALLERY
Royal Middlehaven House, Gosford Street, Middlesbrough, 01642 247 745

Open all year round with free admission, the Python Gallery is a creative development in the heart of the Middlehaven area of Middlesbrough. Launched in July 2007, by Middlesbrough-based development company pythonproperties, the gallery provides quality exhibition space and delivers a rolling programme of shows and events, which have included visual two-dimensional and three-dimensional, performance, installation, multi and time based media. Delivering the very best examples of creativity from this region and beyond, the Python Gallery is establishing itself as a positive venture that engages, inspires and provides a rewarding experience for all who visit.

POP UP STUDIO & POP UP GALLERY
9 Newport Rd. & 148 Linthorpe Rd & 95-97 Albert Rd., Middlesbrough

These high-street spaces that have staged some of the most imaginative and vibrant exhibitions and one-off performances around. There's always something going on with also plenty of items for sale. Worth going back to again and again.

WINKIES CASTLE FOLK MUSEUM
162 High Street, Marske-by-the Sea, Yorkshire, 01642 775 086.

Open 11.30am to 4.30pm Thursday, Saturday & Sunday from Easter to September. Admission: adult £1.50, Under 16 - £0.75, Under 5 – free, Family £4.00.

This is a re-dressed period museum of the history and heritage of Marske. It was founded by a local cobbler in the 1970s and it displays many hand-crafted items that have passed through the palms of the locals. I bet they would high-five the museum now with those same hands to congratulate its success.

ZETLAND LIFEBOAT MUSEUM
5 King Street, Redcar, 01642 494 311.

1 May – 30 September Mon - Fri 11am - 4pm, Sat & Sun 12pm- 4pm. Free admission. The Zetland is the world's oldest fishing boat and it spends its retirement in this lifeboat museum in Redcar. The boat was built in 1802 and has saved 500 lives in its lifetime. It saved an extra life when the museum opened because it allowed local maritime history to be given a second chance.

SUNDERLAND

FULWELL WINDMILL
Newcastle Road 0191 516 9790

Open: 12pm-4pm everyday. Sat – May-Sept,

Sun – all year. The north-east's one and only fully functional windmill. Fulwell was built in 1808 by local mason Mr. Allison who used limestone to achieve the tower's pretty exterior. The windmill now has a visitor centre where any number of interesting windmill facts can be found. Free admission.

THE ART STUDIO
1-3 Hind Street 0191 567 7414
Open: Mon-Fri 10am-5pm. Free admission.
You can't miss The Art Studio on St Michaels Way in Sunderland. Primarily established to enable people with mental health problems to develop their skills. There are some magnificent pieces of work on show and workshops and open days where everyone is welcome.

MONKWEARMOUTH STATION MUSEUM
North Bridge Street,
 M *St Peter's 0191 567 7075*
Open: Mon-Sat 10am-5pm. Sun 2pm-5pm. Free admission. The museum is housed in an original Victorian station building that was commissioned by the famous railway entrepreneur George Hudson. The interactive galleries make learning about the history of travel and transport in Tyne and Wear fun and exciting for children of all ages.

NATIONAL GLASS CENTRE
Liberty Way, St Peter's, 0191 515 5555
M *St. Peter's*
Open: Mon-Sun 10am-5pm. Free admission.
A contemporary building with unique glass roof that you can walk over, situated on the banks of the River Wear. This houses an exciting and thought-provoking programme of exhibitions, workshops, courses, talks and events inspired by glass. Also home to glass production facilities with live demonstrations, craft & design shop, artists' studios, function suites and café/restaurant.

NORTH EAST AIRCRAFT MUSEUM
Old Washington Road, 0191 519 0662

Open: Daily 10am-5pm, £4 adults, £2 children/OAPs.
Houses a collection of military and civilian aircraft (35 aeroplanes in total); displays wreckology and an assortment of engines from 1908.

NORTHERN GALLERY FOR CONTEMPORARY ART
City Library and Arts Centre, Fawcett Street, 0191 561 8407 **M** *Sunderland*
Open: Mon/Wed 9.30am-7.30pm, Tue/Thurs/Fri 9.30am-5.00pm, Sat 9.30am-4.00pm. Free admission. A fantastic major contemporary art space based right in the heart of the city, 50m from Sunderland train station and Metro. The NGCA shows an ambitious programme of contemporary photography, video, painting, installation, sculpture and new media both from around the world and from the north-east. The Project Space provides an important spring-board for new talent, featuring emerging artists alongside established names. And with regular previews, talks, tours, an education room and a new family area, The Drawing Room, the NGCA is definitely worth a look.

THEPLACE
Athenaeum Street, Sunniside, 0191 561 2076 **M** *Sunderland*
Adjacent to the recently developed Sunniside gardens, thePlace is a state-of-the-art business and arts centre in Sunniside. It houses a range of business suites and artists studios, providing artists with performance space and an art gallery, as well as accommodating conference space and meeting rooms. There's also a ground floor café. The building itself comprises a new complex and six refurbished grade II listed buildings. Contact for information on current exhibitions and opening times.

REG VARDY GALLERY
School of Art, Design & Media, University of Sunderland ,

Ashburn House, Ryhope Rd.
0191 515 2128 **M** *Park Lane*
Open: Tues 10am-8pm, Wed-Fri 10am-6pm. Free admission. The very varied programme instigated here aims to reflect developments in the arts locally, nationally and internationally.

RYHOPE ENGINES MUSEUM
The Waterworks, Ryhope 0191 521 0235
Open: Sundays only 2.00pm-4.30pm. Special event weekends 11am-4pm. Call for further details. Free admission. Two fine old beam engines demonstrate the best in Victorian engineering along with displays and exhibitions of Victorian and water-related articles. The engines are actually 'in steam' on Bank Holidays only.

SUNDERLAND MUSEUM & WINTER GARDENS
Mowbray Gardens, Burdon Rd, Sunderland 0191 553 2323
M *Sunderland*
Open: Mon-Sat 10am-5pm, Sun 2pm-5pm. Free admission. In the museum discover the history of the city from its prehistoric past to the present day in exciting displays interpreting the collections with hands-on exhibits and interactive displays. The art gallery features paintings by LS Lowry alongside Victorian masterpieces and artefacts from the four-corners of the world. The stunning Winter Gardens stimulate the senses with over 1,500 of the world's most exotic flowers and plants. The gardens also include exciting water features and a stunning treetop walkway, from which visitors can look down on the plants below.

DURHAM

BEAMISH: THE NORTH OF ENGLAND OPEN AIR MUSEUM
Beamish 0191 370 4000
Open: Mar. 27–Oct. 31 10am-5pm (daily) / Jan. 4-Apr. 1. 10am to 4pm (closed Mons. and Fris.). Closed December.

Adults £16 / Students and 60+ £13 / Children £10 / Family tickets £32/£46 in summer. Tickets are valid for 1 year unlimited trips. Winter prices are reduced.
This unique, open-air museum provides a living, working experience of life as it was in north-east England between the early 1800s and early 1900s. Set in over 300 acres of beautiful countryside, Beamish is replete with working trams, replica streets and more.

DURHAM HERITAGE CENTRE AND MUSEUM
North Bailey 0191 386 8719
Open: June 2pm-4.30pm July-Sept. 11am-4:30pm (daily) / Oct. 2pm-4:30pm (weekends) / April-May 2pm-4.30pm (weekends and Bank Hols.)
£0.50-£1.50
Durham's only dedicated local history museum, this Medieval church retained its original purpose until the 1960s but now plays host to a wide variety of historical pieces from the locality, including a cell from Durham jail.

DURHAM LIGHT INFANTRY MUSEUM AND ART GALLERY
Aykely Heads 0191 384 2214
Open: April-Oct. 10am-5pm (daily) / Nov-March 10am-4pm (daily)
Adults £3.50 / Concessions £2.50 / Children £1.50 (under 4s free). Family (Two adults and up to three children) £9.
The Durham Light Infantry Museum and Durham Art Gallery is one of Durham's most rewarding family attractions. The museum tells the proud story of the Durham Light Infantry - County Durham's own regiment - over 200 years, with particular focus on the world wars. Meanwhile the gallery shows an exciting programme of contemporary art from regional, national and international artists, complemented by a range of artists' talks and workshops.

Sunderland Museum & Winter Gardens

DURHAM UNIVERSITY MUSEUM OF ARCHAEOLOGY
Old Fulling Mill, The Banks
0191 334 1823
Open: Apr.-Sept. 11am-4pm, Oct-March 11.30am-3.30pm Prices: £0.50-£2.50.
The University Archaeological Museum houses ancient pottery and inscribed slabs as well as hosting changing exhibitions on topics ranging from the archaeology of Durham Cathedral to medieval cloth making. Permanent exhibitions include explorations of the Stone Age, Roman, Medieval and Tudor periods in Durham.

DURHAM UNIVERSITY ORIENTAL MUSEUM
Elvet Hill (off South Road)
0191 334 5694
Open: 10am-5pm (Mon.-Fri.) / 12pm-5pm (weekends and Bank Hols.)
Adults £1.50 / Children £0.75 / Families £3.50. Under 5s free.
Full of fascinating objects from Japan, Mesopotamia and even further afield. Highlights include some amazing jewellery, plates, paintings and animal carvings. Also hosts temporary art exhibitions with an Oriental theme.

FOWLER'S YARD
Back Silver Street 0191 301 8726
The Yard comprises of an historic group of buildings overlooking the River Wear in the centre of Durham. The site has been refurbished as a unique development with nine creative workshops for professional artists, craftspeople and creative businesses.

HARPERLEY P.O.W. CAMP MUSEUM
Fir Tree, Crook 0138 876 7098
Open: 9am-5pm (daily)
Originally designed to house low-risk Italian and German prisoners during WW II, the camp now boasts a caravan site, restaurant, farm gift shop as well as the museum itself. Virtually all of Harperley's original structures remain, rendering the site unusual amongst British former concentration camps.

WEARDALE RAILWAY
Stanhope Station, Station Road, Stanhope
01388 526 203
Adults £8 / Seniors £6 / Children £4
All aboard! County Durham's heritage railway offers young and old alike the chance to experience the golden age of rail. Take a trip on a steam or diesel locomotive between Stanhope and Wolsingham within the Northern Pennines. Booking in advance is strongly advised.

From clubs especially dedicated to comedy (and no, we don't mean the region's perennially under-achieving football teams) to grand theatres staging huge West End musicals, the north-east has a veritable abundance of performing "spaces" ready to enrapture enthusiastic audiences. The region is also renowned for breaking new and talented writers, so look out for the many premiers held throughout the north-east.

Northern Stage

BOULEVARD
3-9 Churchill Street, Newcastle
0191 250 7068 **M** *Central Station*
Burlesque meets Broadway here as you join one of the UK's top cabaret entertainers Betty Legs Diamond and her full cast of Broadway dancers for a memorable night out. See stunning costumes, hilarious comedy and fabulous dance routines in this spectacular extravaganza that consists of everything from slapstick comedy to brilliantly choreographed dance routines.

CAEDMON HALL
Gateshead Central Library, Prince Consort Road, Gateshead
0191 4336965
A flexible and intimate venue, Caedmon Hall hosts a plethora of activity from theatre to music, story telling to seminars, gaming workshops and community events. The venue is also available to hire.

CUSTOMS HOUSE
Mill Dam, South Shields
0191 454 1234 **M** *South Shields*
Fabulous theatre complex with restaurant, gallery and cinema in impressive surroundings (right on the Tyne), situated a few miles outside of Newcastle but well worth the trip.

Imaginative programming from touring and local theatre companies to comedy, to band nights (rock, folk, pop etc) to panto.

DANCE CITY
Temple Street, Newcastle
0191 261 0505 **M** *Central Station*
Whether you have been dancing all your life, or are a complete novice, Dance City has something for you. They run classes in a huge range of styles, from tap and tango to ballet and break dance, at different ability levels to suit everyone. It's a great way to meet people and get fit, so get yourself along and have a go. You can have a drink and a bite to eat at Urban Café at Dance City, too.

GATESHEAD HERITAGE @ ST MARY'S
St Mary's Church, Oakwellgate, Gateshead 0191 4336965
In addition to the heritage information on display, this beautiful building hosts a varied programme of lunchtime concerts, craft workshops, evening performances, music and reading group meetings and magical installations.

GATESHEAD OLD TOWN HALL
West Street, Gateshead 0191 433 6965
M *Gateshead*
Hosting theatre, comedy, children's productions, drama and dance workshops all in the

Dance City

Gateshead Old Town Hall

NORTHERN STAGE
FORMERLY NEWCASTLE PLAYHOUSE

Northern Stage is a theatrical powerhouse of creativity. If you're after laugh-out-loud comedy, bold contemporary dance, explosive drama and innovative Christmas shows, then we'll have something for you. You can eat or drink from early morning til late evening, take in some art on our walls or take a tour of the theatre.

FOR MORE INFORMATION VISIT:
WWW.NORTHERNSTAGE.CO.UK

OR CALL
0191 230 5151

Two minutes walk from Haymarket
Metro, behind the new Newcastle
University Building (King's Gate).

Supported by
ARTS COUNCIL ENGLAND

Newcastle City Council

Northern Stage (Theatrical Productions) Ltd Charity No. 700X

stunning setting of this Grade II listed building.

HYENA CAFE
Leazes Lane, Newcastle
0191 232 6030 M *St. James*

This purpose built comedy venue has been running for a good number of years and they certainly know how to pack them in. Every Friday and Saturday (and some Thursdays) sees tip-top comedy acts gracing the boards, both national talent and acclaimed international acts too. They have a late license until 2am.

THE JOURNAL TYNE THEATRE
111 Westgate Road, Newcastle
0844 493 9999 M *Central Station*

A plethora of excellent features at this venue that primarily stages music events, although they often stage children's shows and annual pantomimes. It also has a beautifully restored Victorian interior that houses a colourful history.

LITTLE THEATRE
1-4 Saltwell View, Gateshead 0191 478 1499

Home to The Progressive Players who stage ten productions a year (a good mix of classic plays from the past and modern works) and always to a very high standard.

LIVE THEATRE
Broad Chare, Quayside,
Newcastle 0191 232 1232 M *Manors*

Live Theatre, located on Newcastle's vibrant quayside, is an award-winning new writing theatre with a national and international reputation for its production of new plays and support of new writers. Its unique 160-seat cabaret style theatre means that audiences are never far from the action and its intimate Studio Theatre offers a flexible space ideal for rehearsed readings, acoustic music and family theatre. Highlights include New Writing Studio Sessions where audiences can meet leading writers, watch rehearsed

readings or showcase their own scripts, and live stand-up gigs offering a chance to laugh along to side-splitting comedy from some of the UK's finest comedians. With various discounts available for preview performances, Live Theatre is a night out not to be missed!

MORDEN TOWERS
West Walls (Back of Stowell St.),
Newcastle
0191 477 4430 M *St. James*

Morden Tower is a well-established poetry (and music) venue that was initiated in the 1960s playing host to such greats as Allen Ginsberg, Seamus Heaney and Ted Hughes. A friendly and mixed audience gather regularly in this ancient meeting-place (it's part of the original city walls dating back to 1290) to listen to a wide range of contemporary poets as well as occasional music nights.

NORTHERN STAGE
Barras Bridge, Newcastle
0191 230 5151 M *Haymarket*

Northern Stage is the largest producing theatre company in the north-east of England, and are regarded as one of the top producing theatres in the UK. They have built a reputation for fresh and relevant productions of modern classics that attract audiences of all ages. Their original base of Newcastle Playhouse has been transformed into Northern Stage, a stunning performance space with three stages, and a high-tech acoustic wall that can be removed to create one of the greatest theatrical spaces in the north of England. With amazing work on stage, great visual art and hundreds of intriguing events, Northern Stage is throbbing with excitement!

THE PEOPLE'S THEATRE
Stephenson Rd., Heaton
0191 265 5020

A smallish theatre that puts on very popular local productions (including popular classics

Northern Stage

Peoples Theatre

from Shakespeare, Beckett, Coward etc) and it won't cost you too much to get in either. The theatre also houses the Calouste Gulbenkian Gallery, a small space used by local artists.

THE STAND COMEDY CLUB
High Bridge, Newcastle
0844 693 3336 **M** *Central Station*
This fabulous new, purpose built, comedy venue is a real boon to Newcastle. It's a basement club and aimed at the more discerning comedy fan (stag and hen parties are banned. Hooray!) Small candlelit tables create the right ambience and they run an array of nights from comics just cutting their teeth on the circuit to big hitters from Thursday to Sunday with the likes of Rory Bremner, Mark Watson and Patrick Monahan already going down a storm here. They also have a great bar/restaurant on the ground floor which is open all day. Make sure that this one is on your "must visit" list.

THEATRE ROYAL
Grey Street, Newcastle
0844 811 2121 **M** *Monument*
Newcastle's major theatre and inside and out, it's a real beauty; especially as it's just had a massive, multi-million pound refit (including the kind of comfy seats which your bottom will go ga-ga for). Home of most of the major

productions to hit Tyneside, there's an annual visit by the RSC and Opera North (these usually sell out in advance, so it's worth booking early). In addition there are many West End shows touring either before or after they start their runs in London and an excellent dance programme. There's truly something here for everyone, including one of the best pantomimes in the country – oh yes it is!

ARC
Dovecot St., Stockton-on-Tees
01642 525 199
ARC rarely passes up an opportunity, so its involvement with theatre comes as no surprise. It leaves no theatrical rock unturned, catching comedy, amateur, opera, musicals and drama in its artistic net. A real good 'un - don't miss.

DARLINGTON ARTS CENTRE
Vane Terrace, Darlington, 01325 348843
The Arts Centre provides more independent and experimental theatre than the Civic. It is an outstanding theatrical venue because it constantly searches for challenging visual art. The programming includes musical events, drama, dance and film for the main part.

DARLINGTON CIVIC THEATRE
Parkgate, Darlington,
01325 486555
This is one of the largest theatre venues in the area and there is a high probability that if any major shows travel through the north-east, they will stop here. It is a truly outstanding building and has been since it was opened as The New Hippodrome & Palace of Varieties in 1907.

THE FORUM
Queensway, Billingham,
Stockton-on-Tees
01642 552663
Reopened after undergoing a two year-long refurbishment, the forum is better than ever.

MIDDLESBROUGH THEATRE
The Avenue, Linthorpe, Middlesbrough,
01642 815181
Middlesbrough Theatre celebrates both professional and amateur drama, musicals and pantomime. It also encourages local talent to flourish by working with Middlesbrough College. It has 484 seats, and has been a much loved barer of theatre for many moons.

MIDDLESBROUGH TOWN HALL
Albert Road, Middlesbrough,
01642 729729
Middlesbrough Town Hall caters for school theatre events because many of the other tour-

ing performances play at the Middlesbrough Theatre. They have a wide range of entertainment from classical music, to comedy acts. Previous performers who've visited this venue include Jimmy Carr, The Royal Shakespeare Company and The Arctic Monkeys.

TOWN HALL THEATRE
Raby Road, Hartlepool,
01429 890 000
A beautiful theatre with 400 seats, it provides generous discounts to children, students and the over 60s. Be prepared to see anything from music, comedy or dance.

SUNDERLAND

THE ARTS CENTRE
Biddick Lane, Fatfield, Washington
0191 219 3455
An arts centre that stages numerous events including theatre in their 110 seated auditorium showing the best of amateur productions as well as touring professional companies and loads of great comedy and music.

EMPIRE THEATRE
High Street West, Sunderland 0844 847 2499 M *Sunderland*
They don't make them like they used to! This stunning, grand, in the truest sense, theatre in Sunderland underwent a £4.6m refurbishment

Gala Theatre & Cinema

Empire Theatre - Sunderland

a few years ago. The work has involved major backstage changes to allow larger shows to be performed (including some fabulous West End extravaganzas), while the auditorium has had some new seating and carpeting. The theatre offers an impressive range of events from comedy to opera, from ballet to great Christmas shows. Keep your eyes open for their special discounts.

ROYALTY THEATRE
Chester Road 0191 567 2669
The Royalty is an amateur repertory theatre but very well respected for the quality of its productions and has a varied selection of shows.

DURHAM

THE ASSEMBLY ROOMS THEATRE
40 North Bailey
0191 334 1419
Catering primarily to student drama, the 223-seat Assembly Rooms Theatre lies on the Bailey in the heart of Durham. Predictably, productions tend to coincide with term times though fortunately they are generally open for all to attend and actually of a reasonably decent standard. Oh and look out for the scrumptious ice cream invariably on offer during intervals! Ticket prices vary.

THE CITY THEATRE
Fowlers Yard
0191 384 3720
Owned and operated by the Durham Dramatic Society, The City Theatre houses only 72 seats yet shows at least five full-blown mainstream productions per year. Also sees a number of one-act plays which are entered into the All England Drama Festival.

EMPIRE CINEMA AND THEATRE
Front Street, Consett 01207 218171
The only remaining traditional theatre in County Durham, the Empire Cinema and Theatre is a popular venue staging professional acts and entertainment from all over the UK. A licensed bar is available 45 minutes in advance of all evening shows along with a café serving snacks and drinks. The theatre also has an induction loop system installed in the auditorium and full disabled access downstairs in addition to disabled parking at the front of the building.

THE GALA THEATRE
Millennium Place
0191 332 4041
The centrepiece of Durham's ambitious arts programme, the Gala Theatre houses a state-of-the-art modern theatre, spacious and comfortable café-bar and two cinema screens. Over the last few years Gala has developed a strong reputation for producing high-quality in-house theatre productions alongside a programme that attracts the country's leading theatre companies, comedians, bands and musicians and dance performers.

THE LAMPLIGHT ARTS CENTRE
Front Street, Stanley
01207 218 899
The Lamplight Arts Centre is another multi-purpose venue, offering a range of events and performances sure to cater for all. The main auditorium has a large stage and a seating capacity of 430. The retractable style of the seating offers flexible use of the large amount of available space for live theatre and cinema, tea dances and lavish wedding ceremonies and receptions. On the same floor, a lounge bar combines with a gallery space to produce a casual area to relax in.

CINEMA

Student Nights at ARC

Just behind the High Street in Stockton Town Centre, ARC has the only independent cinema in the area and the best comedy line-ups around.

Make it on your top places to visit, and join us for the best student offers.

Have a good giggle and blow off some study-steam at our fortnightly Catch 22 Comedy Club.

Every gig we have a small number of student tickets available for just £5, but get in there fast they run out quickly!

Use code **Cracking** when booking online or at the Box Office.

Join us for a cracking student offer of £3.50 per ticket every Tuesday for the best in independent, world and blockbusters films. Plus fantastic food and drinks promotions running throughout the year.

Student Night at ARC Cinema

 Supported by ARTS COUNCIL ENGLAND

Stockton-on-Tees

Box Office: 01642 525 199
Book Online: www.arconline.co.uk

Naturally, the region has an abundance of multiplexes showing all of the latest disappointing sequels and ill-advised remakes, but we also have a number of independent cinemas which are renowned throughout the UK for their innovative programming which encompasses art house, classics, foreign films, documentaries and any number of special events.

NEWCASTLE & GATESHEAD

THE CUSTOMS HOUSE
Mill Dam, South Shields
0191 454 1234 **M** *South Shields*
Situated a few miles outside of Newcastle, at the coast, The Customs House is a theatre/art gallery, but they also have a cinema which usually shows all the latest releases.

EMPIRE
The Gate, Newgate Street, Newcastle
M *Monument*
Info line: 08714 714714
Empire's state of the art cinema at The Gate has 12 screens ranging from a 67 to 436 capacity, all with Dolby Surround Sound and the capability to show most formats of film (including 3D).

STAR & SHADOW CINEMA
Crawhall Road, Ouseburn 0191 2610066
M *Manors*
The Star and Shadow Cinema is a truly independent venue, programmed entirely by the volunteers that run it. Expect films from all over the world, oddities and forgotten gems, plus political and social documentary. They often show groups of films, focusing on directors, movements or films from a specific region. The film programme runs Sunday and Thursday evenings. A huge array of other gigs and events also happen throughout the week. A complete and utter gem.

TYNESIDE CINEMA
10 Pilgrim Street, Newcastle 0845 217 9909 **M** *Monument*
A night at the pictures – as it should be! The Tyneside Cinema is THE place to go to in Newcastle if you love film. Based right in the heart of the city, this independent marvel shows the very best movies, mixing mainstream modern greats with the best of films from right across the world and classics of yesteryear. The

Tyneside's screens are also something rather special and are fully licensed too, so you can enjoy a full-blown night out at the flicks in a comfy leather armchair that's something much more than the norm. It's also home to three of the best cafes in town: the legendary Tyneside Coffee Rooms, the super cool cocktail bar/cafe, Intermezzo, and the dinky Tyneside Bar.

ODEON SILVERLINK
Silverlink Retail Park, North Shields
0871 2244 007
Buckets of ice cream, the latest Lucas Ex system, body moulded seats and all the other trappings you'd expect from a multi-screen cinema.

ODEON METROCENTRE
48 Garden Walk, Metrocentre,
M *Gateshead*
0871 2244 007
This cinema – found at the huge Metrocentre complex – will cater for all your IMAX, 3D and other blockbuster needs.

TEES VALLEY

ARC CINEMA
Dovecot Street Stockton on Tees TS18 1LL
01642 525199
ARC is the place to go for the best in alternative, world, independent and British cinema. ARC screens everything from the contemporary, to the retro and classic with a couple of shorts nights thrown in as well. As Tees Valley's only Independent Cinema ARC can't help but be proud to show the best films in one of the cosiest settings in the region.

CINEWORLD
Middlesbrough Lesirue Park,
Marton Road, Middlesbrough.
0870 200 2000.
Ten screens at this multiplex which has

| THE CRACK MINI GUIDE

plenty of fast food outlets nearby if that's your thing.

DARLINGTON CIVIC THEATRE
and Arts Centre
Vane Terrace, Darlington. 01325 486 555
Prices vary depending on film
The Art Centre provides cinema which challenges your mind without challenging your pocket.

ODEON CINEMA
Northgate, Darlington. 0871 224 4007
The Odeon has three screens and can home 850 people between them.

THE REGENT CINEMA
Newcomen, Redcar. 01642 482094
This is a humble cinema with one screen, but it has projected its way into the local's hearts for being a continual source of cinema, and will hopefully continue to do so for many talkies to come.

SHOWCASE CINEMAS
Aintree Oval, Teesside Leisure Park
0871 220 1000.
This is a beast of a cinema, with 14 screens and 2,000 seats.

VUE
The Lanyard, Hartlepool TS24 0XS
0871 224 0240
What do you get when you cross seven screens with 1,807 seats? Vue cinema in Hartlepool!

SUNDERLAND

CINEWORLD BOLDON
Abingdon Way, Bolden Colliery
Box Office: 0871 200 2000
This huge multi-screen cinema just outside of Sunderland has all the usual trappings of such an enterprise. There's an arcade and bar and a pick and mix to die for.

EMPIRE CINEMA
4 Lambton Street, Sunderland
Booking/Info: 08714 714 714
M *Sunderland*
The newish cinema complex has 12 screens and a number of VIP boxes. The cinema also contains disabled points, separate disabled toilets, removable chairs in screens for alternative seating and loop system for the hearing impaired inside screens. It is located only a short walk from all bus routes in Sunderland City Centre.

DURHAM

EMPIRE THEATRE AND CINEMA
Front Street, Consett
01207 218 171
A historic venue with a family-friendly feel that screens both classic film fare and the latest Hollywood releases. Completely renovated in a few years back and now handily fully-equipped with a licensed bar and eatery for all your pre-film drink and snack needs.

THE GALA
Millennium Place
0191 332 4041
As well as being a fantastic venue for catching theatrical events, The Gala also boasts two cosy fully accessible cinemas and very reasonable prices. In addition to the latest Hollywood blockbusters there is a Kids' Club on Saturdays, Golden Days screenings for the over-60s on Tuesdays and world cinema films on some Monday evenings.

LAMPLIGHT ARTS CENTRE
Front Street, Stanley
01207 218 899
Choices are limited given that the cinema portion of the centre only comprises of a single screen. Ticket prices vary although admission to the gallery is free.

There's a vibrant music scene in the region at present with a huge number of great local bands packing out sundry back rooms in a number of pubs. Of course, we also do bigger venues too, with everyone from the latest NME darlings to international superstars regularly appearing throughout the north-east.

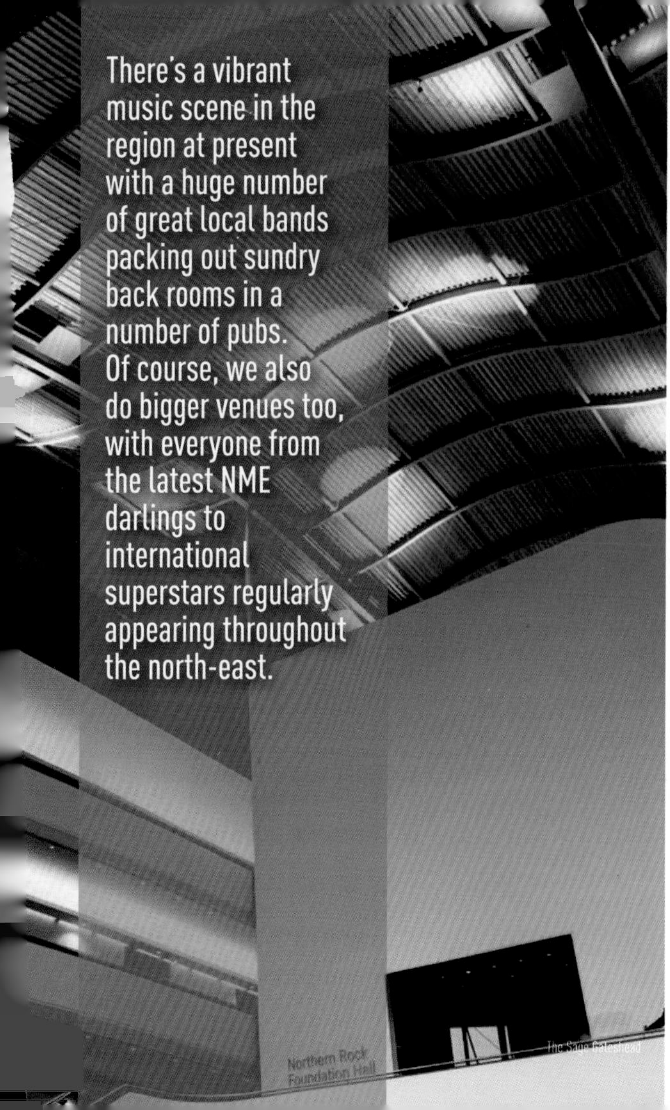

Northern Rock
Foundation Hall

The Sage Gateshead

Cluny 2

Cumberland Arms

NEWCASTLE & GATESHEAD

THE BRIDGE HOTEL
Castle Square, Newcastle
0191 232 6400 **M** *Central Station*
The upstairs room in this smashing, traditional boozer is the place to see anything from top acoustic acts to local bands on the up and up. See pubs section for more info.

THE CLUNY
Lime St., Ouseburn
0191 230 4474 **M** *Byker*
This cracking bar has built up a great reputation for live music and you'll find the cream of local talent - both experimental and traditional - as well as touring national and international acts, including the eclectic likes of everyone from Maximo Park to Evan Dando; Led Bib to The Arctic Monkeys. A real winner. See pubs for more info.

CLUNY 2
Lime St., Ouseburn
0191 230 4474 **M** *Byker*
This superb venue seats 160 and is an ideal place to catch intimate acoustic acts in wonderful surroundings. The bar is a glass-roofed, continental-style café-bar, serving the best premium lagers, wines and high quality spirits and the place is generally an extension of all the great things that The Cluny (see above) does.

THE CORNERHOUSE
Heaton Rd., Heaton, 0191 265 9602
Jazz aficionados will vouch for the reputation of this place, which attracts virtuosos from far and wide. Other types of music are also catered for, as is comedy. See pubs for more info.

CUMBERLAND ARMS
Byker Building, Byker
0191 265 6151 **M** *Byker*
As one of Newcastle's long-standing music venues, The Cumberland Arms offers a great space for live music with a splash of comedy also provided by the fabulous The Suggestibles gigs which are always packed out. The back room gives way to a great variety of regulars each week and this is a pub where you can come and satisfy your taste for indie, rock and jazz through to traditional folk. See pubs section for more details.

GATESHEAD OLD TOWN HALL
West Street, Gateshead 0191 4336965
M *Gateshead*
Eclectic and varied programming from funk & soul clubnights to live jazz, country, blues, world music and Americana plus some of the finest touring bands. Stunning architecture and a flexible capacity mark the Grade II listed Old Town Hall as one of Tyneside's most unique and charming venues.

NEWCASTLE & GATESHEAD MUSIC VENUES

www.thecrackmagazine.com

135

THE HEAD OF STEAM
2 Neville St., Newcastle
0191 230 4236
M *Central Station*

Practically opposite central station, this great pub is set over two floors and stocks a top range of European lagers and fine real ales. Here you'll find some of the best local bands with some splendid national and international touring acts to boot. If it's not live the HOS sound system always plays a cracking mix of funk, soul, dub and indie. A real goodie. Also see pubs.

THE JOURNAL TYNE THEATRE
111 Westgate Road, Newcastle
0844 493 9999
M *Central Station*

This fabulous venue can seat 1100 and has some of the best acoustics around and plays host to everyone from household names to tribute bands.

JAZZ CAFE
25 Pink Lane, Newcastle
0191 232 6505
M *Central Station*

The Jazz Cafe is a very popular little place, which gets heaving thanks to its late licence, good entertainment and laid-back style. Jazz most nights of the week and also look out for

their hot to trot salsa nights. The beret sporting proprietor is a local legend...

METRO RADIO ARENA NEWCASTLE
Arena Way, Newcastle
0844 493 6666 **M** *Central Station*

This massive 11,000 seat arena is the ideal place to catch some of the biggest names around with everyone from Lady Gaga to Shirley Bassey getting their hits out here.

NEWCASTLE CITY HALL
Northumberland Rd., Newcastle
0191 261 2606
M *Haymarket*

Acts appearing at this fine place range from top bands to classical ensembles (and some of the best stand-up comedians touring the larger venues). Check out the local press to find out what's coming up at this great venue and make sure you book early. A northern institution and rightly so.

NEWCASTLE UNIVERSITY
Kensington Tce., Newcastle
0191 239 3900 **M** *Haymarket*

Host to numerous touring NME-type bands, many a good night has been spent leaping around here. Also look out for their club nights which attract some of biggest DJs in the country to the region. The union has refurbished not so long ago so is all nice and shiny.

Journal Tyne Theatre

Darlington Arts Centre

NORTHUMBRIA UNIVERSITY
Sandyford Road, Newcastle
0191 227 4757
 M *Haymarket*
The main hall is one of the largest venues around and plays host to some of the country's best bands. The second stage often provides a useful chance for new bands to show their wares.

O2 ACADEMY
Westgate Rd., Newcastle
08444 77 2000 M *Central Station*
This purpose-built music venue has two stages (one with a capacity of around 2000; the other has nearer 400) and is a great place to catch national and international touring acts.

THE SAGE GATESHEAD
Gateshead Quays, Tickets:
0191 443 4661
Reception: 0191 443 4666
 M *Gateshead*
According to The Times this is: "The most exciting music venue in Britain". We're not arguing! The Sage Gateshead is an international home for music and musical discovery. The curvaceous silver roof houses three main performance spaces with great acoustics, a music education centre that includes a recording studio, a music information resource centre, bars, a newly refurbished brasserie and a café. You can hear all types of music being performed here including world, rock, pop, classical, acoustic, indie, country, folk, jazz, electronica and dance. You can also join in the music-making, both inside The Sage Gateshead and across the whole of the North of England, as a wide range of opportunities to explore and create all kinds of music, for all ages at every level of ability and experience, is on offer. The building itself – designed by Norman Foster - is well worth a visit: entry is free, so pop in and enjoy a beer, or a cup of coffee and a slice of lovely cake while

enjoying spectacular views of Newcastle and Gateshead quaysides.

RIVERSIDE
Quayside, Newcastle
0191 230 1913 M *Central Station*
Superb newish venue that stages live music every Thursday and Sunday with the very best of local and touring bands kicking up a real storm. Also stages great club nights (see clubs section).

TRILLIANS ROCK BAR
Princess Square, Newcastle
0191 232 1619 M *Monument*
Attracting the best rock bands from far and wide, Trillians is legendary in Newcastle and well worth checking out. They've got a great stage and the vibes are always nice and friendly. We're confident that you're going to love this one. See pubs section for more details.

THE TROJAN ROOMS
South Parade, Whitely Bay
0191 251 0080 M *Whitley Bay*
One of the newest music venues in the region and it's down the coast at Whitley Bay. 250 capacity, with great facilities, fabulous sound system and some great bands – what's not to love? Music policy runs from reggae to rock, ska to classic and a bit of jazz. Good stuff.

ARC
Dovecot St., Stockon-on-Tees. 01642 525 199
Big ARC strikes again: the all-rounder of entertainment venues. It provides the musical spotlight for all genres, from orchestral razzmatazz to the unsigned and up and coming: an eclectic and cultural stew and one not to miss.

DARLINGTON ARTS CENTRE
Vane Terrace, Darlington, 01325 348843
The Arts Centre offers an extensive range of musical delights with a huge range of genres covered. And it's a very friendly venue to boot.

DR. BROWN'S
135 Newport Road, Middlesbrough, 01642 213 213
Dr. Brown's prides itself on giving new bands the opportunity to get behind a microphone on Thursday, Friday and Saturday nights.

THE EMPIRE
Corporation Road, Middlesbrough, 01642 253553
Much like a cream egg, The Empire is as good as it is on the outside as it is on the inside. This three-floored art deco Victorian Theatre has been a unique clubbing venue for 18 years

Gala

Liberty's in Town

now and its easy to see why. With regular club nights, Fridays are with Sumo the best rock, mosh and indie night around with regular live acts. Saturday nights are with Metropolis offering five rooms from Indie, electro, pop and RnB. To top it off they offer great gigs from some of the world's top bands on tour. The admission price varies depending on whose playing but you always get your dollars worth!

THE GEORGIAN THEATRE
Green Dragon Yard, Stockton-on-Tees,
01642 674 115
The Georgian is a 200 capacity venue and has seen the likes of the Arctic Monkeys, The Cribs and Lost Prophets boogie under its hat.

THE KU BAR
Prince Regent Street,
Stockton-on-Tees,
01642 860068
The Ku Bar is your reliable venue for your indie, rock and alternative bands. Friday is their usual day of fancy, but don't be surprised to hear the floor moving throughout the course of the week.

LIBERTY'S IN TOWN
266 Linthorpe Rd, Middlesbrough,
North Yorkshire, 01642 231387
A firm favourite with student and regulars alike, Liberty's in Town provides local music intermittently in the course of any given month.

MIDDLESBROUGH TOWN HALL
Albert Road, Middlesbrough.
01642 729729/815181
The Town Hall will never see its facilities go to waste and has opened its threshold to many acts over the years...

THE HARTLEPOOL
COMMUNITY STUDIOS
Hartlepool, Tower Street, Hartlepool,
Cleveland,
01429 424 440
The Studio supports live music in its entirety

Gateshead
Old Town Hall

The Gallery/
Gateshead Central Library

Gateshead Heritage
@St Mary's

Gateshead LIVE

Music
Comedy
Dance
Theatre
Workshops
Festivals
Exhibitions

For the latest information see the What's On section on
www.gateshead.gov.uk

Gateshead
Council

and offers low admission prices to keep the love for the live strong. At the heart of their activities lie two fully equipped acoustically designed recording studios, which offer training courses from introduction to sound recording to DJ skills.

SUNDERLAND

ARTS CENTRE
Fatfield, Washington
0191 219 3455
Superb venue hosting all manner of music nights from every genre that you care to think of.

THE BOROUGH
1 Vine Place, **M** *Park Lane, 0191 514 5675*
A well loved Sunderland pub, which stages some quite storming gigs, usually of a metal variety, and held each Thursday, Friday and Sunday. One of the best in the north-east at what it does.

THE BUNKER
Stockton Rd., **M** *Park Lane, 0870 922 0336*
Studio, rehearsal space and music venue in one, The Bunker has hosted the likes of Bloc Party and Kasabian when they were just on the cusp.

EMPIRE THEATRE
High Street West, Booking Tickets: 0844 847 24 99 **M** *Sunderland*
One of the biggest theatre's in the north and attracting all manner of big shows with musicals, ballets and comedy shows all packing them in here.

INDEPENDENT
36 Holmeside 0191 568 9770
M *Park Lane*
Really superb, independent (naturally) venue which has played host to the cream of up and coming indie music including: Klaxons, Maximo Park, The Futureheads, Pull Tiger Tail etc.

THE KINGS ARMS
Ayres Quay, Millfield,
0191 567 9804
Top quality blues, jazz and folk at this extremely popular bar.

PADDY WHACKS
6-7 Green Terrace
0191 564 1010
M *Park Lane*
Newly refurbished Irish Bar, serving the obligatory Guinness and busker nights, with other live music on weekends.

THE ROPERY
Webster's Bank, Deptford,
M *Pallion*
0191 514 7171
Perfectly located on the riverside, they have bands on most nights of the week.

THE ROYALTY
Chester Rd., University, 0191 565 9930
Another popular pub venue with local bands playing in the upstairs function room.

DURHAM

THE ANGEL INN
53 Crossgate
0191 386 5561
In addition to a fabulous jukebox and a beer garden, this hard-rocking pub also offers performances from a fair amount of local bands throughout the month and acts as the official "pre-bar" for nearby Studio's Skool of Rock night on Fridays.

THE BEAMISH MARY INN
No Place, Beamish, Stanley
0191 370 0237
A traditional, family-run pub since 1897, The Beamish Mary Inn also has live music three times a week or more.

THE BIG JUG
88 Claypath
0191 384 8354
A relative minnow in Durham's music scene, this fine pub nevertheless hosts its own Open Mic evening every Thursday without fail.

THE CITY HOTEL
84 New Elvet
0191 386 9936
Conveniently situated right at the heart of Durham and known to host the occasional Battle of the Bands event in addition to its semi-regular live acts.

DURHAM LIVE LOUNGE
North Road
0191 383 1387
A newish one, this. Situated on the former site of Aussie chain pub Walkabout and the cinema of years gone by, Durham Live Lounge is easily one of the biggest live venues in the city. The acoustics are a cut above and the atmosphere is usually top-notch. A wide variety of bands have been attracted here and with little wonder. Do pay it a visit.

DURHAM UNIVERSITY
Students' Union
Dunelm House, New Elvet
0191 334 1777
Easily the biggest venue on this list, Durham Students' Union is one of the only places in the city to see acts of national significance.

FISHTANK
29-33 Neville Street
0191 384 2685
Tiny though it may be, The Fishtank nevertheless serves up a wide range of live performances from local independent bands and those further afield.

GALA THEATRE
Millennium Place
0191 332 4041
The magnificent Gala Theatre brings the very best live music to Durham, with everything from pop to classical fare served up for your delectation.

HEAD OF STEAM
3 Reform Place, North Road
0191 386 6060
Having taken over from Reform Place a few years back, this lovely place is part of the venerable Head of Steam franchise and, consequently, is renonwned for putting on some gigs by up and coming bands that you wouldn't hesitate in describing as extraordinary. Great stuff.

SHAMROX
91A Claypath
0191 389 4102
A good line in performances by touring regional singer-songwriters of repute.

2 Scotswood Road
Newcastle upon Tyne
newcastles longest running gay bar

Churchill Street
Newcastle upon Tyne
longest running disco bar

42 Scotswood Road
Newcastle upon Tyne
leather, rubber & denim bar

the only
gays
in the village

**visit the only bars that are gay owned
and gay run for gay people**

It's queer up north; especially in Newcastle which has The Pink Triangle, an area not far from the Central Station that contains a number of gay (and gay friendly) pubs and clubs. Lately Sunderland and Middlesbrough have also been starting to make a splash with many more gay nights springing up over the last year or so.

[@NE BAR
1 Marlborough Crescent, Newcastle
0191 260 3841 M *Central Station*
One of the smartest gay bars in the quarter, this light an airy establishment has an eclectic music policy that veers from camp trash to cool house. Well worth checking out mid-week when they have two for one drink offers and is a pre-club venue if you're so inclined.

THE BANK BAR
12 Scotswood Road, Newcastle
0191 261 8880 M *Central Station*
One of the busiest bars in the pink triangle with a variety of different nights to keep you entertained including: Sunday: Greta-La-More (with her blend of camp tunes and drink promos), Ophelia Balls & Raunchie Rusty; Mon, Thurs, Fri & Sat: cabaret night (do your thing) with Raunchy Rusty; Tues: Topkatz Karaoke with Miss Kitty. Funderful.

THE BARON & BARONESS
Times Square, Newcastle
0191 233 0414 M *Central Station*
Think Tom Cruise taking a blood thirsty bite out of Brad Pitt in Interview With A Vampire: chandeliers, candle lit archways, organ pipes, fireplaces, cosy nooks and crannies and carved wooden thrones. Yep, this is a gothic themed bar which attracts a mixed crowd.

BOULEVARD
3-9 Churchill Street, Newcastle
0191 250 7068 M *Central Station*
Burlesque meets Broadway here as you join one of the UK's top cabaret entertainers Betty Legs Diamond and her full cast of Broadway dancers for a memorable night out. See stunning costumes, hilarious comedy and fabulous dance routines in this spectacular extravaganza that consists of everything from slapstick comedy to brilliantly choreographed dance routines.

BLUE CORNER SAUNA
164b Heaton Park Rd., M *Heaton*
0191 240 0122 Mon-Sat 11am-7pm; Sun 12pm-6pm. Out of town this is a relaxed sauna with friendly atmosphere. Facilities include steam room, large sauna cabin, two TV lounges, two shower areas, rest rooms, coffee shop, smoking and non-smoking areas.

EAZY STREET
8-10 Westmorland Rd., Newcastle
M *Central Station*
Newish addition to the Newcastle gay scene and it's a very jolly cabaret and trebles bar with plenty of high jinx with Vicky Pais and co. The student party night on Monday is always well worth checking out.

THE DOG
15 Malborough Cres., Newcastle
0191 221 0775 M *Central Station*
A pretty small pub that has a loyal band of regulars (gay and straight), but don't worry if you're not one of the usual crowd - outsiders are welcome with open arms. The upstairs karaoke is very popular with lesbians.

THE EAGLE
42 Scotswood Road, Newcastle
0191 230 4416 M *Central Station*
Attracts a mostly male crowd over 25. Like its Amsterdam and US cousins, The Eagle has all the trappings you would expect from a gay male dominated space. Think denim, think leather, think rubber. Open late.

ECLIPSE
Eclipse, 48 Clayton Street, Newcastle
0191 222 0183 M *Central Station*
A large bar with great value food during the day. Attracts a mixed crowd which gets more gay at nights and weekends. Upstairs offers a pre-club space which is popular with lesbians.

GOSSIP

Westmoreland Road
0191 261 6824 M *Central Station*
Presented as a sports bar (so there's loads of screens to watch the football), this smart pre-club venue is adjacent to The Powerhouse. Great place for a drink during the week, it offers a great warm-up to the club at weekends.

HEAVENS
Churchill Street, Newcastle
0191 232 2037 M *Central Station*
This place has always attracted the great and the good. Well designed you'll find a young, fun clientele here. A positive feel-good vibe abounds and you'll be able to catch DJs on a weekend.

THE LOFT
10a Scotswood Rd.
0191 261 5348 M *Central Station*
Located above Switch and The Bank, this is a really canny club, offering a large heated roof terrace, well-lit dancefloor and a great selection of some of the scene's most popular nights.

NICE 'N' NAUGHTY
62 Scotswood Rd.
0191 221 2571 M *Central Station*
Shop stocking all of your fruity needs.

NUMBER 52
52 Scotswood Road,
0191 221 189 M *Central Station*
Hooray for this place! Fab steam room, sauna room, hydrotherapy pool, restrooms, video lounge, internet, private courtyard with smoking area and fully licenced refreshment area in this fantastic new establishment which pushes all the right buttons and is consequently proving very popular.

THE POWERHOUSE
0191 261 5348 M *Central Station*
Westmoreland Rd., Newcastle
The largest gay club in the north-east offers

three floors and a roof terrace. They also have a fabulous sound system and offer a wide variety of music depending on which room you venture into. They're usually the first port of call for contestants who get booted off The X-Factor too. A local institution.

SWITCH
4-10 Scotswood Road, Newcastle
0191 230 3863   **M** *Central Station*
During the day Switch offers a warm family atmosphere, serving a wide range of food at affordable prices. By night Switch is transformed into a lively disco bar with DJs mixing up all of your favourite party and chart classics every night of the week.

TOP 2 BOTTOM
85-89 Blandford St., Newcastle
0191 230 4110   **M** *Central Station*
Sun-Thurs 11am-11pm; Fri/Sat 11am-6am
This sauna offers a large stream room, video lounge, TV lounge, jacuzzi and snack bar.

TWIST
Times Square, Newcastle
   M *Central Station*
A very mixed bar, popular in the summer with its outdoor seating area and offers a great selection of food.

THE YARD
2 Scotswood Road, Newcastle
0191 232 2037   **M** *Central Station*
The longest running gay bar in Newcastle and still one of the best. Attracts a wide range of punters from people who have been frequenting it since it first opened, to newcomers to the scene who just love the friendly atmosphere.

ANNIE'S BAR
97 Linthorpe Road, Middlesbrough
07867 564 735
Very friendly pub that has long been at the heart of the Boro gay scene. Monday is free pool night (i.e. the game – you won't need your swimming stuff), Tuesday is karaoke with Chubbs, Wednesday is karaoke with Peter, thrill to Jackie Daniels each Saturday, and on Sunday it's Sheila Bilge.

BASEMENT
Albert Road, Middlesbrough
01642 220 040
Home to Tees Valley's biggest and brashest gay night: Satur-gay. More hands in the air action than anyone could possibly want.

The Eagle

Rhe Bar

BIJOU @ HARVEYS
Linthorpe Road, Middlesbrough
Happening monthly on a Thursday gird yourself for an avant-garde night of fun with the drag DJ Ava Divine.

BLU
Albert Road, Middlesbrough
01642 220 040
There's a variety of nights that you should know about at this place and they are Blu Tuesdays (karaoke with Kris King); Wii Wednesday; Quiz (last Thursday of each month – with cash prizes); Pout! (with DJ Matt Nevin spinning the tunes); Satur-gay pre-party (with DJ Matt Nevin).

THE CROWN
143 Linthorpe Road, Middlesbrough
01642 255 311
Get along here every Tuesday for the lovely Basecamp night which is free entry and runs from 10pm-2am.

THE OAK
23 Newport Road, M'bro
01642 219 748
The "owned by gay people for gay people" Oak is a long standing friendly bar in the Middlesbrough area. It hosts DJ nights and karaoke nights most evenings. Never before has an oak grown in such a loud and proud fashion. Keep on growing!

SUNDERLAND

ARIZONA @ THE POINT
The Point, Holmeside
0191 510 8680
M *Park Lane*
Situated in The Point mega-complex thrill to Miss Ophelia Balls and The Lush Crew every Tuesday.

THE BLACK BULL
309-310 High Street West
0191 567 5702 **M** *Sunderland*
The Black Bull dons its gay head each Tuesday with drag acts and karaoke etc.

CHASE
1-3 Park Lane
0191 567 0753 **M** *Park Lane*
Every Tuesday, until 1am, see what Miss Kitty and guests have in store for you...

DIVA
Galen Building, Green Terrace
0191 567 0760 **M** *Sunderland*
Running every Tuesday from 11.30pm until the wee hours (4am) keeping you company is Frenchy Kiss and Viva La Diva.

LOLA'S
17 Vine Place
0191 564 1536 **M** *Park Lane*
Like all the gay nights in Sunderland this is held on Tuesday nights and Lola's is where you can get down to DJ Gerard Purvis.

LUMA
15-17 Derwent Street
0191 514 5111 **M** *Sunderland*
Luma-Licious and Vicky Paris are your passport to pleasure here every Tuesday night.

RUSH
24 Vine Place
0191 514 3800 **M** *Park Lane*
DJ Skippy will be spinning a selection of tunes to make your hips positively swivel at this place every Tuesday.

TTONIC
12-14 Vine Place
0191 565 5755 **M** *Park Lane*
Ttonic goes gay on Tuesdays with a friendly and welcoming atmosphere. With resident drag queen too.

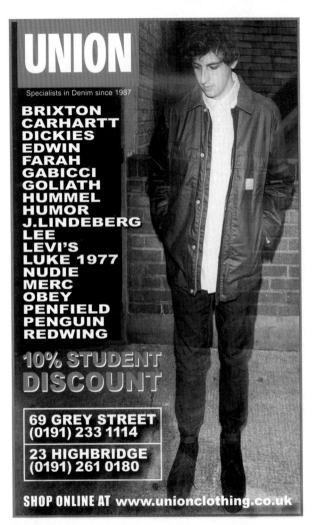

UNION

Specialists in Denim since 1987

BRIXTON
CARHARTT
DICKIES
EDWIN
FARAH
GABICCI
GOLIATH
HUMMEL
HUMOR
J.LINDEBERG
LEE
LEVI'S
LUKE 1977
NUDIE
MERC
OBEY
PENFIELD
PENGUIN
REDWING

10% STUDENT DISCOUNT

69 GREY STREET
(0191) 233 1114

23 HIGHBRIDGE
(0191) 261 0180

SHOP ONLINE AT www.unionclothing.co.uk

From out of town, mega-shopping complexes, to the dinkiest of boutiques the north-east likes to shop. We have a huge variety of fashion emporiums from some of the biggest and best designer stores in the UK, to some rummage-tastic vintage shops. We also have some great independent record and book outlets and the kind of markets which you could happily lose a day at.

NEWCASTLE & GATESHEAD SHOPS & MARKETS

NEWCASTLE & GATESHEAD

SHOPPING CENTRES

CENTRAL ARCADE
Grainger Street, Newcastle
M *Monument*
A quiet beautiful shopping thoroughfare containing fashion and beauty stores as well as the fabulous music shop Windows (see music section for more details).

ELDON GARDEN
Percy Street, Newcastle
0191 261 0117 **M** *Haymarket*
Linking to Eldon Square is the Eldon Garden Shopping Centre, which offers an extensive collection of designer brands and fashion labels in a stylish environment, as well as specialist outlets for interiors, jewellery, gifts and home electronics. Added to this are opportunities to pamper yourself while out shopping, with a beauty salon, two hair salons and three relaxing pavement style eateries.

ELDON SQUARE
Central Newcastle
0191 261 1891 **M** *Monument*
Newcastle's main shopping area is this very well designed arcade. Encompassing all the main high street stores, there's also restaurants, cafes, book, stationary and video game stores as well as independent clothes and shoe shops. The recently opened St Andrew's mall section has also brought new stores to Newcastle, such as Apple, Guess, Superdry and Hollister. There are many entrances; the main one is Northumberland Street but they're also at Grainger Street, Monument and the bus station off Percy Street - so you can't miss it!

METROCENTRE
Gateshead 0191 493 0219
Metrocentre is officially the largest shopping complex in Europe. It contains over 330 shops including big high street names and fashion labels, to smaller, specialist shops unique to the centre. Metrocentre is more than a shopping experience however: new leisure facilities include six new restaurants, adding to the 50 plus places to eat, the only Odeon IMAX cinema in the region and a Namco Funscape family entertainment complex, complete with ten pin bowling and dodgems.

MONUMENT MALL
Newcastle 0191 233 2323
M *Monument*
Situated next to Grey's Monument, right in the centre of town, this three-storey shopping arcade and food mall is an excellent modern structure. In keeping with the appearance of old Newcastle it has a beautiful glass dome situated directly above the Monument Metro Station.

ROYAL QUAYS OUTLET
Coble Dene, North Shields
0191 296 3743 **M** *Percy Main*
Royal Quays is a unique shopping environment situated about 10 miles away from Newcastle. A massive refurbishment programme has attracted some of the biggest brands around - all offering up to 60% off recommended retail prices every single day. If you love shopping, you'll enjoy browsing in their huge range of stores.

FASHION

AL'S
3a Cheltenham Terrace, Heaton, Newcastle **M** *Chillingham Road*
Just off Heaton Road (and recently opened) is this charming emporium which stocks gentleman's vintage wear, assorted accessories and vinyl. It's all rather delightful.

ALL SAINTS
33 Market St., Newcastle
Eldon Square, Newcastle
0191 221 1320/ 0191 211 2910
M *Monument*

Funky urbanwear for men and women from this ever popular chain.

ATTICA
2 Old George Yard,
off High Bridge, Newcastle
0191 261 4062 **M** *Monument*
Period clothing from the 20s to the 80s, this treasure trove has everything from a brilliant selection of cool vintage clothes, including a great range of dinner jackets, ballgowns and footwear, to furniture and artefacts for the home. Check out the 50s & 60s glassware and lamp selection. Recently celebrated 25 years in the biz and still a goodie.

BEST VINTAGE
14 High Bridge, Newcastle
0191 261 8500 **M** *Monument*
This is a huge store stocking a fantastic array of quality second hand gear and accessories. Not only that, they also do up old and unwanted textiles in an inventive and creative way, customising their way into our hearts. A pocket-pleasing palace of great clobber.

BETWEEN THE BUTTONS
8 St Mary's Place, Newcastle
0191 261 6671 **M** *Haymarket*
This store prides itself on recycling old clothing, fabric, jewellery and accessories in partenership with students from Newcastle college to support new designers and bring life back to old products. If you want to alter or customise their products this is a service they also offer. Brill.

CRUISE
1-6 Princess Square, Newcastle
0191 261 0510 **M** *Monument*
This huge shop specialises in designer names for both men and women. Gear by designers such as Cavalli, D&G, Jimmy Choo, Sass and Bide, True Religion, Hugo Boss, Prada etc - there's also a good selection of shoes and accessories. Can be pricey but great sales.

CRUISE JEANS
15-17 Princess Square, Newcastle
0191 260 2601 **M** *Monument*
Another two floors of swanky Cruise style goodness for lads and lasses in need of a wide range of labels and denim.

DEEP
51 High Bridge
This little beauty is one of the newest additions to Newcastle's vintage shops range. Already with stores in Middlesbrough and York, this is bound to become a favourite haunt for anyone in Newcastle looking for good retro pieces. Whether it's Levi's cut-offs or printed

End Hunting Company

DEEP

dresses they have plenty to offer and what we love most is that their prices aren't going to break the bank.

EDEN
6 Brentwood Avenue, Jesmond, Newcastle 0191 281 7929 M *Jesmond*
Recently relocated, a concept store that hopes to deliver noticeable and different fashions. Carrying labels such as Betty Jackson, Theory and D'Exterior. Also includes a range of bags and jewellery from equally renound designers like Anya Hindmarsh and Yvonne Christa.

EDO JESMOND
13a Clayton Road, Jesmond, 0191 239 9666 M *Jesmond*
Menswear store full of brands such as Belstaff, Oiler and Boiler, Calabrese and Robert Graham. And they've even started designing their own shoes! Nice one for the boys indeed.

END
4-6 High Bridge, Newcastle 0191 261 9327
M *Monument*
This top notch store is a real magnet for the region's style conscious lads. They stock a real cool list of top labels including: Nike, Adidas Originals, Levi's Vintage, Lyle & Scott, Fred Perry, Clarus Originals, Nom De Guerre, A.P.C., Sergio Tacchini, Trainerspotter, Money, Baracuta, Better Off Dead, Billionaire Boys Club etc. Set over two floors, End is a real winner.

END HUNTING COMPANY
High Bridge, Newcastle 0191 230 3629 M *Monument*
Some more fashion finesse from the people behind End (see above) which has the feel of a hunting lodge with its wood panelled walls, roof beams and huge fireplace. And the clothes? Think rural chic and Americana inspired comfort with some top brands including Barbour's much sought after, and very fab, Japanese collection as well as stuff from Fila to Commes des Garcons to Adidas Consortium to Nigel Cabourn. Cool.

EXCLUSIVE FOOTWEAR
8-12 Shakespeare Street, Newcastle 0191 232 7610 M *Monument*
Wide range of footwear for both men and women from purveyors of quality shoes including Oliver Sweeney, Gant, Cheaney, Jeffrey West, Converse, Bourne and more. They also stock a good children's range as well as bags and other accessories.

FAT FACE
141 Grainger Street, Newcastle 0191 260 3429 M *Monument*
You know the score here. Clothing for lads and lasses who reckon they're down with the skiers, surfers and general active, outdoor types.

FENWICK
Northumberland St., Newwcastle 0191 232 5100 M *Monument*
Spread over five floors this department store is a local institution and has a plethora of fashion for both women and men as well as a huge range of cosmetics (and TVs and computers and furniture and greeting cards and food and just about everything else). Look out for their legendary Christmas window display (another local institution).

FLIP
1st Floor, 104 Westgate Road, Newcastle 0191 233 1755 M *Central Station*
Something of a local legend; this is Newcastle's longest established vintage store, specialising in "Americana" both vintage and new. With baseball jackets and boots, Hawaiian and flannel shirts, bowling gear and bandanas, you're sure to find what you're looking for. Check 'em out!

FREEFALL
24 High Bridge, Newcastle,
0191 231 2156 **M** *Monument*
Cool little shop selling some of the
funkiest, most interesting gifts and
fashion accessories around. Some of
the brands stocked include Paper Plane,
Moomin, Dandy, Scaramanga Satchels, Vans
Backpacks, New Era Caps, King Apparel and
Rocawear. New stock arrives weekly.

FROCK-A-HOLIC
21 Newgate Centre, Newcastle
0191 232 6119 **M** *Central Station*
Hidden away in the Newgate Centre is this cute
little shop which fuses vintage with boutique.
They stock both high street stuff along with
designers like D&G and Karen Millen, taking
pride in the good quality of their "pre-loved"
garments.

HAVETOLOVE
1-3 Hawthorn Road,
Gosforth, Newcastle
0191 213 1155 **M** *South Gosforth*
Very flamboyant and individual boutique
stocking super-chic French label Manoush
and American Retro, as well as staples such
as Made in Heaven jeans.

H & M
42 Northumberland Street, Newcastle
104-108 Grey Street, Newcastle,
0844 736 9000 **M** *Haymarket*
Well known chain but still a boon - cheap,
funky and some right bargains for lads, lasses
and kids. Great accessories and make-up too
at pocket pleasing prices.

JAEGAR
130 Grainger Street
0191 244 9738 **M** *Monument*
Part of the global fashion company, this is a
relatively new addition to Newcastle, offering
beautifully made, luxury women's wear.

JULES B
46 Acorn Rd., Jesmond
0191 281 7855 **M** *West Jesmond*
Upmarket shop stocking most well-known designer labels for men and women.

ME ME ME
26 Eldon Garden, Newcastle
16 Acorn Road, Jesmond, Newcastle
0191 261 0362/ 0191 209 4898
M *Monument / Jesmond*
A shopping haven for bags, jewellery and accessories, such as Pandora charms.

OFFICE
136-138 Grainger Street, Newcastle
0191 261 7277 **M** *Monument*
Superb for trainers – with those just released items being a speciality – as well as more dressy footwear and casual wear. For both men and women and a real goodie.

REISS
133-137 Grainger Street, Newcastle
0191 230 4999 **M** *Monument*
Understated chic for men and women set over two floors.

RETRO CLOTHING
2 High Bridge, Newcastle 0191 231 4226 **M** *Central Station*
Great store selling both gorgeous vintage and new pop clothing. Definitely worth a rummage.

RUBY & FRANK
4 Percy Park Road, Tynemouth
0191 259 6290 **M** *Tynemouth*
Well hello Dolly! This superb emporium pulls off the rare trick of being able to provide quirky, individual clothing and accessories, with original designs, at very reasonable prices. It's easy to reach (just hop on the Metro) and we're stamping this with a "Must Visit". Plenty of under-the-radar labels and very friendly staff to boot.

SCHUH
9-15 Blackett St., Newcastle 0191 267 4633
Unit 15, 31 St Andrews Way, Eldon Square Newcastle: 0191 231 4092 **M** *Monument*
Excellent range of shoes from their own make 'Schuh Clothing for Feet' that sit alongside the likes of Adidas and Dunlop to the more casual Dr. Marten's, Kickers, Bronx, Vans, DC and Nike amongst others. Also stock funky accessories including some yummy bags...

SCORPIO
Grainger Market, Newcastle
0191 232 0882 **M** *Monument*
Stocking those famous foot stalwarts, Dr. Martens, Scorpio also feature Caterpillar, Dealer Boots, Fly, Underground, Fit Flops, Vans, Iron First, Blow Fish, Iron Fist, Dude, Yoma, XTI and Tuk etc.

TK MAXX
Monument Mall, Newcastle
0191 261 0404 **M** *Monument*
Huge store that sells discounted gear from clothes to vases to shoes to underwear. It's often worth having a wade through the racks upon racks of clothes for the odd bargain and there's often a fair bit of cheap designer gear (SO last season though darling) - if you're that way inclined.

TRICKLE CLOTHING
35 High Bridge, Newcastle
0191 231 4789 **M** *Monument*
Another new shop on High Bridge offering trendy clothes for fashion conscious blokes. They offer a brilliant selection of designers and are currently the only place in Newcastle stocking Cheap Monday jeans. Definitely worth a visit.

Stretch your student budget

With over 330 stores, 50 restaurants and the largest selection of student discounts under one roof. Metrocentre is a must for stylish students. We're also home to a 12-screen Odeon Cinema, featuring the only IMAX theatre in the region, and the Namco Funscape, complete with bowling and dodgems.

To keep up to date with the latest student offers and competitions, follow us:

Facebook @metrocentreSHOP

Twitter @metrocentreSHOP

Larger than life for 25 years
metrocentre 25
www.metrocentre.uk.com

TRIPLE S
96-98 Grainger St., Newcastle
0191 230 1186 **M** *Monument*
Upper Blue Mall, Metro Centre
Upper Green Mall, Metro Centre
0191 460 4997/ 0191 460 1808
Names names names… Bench, Carhartt, Superdry, Vila, Fred Perry, Delicious, Amplified, Pop Vintage… the list is almost endless. With labels like these for both men and women this shop will have you dressed up and lookin' street stylee in no time as long as you've got the green, geezer.

UNION
69 Grey St., Newcastle
23 High Bridge, Newcastle
0191 233 1114 / 0191 261 0180
M *Monument*
If specialist denim and great casual wear is what you're after then look no further than the marvellous Union. Two stores stocking brands such as Carhartt, Edwin, Lee, Levis, Humor, Penfield, Luke 1977, Nudie, J.Lindeberg, Marshall Artist, Crojack, Obey, Farah Vintage to name but a few. Footwear and accessories are also sold here so you'll be sorted for whatever you fancy.

USC
26 Blackett Bridge, Eldon Sqare
0191 221 0009 **M** *Monument*
Providing the latest designer brands like Firetrap, Abandon, Gio-Goi, Diesel and Yumi, USC tends to be a little more cutting edge than general high street shops. But, because of the nature of their designer gear, their stock comes and goes quickly, so if you spot something you really, really like: snap it up quick!

VIVIENNE WESTWOOD
1 Hood St., Newcastle
0191 260 5220 **M** *Monument*
Lovely array of slinky and off-beat pieces from La Westwood for both men and women. Quality stuff.

FURNITURE

GREY BEAR
19 High Bridge, Newcastle
0191 232 3822 **M** *Monument*
Grey Bear is a brand new retailer situated on the cobble street that links Grey Street to the Bigg Market and it provides both new and vintage homeware for all occasions.

POSHED UP FURNITURE & THINGS
31 Heaton Hall Road, Newcastle
0191 265 6304 **M** *Chillingham Road*
Hand decorated vintage furniture shop that can be found in the lovely Newcastle suburb of Heaton. Not the biggest, but packed with interesting stuff and they also offer a poshed up furniture decorating service.

RECYCLE YOUR FURNITURE
Unit 1, 1 Stepney Rd., Ouseburn, Newcastle
0191 222 0212 **M** *Manors*
Fabulous place that saves furniture destined for the junk yard to creatively "re-funk" them into something fresh and different. Lovely stuff.

ARTS, CRAFTS & PHOTOGRAPHIC

BLACKWELL'S
141 Percy Street, Newcastle
0191 232 6421 **M** *Haymarket*
Newcastle's premier art shop caters for professional, amateur and students alike. A wide range of art and design materials found in store at competitive prices and great deals all year round!

DETAILS AT NEWCASTLE ARTS CENTRE
67 Westgate Road, Newcastle
0191 261 5999 **M** *Central Station*
A shop in the Newcastle Arts Centre which sells artists' works, handmade jewellery, pottery, glass and cards. This brilliant craft shop, pottery studio and purveyor of the

Free Fall

Grey Bear

region's largest selection of artists' materials is a complete winner. Students can also get a discount with an NUS card and most of their prices are less than the manufacturers' retail price anyway. They also offer a picture framing service.

DISCOVERY MUSEUM
Blandford Square, Newcastle
0191 232 6789 **M** *Central Station*
This shop sells an array of unique gifts for all ages, including toys for children, souvenirs from the museum and local history items.

GREAT NORTH MUSEUM: HANCOCK
Barras Bridge, Newcastle
0191 222 6765 **M** *Haymarket*
A range of themed gifts from dinosaurs to Romans and the ancient Egyptians.

JESSOP'S
23 Newgate street, Newcastle
0845 458 7228 **M** *Monument*
Stocks leading camera, camcorder and digital brands and offers developing, printing and equipment repair.

LAING ART GALLERY
New Bridge Street, Newcastle
0191 232 7734 **M** *Monument*
Presenting a selection of unique makers to the region, this craft shop is perfect for

special gifts or treats. It is also a great stop for cards, stationery, books and a range of locally-themed items.

SHIPLEY ART GALLERY
Prince Consort Road, Gateshead
0191 477 1495 **M** *Gateshead*
This craft-inspired shop stocks an array of unique handmade gifts, cards and jewellery. All sales help support the Gallery.

REORD SHOPS

BEATDOWN RECORDS
Basement Unit, Clarendon House,
Bewick Street, Newcastle
0191 261 8894 **M** *Central Station*
The fabulous Beatdown Records has two stores in Newcastle. The flagship is on the corner of Clayton Street and Bewick Street and covers all genres from rock and pop, metal, punk, jazz and blues and lots more besides. It also houses their legendary collectors' vinyl selection. They also have another Newcastle store (19a Ridley Place – 0191 221 2113) which is slanted more towards drum & bass, dubstep, hip-hop, house, electronica and indie stuff.

FORCE 10 RECORDS
Unit 2, The Basement, Bewick St.,
Newcastle 0191 221 0328
M *Central Station*

Top notch independent shop specialising in fast and hard euro-style dance music. What's not to love?

HMV
56/58 Northumberland Street, Newcastle. 0843 221 0275
M *Haymarket*
MetroCentre, 22 Cameron Walk, Gateshead. 0843 221 0198
You'll know this one, right?

J G WINDOWS
1/7 Central Arcade, Newcastle
0191 232 1356 **M** *Monument*
16 Garden Walk, Yellow Mall, Metro Centre 0191 493 2244
Excellent jazz, classical and pop sections as well as sheet music. Windows also stock a wide variety of instruments and accessories as well as being very competitively priced.

R.P.M. MUSIC
Unit 4, Old George Yard, Newcastle
0191 221 0201
M *Monument*
One of our faves, RPM caters for all specialist genres: hip-hop, indie, classic rock, jazz, reggae, blues, leftfield etc. They also sell tickets for concerts and they now hold outdoor events in the Courtyard, featuring bands and DJs! The independent spirit truly lives on in this real goodie which also has an amazing vinyl selection. Seek it out (it's beside the Old George pub).

REFLEX
23 Nun Street, Newcastle
0191 260 3246
M *Monument*
Stocking everything from chart toppers to rare imports, Reflex has a huge range of CDs. Merchandise includes record storage and accessories etc and they're also a ticket outlet and a mail order service too.

STEEL WHEELS
8 St Mary's Place, Newcastle
0191 261 6671 **M** *Haymarket*
After two years focussing on their online shop, Steel Wheels are back in a bricks and mortar address. They've got cascades of both vinyl and CDs to look through and some bargain prices as well. For die hard fans there's also some autographs and memorabilia to tempt you. Also featuring Between The Buttons clothing store (see above).

MUSICAL EQUIPMENT

GUITAR GUITAR
27 Grainger Street, Newcastle
0191 261 1568 **M** *Central Station*
Got guitar needs? Then look no further. 3,500sq feet of guitar nirvana is right here in Newcastle. They stock over 600 electric, acoustic and bass guitars and the knowledgeable staff are second to none and happy to answer any questions you may have.

THE GUITAR SHOP
3 Old George Yard, Newcastle
M *Central Station*
Does what it says on the tin! Specialist guitar shop with friendly staff.

NEWCASTLE DRUM CENTRE
10-12 Akenside Hill, Newcastle
0191 221 0301
M *Central Station*
More kits and cymbals than you can shake your drumsticks at, with a special dealing in Sabian and Zildjian cymbals.

NEWCASTLE MUSIC
71 Westgate Road, Newcastle
0191 221 0595
M *Central Station*
Instruments to suit almost any taste here, especially of the woodwind, brass and string variety. You can also grab some sheet music.

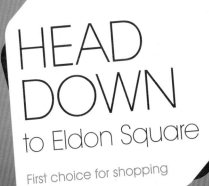

RICHER SOUNDS
94-96 Clayton Street, Newcastle
0333 900 0032 **M** *Central Station*
With stores up and down the country you probably know about this little gem if you're into your music. Excellent range of Hi-Fi equipment and home cinema stuff. The friendly staff know their stuff and their prices are usually second to none. This store was voted Which's best retailer for 2010!

SOUNDS LIVE
27-29 Dean Street, Newcastle
0191 487 9317 **M** *Central Station*
Guitars, amps, keyboards, recording, P.A.s, DJ products. Simply bags of stuff on offer and the staff are well informed.

SOUNDWARE
1 Starbeck Avenue, Newcastle
0191 260 3333 **M** *Jesmond*
At Soundware they specialise in music technology products which enables them to offer musicians, producers and DJs all types of experience levels with a wide range of music-making solutions at low prices. Packed with the latest Pro Audio, computer music, PA and DJ gear.

J G WINDOWS
Central Arcade, Newcastle
0191 232 1356 **M** *Monument*
Loads of instruments here and particularly good on the keyboards.

BOOKS

THE BACK PAGE
56 St. Andrews St., Newcastle
0191 261 5005 **M** *Monument*
The only shop of its kind in the north-east, The Back Page specialises in sports books (all sports catered for) and also stock a huge range of sporting memorabilia, including autographs, dvds, fanzines, football programmes etc. A veritable treasure trove.

BOOKS FOR AMNESTY
92 Westgate Rd., Newcastle
0191 222 0920 **M** *Central Station*
Fantastic second hand bookshop which has an ever changing stock of books from all genres (including collectibles) along with cards, maps and music. All proceeds go to Amnesty International.

BLACKWELL'S BOOKSHOP
141 Percy Street, Newcastle
0191 232 6421 **M** *Haymarket*
First choice for all your essential texts for

Flip

Chic Antique

University & College, ideally situated between Newcastle Uni and Northumbria. Stockists of all academic disciplines and also a wide range of general books and a premier art store too.

FORBIDDEN PLANET
59 Grainger Street, Newcastle
0191 261 9173 **M** *Central Station*
Brilliant shop catering to every whim of comic/toy fans. From Star Wars to wrestling, they stock recent issues of all comics imaginable and also carry a vast range of toys, graphic novels, cards, DVDs, books, posters, and assorted fanzines.

TRAVELLING MAN
43 Grainger Street, Newcastle
0191 261 4993 **M** *Monument*
Lovely comic shop stocking all the latest titles with plenty of independent and locally produced stock too. There's also a large range of graphic novels as well as a comprehensive roll-playing game section.

WATERSTONES
Emerson Chambers, Blackett St.,
Newcastle 0843 290 8503 **M** *Monument*
Very traditional decor with piles of books on top of tables, on shelves and just about anywhere where there's leg room. Very good ordering service.

ADVENTURE@ FREEMANS
1 Bigg Market, Newcastle
0191 233 1572 **M** *Central Station*
Stocking multitudes of outdoor clothing and footwear, including a full range of camping equipment, rucksacks, sleeping bags, tents, swiss army knives, multi tools, binoculars, waterproofs, maps, camouflage and hunting clothes. What more do you need?

BAGNALL & KIRKWOOD
28 Grey St., Newcastle
0191 232 5873 **M** *Monument*
Pick up some classy outdoor gear here from country clothes to treks into the wilderness. Also has a load of fishing gear.

COTSWOLD OUTDOOR
60-62 Northumberland Street,
Newcastle
0191 221 2709 **M** *Haymarket*
Big new store on Newcastle's main shopping street (reached by some escalators) and stocking a huge range of equipment (including watersports equipment) and tents as well as a boot fitting service and all the gear you're ever going to need for any type of outdoor pursuit.

Amnesty Books

Guitar Guitar

LD MOUNTAIN CENTRE
34 Dean Street, Newcastle
0191 232 3561   M *Central Station*
Clothing and equipment for a multitude of outdoor activities stocking the usual brands of Berghaus, Salomon, and North Face.

NORTHERN RUNNER
52 Low Friar Street, Newcastle
0191 261 4322   M *Central Station*
A specialist shop for the serious runner or the beginner, Northern Runner will provide all of your running/all terrain running needs. They stock every type of running shoe you could ever want (spikes, specialist athletic shoes, hiking footwear) as well as suitable clothing and accessories including jogging gear and all weather jackets. All the major labels are available including Asics, New Balance and Odlo. Referrals for sports physiotherapy sessions can be made through the store and you can even book a podiatrist to tend to those poor tootsies.

TISO
100-104 Grainger Street, Newcastle
0191 222 0020   M *Monument*
At a huge 5000sq ft the store is spread over two floors providing the ultimate destination for outdoor enthusiasts, with clothing and equipment from top brands such as The North Face, Columbia, and Vango. They also have an extensive watersports section and are Berghaus Approved footwear specialists.

WILD TRAK
60/62 St. Andrews Street, Newcastle
0191 261 8582   M *St. James*
If ever you're after some outdoor equipment, then look no further than the north's largest specialist store. Everything from lightweight camping to mountaineering, climbing to trekking is catered for, and their expertise has seen them supplying major expeditions over the last 30 odd years.

MARKETS

FARMERS' MARKET
M *Monument*
Meat, cheese, bread, preserves and condiments, all produced within a 50 mile radius are available on the first Friday of each month in this market held from 9.30am-2.30pm next to Grey's Monument in the centre of Newcastle.

GRAINGER MARKET
M *Monument*
This covered, city centre market is a piece of Newcastle history opened as it was in 1835. It's now a Grade I listed building and inside there are plenty of stalls with fresh produce being a speciality from a plethora of butchers and greengrocers. There are also stalls selling books, CDs, clothes and shoes, cards, video games, specialist coffee and food.

ARMSTRONG BRIDGE
Each Sunday from 10am-4pm this beautiful iron bridge which spans Jesmond Dene is resplendent with artists and crafts people selling their wares providing the ideal place to pick up something a little out of the ordinary.

NEWCASTLE QUAYSIDE
M *Central Station*
On Sunday (9.30am-4pm) the normally reasonable streets of the Quayside are transformed into a heaving mass of shoppers and stall holders. It's had a marvellous spruce up over the last few years or so and you can now purchase all manner of quality arts and crafts. Well worth checking out.

SOUTH SHIELDS
Market Square   M *South Shields*
You can either get a Metro to this market or take the more unusual route and go by the Passenger Ferry from North Shields. Excellent Flea Market on Fridays, where it's advisable to get there early and traditional stalls on Mondays and Saturdays.

TYNEMOUTH STATION

M *Tynemouth*

This market couldn't be easier to get to. Jump on the Metro to the coast, hop off at Tynemouth Station and you're there. Every weekend, this quiet, restored Victorian station comes to life with the hustle and bustle of hundreds of bargain hunters. Beneath the glass and wrought iron canopies of this beautiful listed building, you'll discover plenty of stalls weighed down with tempting goodies. On Saturday people search for antiques, bric-a-brac and books, while on Sundays the focus changes to crafts, household and practical items (as well as CDs/DVDs etc). Every third Saturday of the month the market is joined by local farmers selling their fruit, vegetables, meat, cheeses and home-baked cakes and bread. There is also a dedicated book fair four times a year. So why not make a day of it as there are places to eat and drink there, too. Open 9am to 4pm. For information on booking a stall, tel. 01670 536911.

SHOPPING CENTRES

CAPTAIN COOK SQUARE

Captain Cook Square Management, 16 Newport Crescent, M'bro 01642 221 873

The courtyard of Captain Cook Square will provide a breath of fresh air if Wilkinsons gets a little hectic or if TK Maxx is causing maximum stress.

CASTLEGATE SHOPPING CENTRE

3rd Floor Walker House, Stockton on Tees 01642 672 783

Open Mon-Sat 9am-5.30pm, Sun 10am-5pm. This is the more bargain-based shopping centre in Stockton. It has the discounts stores, the pound stores and the markets within its walls.

THE CORNMILL CENTRE

Priestgate, Darlington 01325 369 111

Open Mon-Sat 9am-5.30pm, Sun 10.30am-4.30pm. This has all the high street favourites boasting 50 shops including Waterstones, Dorothy Perkins and Primark. It's a grand place to find shelter when it's raining, but be prepared to lose a buck or two.

DUNDAS ARCADE

Dundas St, Middlesbrough, Cleveland 01642 230 800

Changes

Ding Dong Vintage

The Bridges, Sunderland

Eleven

Only Dundas Arcade could have a tattoo parlour next to a butchers. Perfect. Ask and the in-shops shall provide.

THE MALL
Mall Management. 85 Grange Rd, M'bro 01642 244 682
Open Mon- Sat 9am-5.30pm, Sunday 10.30am-4.30pm. The Mall is home to Topshop, H&M, HMV, Boots and many more besides... all the big names under one big roof. It used to be called The Cleveland Centre, so if you want to fit in with M'bro, you should refer to it accordingly.

THE HILL STREET CENTRE
Management Suite, Hill St Shopping Centre, M'bro 01642 211 123
Open Mon- Sat 9am-5.30pm, Thurs 9am- 7pm, Sunday 10.30am- 5pm. This is The Mall's main competition. It has Debenhams, Primark, Superdrug and Erin O'Conner's favourite hang-out, Marks and Spencers. It has two Greggs, just in case you need to stock up on your sausage rolls. It'll be a while before this centre is over the hill.

QUEENS ARCADE
Queens Street, Darlington 01325 484 126
This is more petite than The Cornmill Centre, but you can buy food, stationary, music and books from here.

TEESSIDE RETAIL PARK
Take A19 / A66 turnoff for Stockton / Thornaby
This a good place to go for washing machines, sofas and other bulky buys. It has various clothing stores, so at least you can go shopping while Dad decides whether to buy the white fridge or the silver fridge. There is also a cinema, a casino and a bowling alley; plenty of memories to be made.

WELLINGTON SQUARE
21 Wellington Street, Stockton on Tees 01642 607 782
Open Mon-Sat 9am-5.30pm, Sun 11am-5pm. Not quite brand-spanking new, but near enough, Wellington Square is Stockton's shopping saviour. There are over 40 stores including River Island, Topshop and WHSmith. If it's high street, you'll find this square giving it a bit of welly.

FASHION

BOX CLOTHING
24 Newport Rd., M'bro 01642 808 592
Blokes' shop stocking labels along the lines of G-Star, Gio Goi, Firetrap, and Diesel.

CHANGES
3 Newport Crescent, M'bro 01642 247 335

Psyche

Triads

This is a small designer boutique built by men for men. The clothing can get a little jazzy but it's a good place to go if you want a change.

DEEP
153 Linthorpe Road M'bro
01642 222828
Whether you're male, female or a retro cross-dresser, you'll be able to kit out your can in this shop. There are two floors of polyester prizes and woollen wonders. They sell hand-made modern dresses or old school tea dresses, and they have so many Levi's jeans and t-shirts for the chaps that you're bound to get lost in the depths of the deep! Don't worry about taking a life jacket though, because there are plenty of leather ones inside.

THE HOUSE
69 High Street, Yarm   01642 790 852
If only this was actually a house. It would be the best house in the world; far better than the Disneyland castle. Mickey and Minnie Mouse cannot provide you with Armani, Betty Barclay and Paul Smith. It's situated on Yarm's famous High Street, which is basically a stamp of the quality of this place. Just look at their window boxes...fabulouso!

PSYCHE
175 - 187 Linthorpe Road M'bro
01642 888 333

Psyche stocks an insane amount of designer brands among its three floors. It is effectively a designer department store on a par with Harvey Nichols and the such. It has cafes and beauty salons too, if the shopping experience all gets too much for your psyche. It continues to be a flamin' hot fashion hot spot.

RED SQUARE
159 Linthorpe Road, M'bro
01642 254 825
Considering the name, this shop is for anyone but the squares. It's been trading on the streets of Teesside since 1990, bringing names such as Carhartt, Pretty Green, New Balance and Lacoste to the thirsty shop-hopper that lies in the heart of every male.

ROCKET RETRO
Zero Baker St, M'bro 01642 224 264
Recently moved to a new premises, this place has got bigger and better. On the ground floor you'll find stacks of great vintage clothes, then on the first floor there's vintage furniture and bric-a-brac. Perfect if you're in the mood for a rummage.

TRIADS
54/56 Albert Road, M'bro
01642 254 124
Triads began in 1988, fighting through hairspray and shoulder pads in order to bring

men's fashion into the next generation. This is Middlesbrough's premier fashion dealer, as it always pushes for the innovative over the mainstream. It deals with Levi's Vintage, Maharishi, Hugo Boss, Evisu and many more designer brands. Unlike other stores, Triads' prices reflect the quality and the originality of every product. The clothes reflect more than just the fashion of the moment, but it works with other influences, like music, art and film. To say that this store is on the pulse is a huge understatement. It's all over the pulse like a mother-tootin' stethoscope.

TRIADS II
182, Linthorpe Rd, M'bro
01642 249 989

Triads II is on two floors: the ground floor is where luxury mainline menswear collections weave their magic and the first floor is all about the women. It opened in 2003 following the success of its brother store on Albert Road. Men can pick from Vivienne Westwood, Gucci and Prada Sport, whereas the women can dabble in Alexander McQueen, John Galliano and Cavalli. Oh yes indeed. Triads II is the first port of call if you want to make the distance between you and the catwalk that little bit smaller.

YAKUZA
170-172 Linthorpe Rd, M'bro
01642 879 009

Are you tired of working out only for your body to be hidden under pesky clothes? Yakuza has the answer; tight t-shirts and bright colours. This is most definitely a store for the metrosexual man. Yakuza will have everything you could ever want to compliment your tan, with stuff from brands like Gabicci, Money Denim, and Replay.

ARTS AND CRAFTS

ARTMART
Regent House, Prince Regent St,
Stockton-on-Tees   01642 678040

Artmart recently moved into a plush new building which some people have described as "soulless" in comparison to the old shop on Norton Road. Whether it has a soul or not, it has art supplies by the truckload...and it's opposite the ARC, so deal with it because it's corking.

ART SHOP
11-12 Bondgate, Darlington
01325 465484

Art Shop does exactly what it says on their metaphorical tin. No slogans, no puns, just pure art materials in your face.

CRAFTY INDIVIDUALS
7 Sideling Tails, Yarm,   01642 789955

This really does tick all of the quality boxes when it comes to quality arts and crafts. A real goodie.

JARRED'S
Bright Street, Middlesbrough,
01642 217451

Jarred's sells office equipment so if you're after office equipment and in Middlesbourgh then Jarreds is a suitable option.

JESSOPS
7 Newport Rd, Middlesbrough
01642 230707

Clickety-click! It's the UK's favourite camera store. It's got everything you and your camera need, from lenses to tripods to carry cases. Developing? Of course Jessops develops your photos, silly.

MARKETS

DARLINGTON MARKET
01325 388691
Monday and Saturday Outdoor/ Monday-Saturday Indoor

Darlington "the daddy" Market has 150 stalls and is unrivalled. It works the outdoor and the indoor which will keep any market mogul happy.

GUISBOROUGH MARKET
High Street 01287 651601 Tuesday, Thursday and Saturday
I used to dislike this market as a child because it had so many stalls! What I believed to be an enjoyable trip to Guisborough with the parents turned into a trek around bag stalls, crafts stalls and stall stalls. Now I am older and wiser, I realise that this is a sign that this market is a good 'un.

MIDDLESBROUGH FARMERS MARKET
Captain Cook's Square, every first Tuesday of each month
Everyone is banging on about buying local produce, so why not attend Middlesbrough Farmer's Market every first Tuesday of every month and bang the gong for British stuff.

NORTH ORMESBY MARKET
Market Place, North Ormesby, Middlesbrough, TS3 6HR 01642 244564 Tuesdays and Saturdays
Locally knows as "Doggy Market", this market shakes its things Tuesdays and Saturdays. Expect typical market stalls and a few obscure things besides.

STOCKTON MARKET
01642 527569 Wednesday, Friday and Saturday
Clothes, meat, things for the house and fresh air: no wonder Stockton Market has been going since 1310.

THORNABY MARKET
Thursdays 01642 527569
This is one of the area's smallest markets, but it will still satisfy your market munchies.

MUSIC STORES

BANDLAND MUSIC
Sedgefield Way, Portrack Interchange Business Park, 01642 605 444
Bandland has the largest selection of percussion in the north-east, so it's easy to see how it has drummed up so much support. It has been trading for 30 years and prides itself for its thorough range of musical delights.

HOBBIES RECORDS
1a Coral Street, Saltburn-By-The-Sea, 01287 625196
This is a great store for new and second hand records. It's a little difficult to get there, but it's worth it if it's sunny because you'll be able to make a day of it in the seaside town of Saltburn. If you choose to chill on the beach after your record splurge at least you can use them as a sun-shield. You - 1, damaging UV rays - 0.

MIDDLESBROUGH MUSIC CENTRE
61 Newport Rd., M'bro 01642 226977
This is Middlesbrough's most trusted music store. It specialises in guitars, amps, keyboards and drums, but it has plenty more inside. If you are inspired by Mark Ronson's brass, then you can at least try and recreate his success by purchasing from the Middlesbrough Music Centre, or the MMC, as I am now going to refer to it.

SOUND IT OUT RECORDS
15a Yarm Street, Stockton 01642 860 068
Great shop stocking new and second-hand vinyl and CDs ranging from jazz to hardcore dance. They usually hold about 60,000 items so always worth a rummage.

OTHER TOURS
5 Errol St, Hartlepool, 01429 262225
Every day is Independence Day for this independent record store in Hartlepool. It's the "other" in comparison to chain stores, I'm guessing. They sell loads of gig tickets too.

PLUCK AND STRUMMIT
Enterprise Mall, Morton Park Way,
Darlington   01325 387660
Give us a tune...a tune on my instrument, that
is. They tune, they repair, they sell.

STEVEN JAMES GUITARS
165 Linthorpe Road, M'bro
01642 867 510
This may shock you, but Steven James Guitars
sells guitars: electric guitars, acoustic guitars,
bass guitars, vintage guitars. If you've got a
spare £1,000, you can buy a vintage 1973
Gibson SG with Bigsy and rock out like David
Cassidy circa "Daydreamer".

SUNDERLAND

SHOPPING CENTRES

BRIDGES SHOPPING CENTRE
Market Square, Sunderland 0191 510
8581 **M** *Sunderland*
The Bridges shopping centre has now
doubled in size and is home to over 100
top name stores including Debenhams,
Topshop, H&M, HMV, Triple S, River Island,
Bank, Disney, Toymaster, Pandora, La Senza,
Blue Inc, JD Sport and loads more. It's a
shoppers' paradise.
Open daily 9am-5.30pm, Thurs 9am-8pm,
Sun 11am- 5pm.

FASHION

APHRODITE
8 Vine Place
0191 567 5898 **M** *Park Lane*
Ultra modern store specialising in designer
menswear and accessories. They offer a great
range of well known brands alongside new and
innovative designers. Well worth a visit with
plenty of friendly staff to help you find what
you're looking for. Not quite a Greek goddess
but definitely a place you'll love.

CORNER 93
Station Road, Fulwell
0191 548 5778
Stocked full of vintage finds this little store
only opened in 2009 but is thriving. Offering
second hand pieces from high-end names as
well as designers. The store owner also buys
pieces from clients so it's the perfect place
to bring in your retro finds that you don't
want anymore.

DR. FUNKENSTEIN
23 Derwent Street, **M** *Park Lane*
0191 567 1971
1 Front Street, Whitburn 0191 529 5333
Both stores stock fancy dress including all
kinds of crazy outfits that are guaranteed to
make you stand out at a costume party. The
Derwent Street branch also sells 60s and
70s clothing and alternative/gothic clothing.

ELEVEN
56 John Street 0191 564 1155
M *Sunderland*
Three floors of class clobber in 19th century
Georgian architecture. Eleven offers a brilliant
range of menswear, stocking the likes of Levi's
Vintage, Folk, John Smedley, Paul Smith,
Universal Works, Stone Island and Moncler.
One of the very best shops of its type in the
north-east, they even offer a bespoke tailoring
service. Trendy.

NORTHERN THREADS
14 Ocean Rd., South Shields
0191 300 6935 **M** *South Shields*
Just a short Metro ride away, Northern Threads
is a fantastic store for men stocking labels
straight from the cutting edge including G-Star,
Lyle & Scott, Duffer, Boss, Evisu, Junk de Luxe,
Gabicci, Jack Jones and loads more.

SOUL RETRO
2 Derwent St.,
0191 567 1300 **M** *Park Lane*
Nice little store that stocks a range of

accessories for men, from Flossy's and plimsolls to Northern Soul bags.

T.K. MAXX
Unit 2, The Bridges 0191 514 4484
M *Sunderland*
Vast store that sells end of season clothes and interior stuff with anything from rugs to vases to bed-linen on offer. Designer bargains galore.

TUCCI
The Bridges Shoppig Centre
0191 567 2453 **M** *Sunderland*
Independent clothes shop for men and women stocking the latest, hippest labels from Paul and Shark, Paul Smith, French Connection and Lacoste.

YAKUZA
24 John Street 0191 564 1825
M *Sunderland*
Great menswear store stocking well known designer brands like Diesel, Barbour, and Religion.

CITY ART
23 Vine Place 0191 565 9254
M *Park Lane*
Local scene pictures and prints, arts & crafts, hobby and needle craft. You can find any high quality art supply from painting materials to card making equipment. It's like art heaven.

CHARLES EAGLES & SON *5 Maritime Street*
0191 567 0317
Family run photography store selling all things relating to cameras. They stock both new and second hand cameras as well as every kind of accessory you could think of. They also offer 10% student discount on film and paper, lovely.

JESSOPS
56 Fawcett Street 0191 510 0881
M *Sunderland*
Stocks leading camera, camcorder and digital brands and offers developing, printing, equipment repair and instant passport photos.

RECORD SHOPS

HOT RATS
37 Stockton Road 0191 567 2099
M *Park Lane*
Collector's paradise, mainly because it's so cheap and friendly. New and used indie/rock etc LPs, CDs and one of the few still selling vinyl. Also stock concert tickets, selected books, DVDs, comic imports, t-shirts and offer a free valuation service.

MUSICAL EQUIPMENT

ALENIA'S MUSICART
314-315 High St. West 0191 567 2004
M *Sunderland*
Fairly new shop, stocking instruments, accessories and music sheets. All stock is brand new. They also sell the work of local artists.

SUNDERLAND MUSIC
4/5 Tavistock Building, Borough Road
0191 564 1693 **M** *Sunderland*
Sunderland Music specialises in new and second-hand drum and percussion. Repair and hire service also available and a 10% student discount.

BOOKS

WATERSTONES
Unit 31, Walworth Way, The Bridges
0191 567 4331 **M** *Sunderland*
Part of the national chain, this is one of the smaller branches with a nice little Costa upstairs.

OUTDOOR PURSUITS

LAMBS BIKES
25 Claypath 0191 384 0319
M *Sunderland*
Loads of bikes for sale and hire along with every accessory you could ever need and a repair service too.

GREAT OUTDOORS
9 The Bridges, 0191 567 2727
M *Sunderland*
Leading brands in outdoor wear, boots, camping, and work wear.

MARKETS

JACKIE WHITES
The Bridges Shopping Centre
M *Sunderland*
General market with any amount of bits and bobs up for grabs Mon-Sat.

THE OUTDOOR MARKET
Park Lane **M** *Park Lane*
Although small in size it still has everything you could want from a market, including fish stall, DVD stall and pet stall.

DURHAM

SHOPPING CENTRES

THE GATES
1 Framwellgate Bridge 0191 386 9363
Representing many of the high street chains, The Gates also houses a few specialist shops selling luxury items. While the closure of anchor store Waitrose a couple of years ago was a shame, there's still just about something for everyone.

DALTON PARK
Murton, Co. Durham 0191 526 6157
The north-east's newest shopping extravaganza is a 'shopping village' near Sunderland set in amidst 55 acres of parkland and chock-full of factory outlets, most offering big discounts on all your favourite big-name brands. Worth the journey for the innovative layout alone.

FASHION

BOX CLOTHING
10 Elvet Bridge 0191 383 0115
Replay, Diesel, G-Star, Ted Baker and Lacoste are but some of the designer labels on sale in this three-floored shop for blokes. Also stocks a cool range of accessories from shoes to sunglasses.

DING DONG VINTAGE
45 The Gates 07887 563 409
This must be one of the very best vintage shops in the whole of the north-east and stocks a superb range of stuff taking in everything from shoes to dresses, coats to jackets. Also loads of great accessories. The last time we popped in they had some gear that used to belong to Vivien "Gone With The Wind" Leigh... Now that is quality!

FAT FACE
Unit 4, Prince Bishop's Shopping Centre 0191 384 8396
Top-notch urban clothing for lads and lasses in a shop jam-packed with goodies.

GAVIN SHELLEY JEWELLERY
Saddler's Yard
0191 383 1221
Contemporary - mainly silver - jewellery, this place is certainly good for a browse but it's also worth noting that repairs and commissions are undertaken too.

THE GEORGIAN WINDOW
50-51 Saddler Street 0191 384 8890
Jewellery, frames, posters, clothes and accessories, many with a Celtic bent. Quite possibly the finest ladies' accessories shop in Durham.

J. TROUGHEAR SUIT HIRE
10 Sherburn Road 0191 386 1648

If you're attending a formal function in the area, why buy a suit when you can hire one from here? This little shop has over 20 years' experience in lending suits and tuxedos at competitive rates to students and professionals alike.

JACK WILLS
40 Saddler Street 0191 383 9685

Billed as the 'English Abercrombie and Fitch,' Jack Wills has for many years prided itself on styling the nation's well-heeled youngsters at an enormous cost with its ranges of polo shirts, trousers, skirts and more.

MUGWUMP
37 Saddler Street 0191 386 1282

Slightly more mature women's clothing and a veritable Aladdin's Cave of trinkets and nick-nacks. Cards, jewellery, glassware, lotions and, for the trendy, the Alessi range of accessories.

OXFAM BOUTIQUE
18 Elvet Bridge 0191 384 7440

The first of its kind in the UK, this classy Oxfam outlet specialises in boutique clothing, which means that the finest vintage clothing is sourced from all over the country for the benefit of discerning Durham ladies and gents. Also carries a range of accessories.

PERSONA
23 Elvet Bridge 0191 375 7755

A unique, independent women's clothing retailer whose handmade corset collection is perhaps its most exclusive offering. With various fabrics, colours and styles to chose from plus a made-to-order service, Persona can probably create a one-of-a-kind outfit just for you.

SCORPIO SHOES
70 Saddler Street 0191 384 5122

Something of an institution amongst Durham students and alumni, this fine little shoe emporium has been around for years and is still crammed with perennial favourites like Dr Martens, Vans and Converse along with more unusual fare.

TRIPLE S
32 Silver Street 0191 384 3902

Durham's outlet of the north-east skate chain carries jumpers, t-shirts, hats, sunglasses and more from the usual suspects, including Etnies, Bench, Carhartt and Superdry.

VAN MILDERT MEN
Elvet Bridge 0191 384 8508

If you're into men's designer gear check out this store; it has a raft of great clothes from the likes of Junk Food, Prada and Karl Lagerfeld and accessories from Dunhill Sunglasses, Emporio Armani and more.

VAN MILDERT WOMEN
Elvet Bridge 0191 384 8500

Right next to the above is a real treat for the ladies, with even more designer clobber from the likes D&G, Vivienne Westwood, Belstaff and See by Chloe. Like its male-orientated counterpart, the shop also stocks a wide range of accessories including bags, sunglasses and jewellery from Paul Smith, Guess and Juicy Couture.

INTERIORS

GATEWAY WORLD SHOP
Market Place 0191 384 7173

Adjacent to St. Nicholas' Church, this venerable Fair Trade shop stocks a range of food, clothes, pottery and fabrics from the Developing World. The jewellery in particular is worth a gander.

ARTS, CRAFTS & PHOTOGRAPHY

The Art Shop and Kemble Gallery
62 Saddler Street 0191 386 4034
This quaint multi-levelled shop stocks original paintings and prints downstairs as well as a wide variety of artists' materials up above. Also offers a reasonably-priced picture framing service.

CHAS EAGLES AND SON

4 The Gates 0191 383 0813
Another of Durham's evergreen independent specialists, this photography retailer has been going since 1990 and still stocks everything from digital SLR cameras through to accessories like tripods and filters.

SEASONS GALLERY AND FRAMING

14 Church Street 0191 386 0222
A neat little gallery space, albeit a bit out of town, with an interesting business in framing and artwork.

MUSIC

HMV

Unit 14, Prince Bishops Shopping Centre 0191 370 6460
Following the closure of Music Zone and then beloved North Road independent Dam (formerly Concepts), HMV is lamentably now Durham's only music outlet. Still, the chain store does a competent enough job in peddling a wide variety of music genres, though its selection seems to get smaller with each passing month.

MUSICAL EQUIPMENT

E.B.G.B. MUSICAL INSTRUMENTS

The Avenue Corner, The Avenue
0191 384 5813
Musical instrument shop that sells everything from said instruments and amps to strings and sheet music. You can also get your guitar repaired here after that attempt to play along to Jimi Hendrix with the thing behind your head goes awry.

THE GUITAR LOFT

113 Gilesgate 0191 383 0636
Speaking of guitars, this diminutively-proportioned shop carries a small but varied range of acoustic and electric guitars in addition to catering for repairs, with knowledgeable staff invariably on hand to lend some advice.

BOOKS

OXFAM BOOKS AND MUSIC

12 Elvet Bridge
0191 384 6366
Just opposite its new Boutique counterpart on Elvet Bridge, this charity shop continues to sell Fair Trade products and shelves of second-hand books of all genres. Especially worth a visit before term begins and the students go in search of course books.

WATERSTONES

69 Sadler Street 0191 383 1488
Multi-level chain bookstore that does a roaring trade thanks in no small part to the constant influx of students into the city. Carries an impressive range for its size and staff are quite happy to order items for you from afar.

OUTDOOR

CYCLE FORCE 2000

87 Claypath 0191 384 0319
Loads of bikes for sale and hire along with every accessory you could ever need and a repair service too.

TRACK 'N' TERRAIN

21A Elvet Bridge 0191 384 3758
This outdoor pursuits store will meet every one of your track and terrain needs. Stocking Helly Hansen, Low Alpine and Mizuno amongst other leading brands, this is the place for adventurous spirit to find accessories for a life spent out in the wild.

CHESTER-LE STREET MARKET
Market Square
On Saturdays this is an absolute bargain-hunter's paradise. Remarkably like a car-boot sale, except not as cheap and with enough random stuff to buy 'til your heart's content. Tuesdays and Fridays offer a more general market with great home-cooked pies.

DURHAM INDOOR MARKETS
Market Place 0191 3846153
Like most indoor markets, there's an eclectic mix of stall holders here, selling everything from fresh meats to leather shoes through to American Indian art and cookware. The most interesting are the Durham Pipe & Tobacco Shop, selling pipes for both the distinguished gentleman and the student stoner, along with the Wonka-tastic Humby's Sweet Shop.

DURHAM MARKET PLACE
0191 384 6153
In the very nice surrounding of Ye Olde Worlde Durham Market Place, cobble stones and all, this market on Saturday mornings and Bank Holidays gets very busy and sells basic goods, including good fruit and vegetables, plants, clothing and the like. On Sundays there's also an art market down from Elvet Bridge overlooking the River. Also worth noting is the thriving Farmers Market, which takes place on the third Thursday of every month.

The region has many passions (hey, we're passionate people) but surely one of our most heartfelt is for sport. The north-east has some of the best supported football clubs in the country (despite not winning anything since the days of colour TVs being a novelty) but that's just the football side of things. We have just about every sport imaginable available for you to either watch or try out for yourself.

Eldon Leisure

CITY POOL
Northumberland Rd., Newcastle
0191 232 1981 **M** *Haymarket*
The main public pool in Newcastle has a variety of different classes as well as some ornate Turkish baths.

EAST END POOL
Hadrian Sq, Byker 0191 278 8444 **M** *Byker*
This excellent facility has two swimming pools, a sauna, fitness suite and fitness classes.

ELDON LEISURE
High Friars, Eldon Square, Newcastle
0191 277 1277 **M** *Monument*
In the heart of Newcastle, Eldon Leisure is well equipped for a huge array of sport and fitness activities. Includes Impulse Fitness offering a comprehensive range of cardiovascular and resistance equipment for all ages and ability levels.

GATESHEAD INDOOR BOWLING CENTRE
Gladstone Terrace, Gateshead
0191 433 5750 **M** *Gateshead*
Non-members and beginners are always welcome and free coaching sessions can be arranged for individuals and groups.

GATESHEAD INTERNATIONAL STADIUM
Neilson Road, Gateshead
0191 433 5700
M *Gateshead Stadium*
Gateshead International Stadium has a wide range of facilities, both indoor and outdoor, parking for up to 400 cars, and is fully equipped for people with disabilities. As well as hosting international and major events, the renowned stadium offers many activities and courses, which can be booked by the hour, including: 5-a-side football, netball and basketball. It

is also possible to use the running track and the multi-gym equipment.

THE LIGHTFOOT CENTRE
Wharrier Street, Walker, Newcastle
0191 278 2800 **M** *Walker*
A great facility in the heart of Walker with a wide range of fitness and sporting facilities including a traditional fitness suite, large free weight area and kids gym.

NEWCASTLE CLIMBING CENTRE
St. Marks Church, 285 Shields Rd.
Newcastle 0191 265 6060 **M** *Byker*
The premier indoor climbing venue for Tyneside and the north-east and one of the best climbing venues in the UK. Situated in the former church of St Marks the listed building provides a spectacular climbing environment with an internal height of 15 metres and over 1200 square metres of climbing walls for roped climbing and bouldering.

NEWCASTLE EAGLES
Metro Radio Arena,
Newcastle 0844 493 6666
Get the dunk! The Newcastle Eagles are Newcastle's Championship winning basketball team.

NEWCASTLE FALCONS
Kingston Park, Brunton Rd., Newcastle
0871 226 6060 **M** *Kingston Park*
This lovely rugby ground is right next to Kingston Park Metro station and so is a doddle to get to. And this is where you'll want to be if you want to check out the region's premier rugby union team, the Newcastle Falcons.

NEWCASTLE GREYHOUND STADIUM
Fossway, Newcastle
0191 210 5300 **M** *Chillingham Rd*
Newcastle Greyhound Stadium hosts both greyhound racing and speedway and has gained an enviable reputation for excelling in both. The stadium pulls out all the stops when it comes

Pure Yoga

Eldon Leisure

to staging greyhound racing and really lets you make a night of it and they have great packages where you can get three-course meals and a reserved seat. Whether you're a hardened fan, just like the occasional flutter, or simply enjoy the excitement, Brough Park delivers on every count. The meetings are usually on Tuesday, Thursday and Saturday. Newcastle Stadium is also home of the Newcastle Diamonds, one of the top speedway teams in the country who have home matches on Sunday evening during the season.

NEWCASTLE RACECOURSE
High Gosforth Park, Newcastle
0191 236 2020
Newcastle Racecourse, set in the impressive 812 acre High Gosforth Park Estate, is the north-east's premier racecourse and is home to many prestigious events, including the Northumberland Plate Festival, Beeswing Ladies Day and the Fighting Fifth Hurdle. There are 30 race meetings per year over the flat and jumps seasons, including weekend and evening fixtures, with concessionary prices available for students.

NEWCASTLE UNITED FOOTBALL CLUB
St. James' Park, Barrack Rd.,
Newcastle 0191 261 1571 **M** *St. James*

The long journey to silverware at St. James' makes the quest for the Holy Grail look like a stroll in the park. And then there is the almost constant behind the scenes turmoil which tends to keep United on the front pages more than the back. That said, St. James' Park is one of the best - and biggest - grounds in the country and when United are actually on song, there's not too many better places to be.

PURE YOGA NORTH EAST
Newcastle Buddhist Centre, 3rd floor,
Carliol Square, Newcastle
0191 271 3406 **M** *Monument*
Ethical disciplines, self observation, posture, breath control, sense withdrawal, concentration, meditation and a state of joy and peace...

WHICKHAM THORNS OUTDOOR ACTIVITY CENTRE
Market Lane, Dunston, 0191 433 5767
Ski slope, skatepark, indoor and outdoor climbing, assault course, orienteering, archery and mountain biking are just some of the facilities available at this leisure complex which provides opportunities for groups or individuals to participate in a range of outdoor activities not usually found so close to urban areas.

WET 'N' WILD WATERPARK
Royal Quays, North Shields
0191 296 1333   **M** *Meadow Well*
Wheee! Wet 'N Wild is the UK's largest water fun park and they have oodles of attractions.

THE ACKLAM SPORTS CENTRE
Acklam Sports Centre, Hall Drive, Acklam
01642 822 357
In a nutshell, facilities include three sports halls, a swimming pool, a flood-lit artificial football pitch, 12 tennis courts and eight netballs courts.

BILLINGHAM FORUM
The Causeway, Town Centre, Billingham, Stockton-on-Tees
01642 551 381
The forum is currently closed due to major refurbishment work, it is expected to reopen in April 2011.

CASTLEGATE QUAY
Watersports Centre
Moat Street, Stockton-on-Tees
01642 528 689
This is the probably the north-east's best equipped sailing and paddling centre.

THE CLAIRVILLE STADIUM
Clairville Stadium, Park road South, M'bro 01642 246 767
An athletic based centre fitted with state of the art cardiovascular and resistance equipment. There is a running track, and sauna area.

ESTON SPORTS ACADEMY
Normanby Road, South Bank, M'bro
01642 452 488
It has a main pool, a teaching pool, a sports hall, a gym, an energy club dance studio and various beauty therapy treatments.

HOLLYWOOD BOWL
Teesside Leisure Park, Stockton-on-Tees
01642 633 666
As well as plenty of bowling lanes this place has arcade games, air hockey and a bar.

THE NEPTUNE CENTRE
Ormesby Road, M'bro 01642 230 106
The Neptune Centre has been making waves since 1998 because of its community swimming facility aka a pool.

THE ORMESBY SPORTS COMPLEX
Ormesby Comprehensive School, Stockwith Close, M'bro 01642 466 866
This place has a small sports hall which is the location for all your martial arts, climbing and trampolining needs. The aerobics room is self-explanatory, as is the multi use games area.

THE RAINBOW LEISURE CENTRE
Parkway Centre, Coulby Newham
01642 592 800
An expansive place where badminton, football, roller hockey, martial arts, trampolining, squash, spinning and swimming are very much the order of the day.

RIVERSIDE STADIUM
Middlesbrough 0844 449 6789
Middlesbrough FC play here. It has a 35,000 capacity, and if you can afford a ticket, you should be able to get a seat without too much problem.

SALTBURN SURF CENTRE
Pier Car Park, Saltburn 01287 625 321
Top surfing action ahoy at this well appointed venue.

THE SOUTHLANDS CENTRE
Ormesby Road, M'bro 01642 300 428
The Southlands is similar to the Rainbow Leisure Centre in its facilities. It offers football,

Tees Barrage

Saltburn Surf Centre

badminton, basketball, trampolining, table tennis, a rollerdisco (I know!) and a countless number of fitness classes, which is the centre's forte. They welcome all the family and it also operates the X4 Health and Fitness like the Rainbow Centre, so there's no excuse for Middlesbrough to be obese, is there?

SPLASH
Church Road, Stockton-on-Tees,
01642 527 272
Splash has been designed to make the kids go wild. It's bright. It's spacious. It has themed flumes! And wave machines! And a spa pool! And a learner pool! But Splash has got lots more to offer. There's a split-level gym over 75 machines to work every part of your body with a range of cardio and strength/tone machines. An activity room with 2 badminton courts, an interactive zig-zag sports wall.....think a giant a wii and you wouldn't be far off the mark... BRILLIANT! There's fitness and martial arts classes, dance classes, trampolining, soft play, and much more. And if you get peckish after all that cardio, there's a café on site offering a large range of hot and cold snacks.

STOCKTON SPORTS CENTRE
Talbot Street, Stockton-on-Tees,
01642 528 282
5-a-side, badminton, netball, volleyball and basketball. The centre also has six squash courts.

THORNABY PAVILION
Wrightson House, Thornaby,
Stockton-on-Tees,   01642 760 971
Refurbished recently, this offers a plethora of leisure from Baby Gym to gymnastics, fitness classes, squash, badminton, yoga and five-a-side football.

TEES BARRAGE INTERNATIONAL WHITE WATER CENTRE
Tees Barrage Way, Tees Barrage,
Stockton-on-Tees   01642 678 000
This is a superb facility for white water sports because it is so specialised. It offers flat-water facilities for the people who are as acquainted with water as a cactus. The white water is for the professionals, so if you don't consider yourself a pro, say no!

SUNDERLAND

SUNDERLAND COMMUNITY
North Sports Complex
Kingsway, Downhill, Sunderland
0191 553 6915

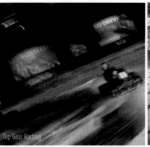
Top Gear Karting

Sunderland Aquatic Centre

A 160-acre site including nine grassed football pitches, one floodlit artificial football pitch and a BMX Track. The site has recently been developed to include a bowling green and multi use games area, also includes a gymnasium.

HOUGHTON SPORTS CENTRE
AND WELLNESS GYM
Station Rd., Houghton-le-Spring
0191 553 6465
This sports centre includes facilities for 5-a-side football, solarium, and indoor and outdoor bowls. Activities include: badminton, 5-a-side, table tennis, gymnastics, bowls, and aerobics, weight training, sunbeds, basketball, netball, karate and gymnastics. Also including new classes, boxer fit, circuit training, taekwando, aikido, kick boxing, pilates and 'fit for kids'.

THE NORTH EAST DIVE ACADEMY
1 Pier Cottage, Marine Walk,
Sunderland 0191 567 7777
At North East Diving Academy (NEDA) every type of diver is catered for, from the individual novice to the most advanced technical dive team. They offer a full range of diving equipment, sales, servicing and rental in addition to PADI and IANTD training courses. They are also the north's only full Nitrox and Trimix filling station providing air to 350 bar as well as tank testing.

PUMA SUNDERLAND TENNIS CENTRE
Silksworth, Sunderland 0191 553 5901
This centre has been designed primarily as a tennis centre, with both indoor and outdoor courts. But they also have weight training/ fitness studio and a soft play area as well as cafeteria, bar and function facilities.

TETLEY'S SUNDERLAND STADIUM
Newcastle Rd., Sunderland
0191 568 6200 East Boldon
This 1700 capacity stadium is one of the best places to enjoy top quality dog racing. It also has a restaurant and 'Northern Lights', which provides an excellent view of the racing, five bars and 'Trapz' nightclub.

SEABURN CENTRE
Whitburn Rd. 0191 553 2600
This centre comprises mainly of a two-court sports hall, weight training/fitness studio and soft play area. Activities include: Badminton, 5-a-side, soft play, and table tennis, weight training, aerobics, volleyball, basketball, netball, and karate.

SILKSWORTH SPORTS COMPLEX
Silksworth Lane, Sunderland
0191 553 5785
This is a fantastic 167 acre site which includes four grassed pitches, two floodlit artificial

football pitches, watersports lake, athletics arena, fishing lake, BMX track and a brilliant dry ski-slope. This quite superb facility (including two nursery slopes) is floodlit, 165 metres long and offers year round recreational skiing and snowboarding, as well as tuition courses for all age groups and abilities.

STADIUM OF LIGHT
Sunderland 0191 551 5000
Ⓜ *St. Peters*
This 48,300 seated stadium is where Sunderland Football Club plies their trade. Situated by the banks of the river Wear, it has been home to the "Black Cats" for over ten years now. The ticket hotline can be reached on 0871 911 1973.

SUNDERLAND AQUATIC CENTRE
Wearmouth, Sunderland 0191 561 6161
Ⓜ *St. Peters*
Built next door to the Stadium of Light, this pool is the only one of its kind between Leeds and Edinburgh. It features the region's first 10 lane 50m pool as well as a spectacular diving pool with five-metre, three-metre and one-metre platforms. The centre also has two Wellness exercise studios, a split-level Wellness centre, a cardio-cycle zone, kinesis zone and free-weights zone for everyone to enjoy.

SUNDERLAND MARINA
and Activities Centre
North Dock, Sunderland 0191 514 4721
Originally constructed by Brunel in 1837, the Dock has been renovated and extended to provide the modern Marina we now enjoy. Sunderland Marina aims to provide top class facilities combined with friendly, efficient service. The Marina is staffed 24/7, all year round and consists of 113 fore-and-aft moorings, 26 berths and 88 fully serviced pontoon berths.

SUNDERLAND WALL
Doxford Works, Pallion Quay, Sunderland
0191 514 4234
Sunderland wall has some of the best route setters in the country, testing the ability of beginners and top climbers alike. At 23m high, you will not find a better competition wall in the UK and probably Europe!

WASHINGTON LEISURE CENTRE
Town Centre, Washington 0191 219 3400
This centre, situated adjacent to 'the Galleries' shopping centre offers a range of activities taken by fully qualified instructors.
Facilities include swimming pool with aqua slide, sports hall, squash courts, soft-play and a Wellness Gym offering first class fitness equipment and a range of classes.

DURHAM

CHESTER-LE-STREET LEISURE CENTRE
Burns Green, Chester-le-Street
0191 388 6673
8am-10pm (Mon.-Fri.) / 9am-5:00pm (Weekends) A sports centre with a wide range of both wet and dry facilities, including two swimming pools, a fitness suite, a sauna and squash courts.

DURHAM CITY AFC
The Arnott Stadium, Belmont Industrial Estate
If you consider yourself a real football fan, come on down to Arnott Stadium on a match day to support Durham City AFC in their bid to climb the Football League. The club were champions of the First Division North a few seasons ago and are looking to move onwards and upwards.

DURHAM COUNTY CRICKET CLUB
County Ground, Riverside,
Chester-le-Street 0191 387 1717
The former County Champions, Durham County are based just down the road from Durham City and ply their trade throughout the summer months. Alternatively, take in an England One Day International or Test Series at the club's magnificent Riverside stadium.

FREEMAN'S QUAY LEISURE CENTRE
The Sands, Durham
0191 301 8306
6:30am-10:30pm (Mon.-Fri.) / 8am-7:30pm (Weekends) A multi-million-pound leisure facility right in the heart of Durham, Freeman's Quay Leisure Centre is doubtless the plushest of all the sports amenities in this list. Houses a 25-metre, 8-lane swimming pool, a learner's pool, a dance studio and a gym furnished with 130 workstations and personal entertainment facilities.

THE GRAHAM SPORTS CENTRE
Maiden Castle, Durham 0191 334 2178
Durham University's considerable sporting achievements are thanks in no small part to this venue, its own sports centre, which boasts everything from a high-performance weights room to a four-lane athletics track. Facilities are generally monopolised by students during term-time but are available to the public at various times for a small cost.

MEADOWFIELD SPORTS
and Leisure Centre
John Street North, Meadowfield
0191 301 8304
8am-10pm (Mon.-Thurs.) / 8am-9pm (Fri.) / 9am-5:30pm (Weekends)
Another fitness centre furnished with an array of facilities and activities to cater for all ages and tastes, including a main sports hall, squash courts, a fitness suite with built-in entertainment options, a weights room and artificial turf football pitches. Childcare is also available.

RIVERSIDE SPORTS COMPLEX
Riverside South, Chester-le-Street
0191 389 0986
The venue has something for everyone, from a first-class cricket stadium and full-size running track to the region's only outdoor water play area for children.

ROSEBERRY GRANGE GOLF COMPLEX
Grange Vila, Chester-le-Street
0191 370 0670
Opened in 1987 on the site of what used to be part of West Pelton Colliery, Roseberry Grange Golf Complex comprises of an 18-hole course, a floodlit driving range and a superbly-appointed clubhouse that provides a bar, excellent catering and a shop. Though the golf course is open to the public, Roseberry Grange Golf Club is also based here.

SHERBURN LEISURE CENTRE
Front Street, Sherburn Village
0191 3018305
A popular local sports centre providing a good range of activities including exercise classes (such as mature keep-fit, ladies' badminton, step aerobics and line dancing), self defence (kick-boxing and taekwondo), toning classes, football, roller-skating and gymnastics.

TOP GEAR KARTING
13 Rennys Lane, Durham
0191 386 0999
Open 1pm-9pm (Mon.-Fri.) / 9am-7pm (Sat.) / 10am-6pm (Sun.)
A fully-fledged go-kart course is what's on offer here, with a 200-metre-plus track length that provides ample opportunity for overtaking foes and an indoor setting that beats the weather and keeps things safe.

Ok: you've totally spent-up with shopping expeditions, pub crawls, clubs (sporting and dance-oriented) and now you just want to kick back and relax. Where better than in one of the region's many, many open spaces?

There's a huge variety of parks and gardens to be found among the more urbanised areas of the north-east, all just crying out for you languid presence...

Derwent Walk Country Park

BEWICK ROAD PARK
Bewick Road, Newcastle

There's been a major, 12-month transformation of this space which boasts wide open views across the Team Valley, new seating, a shaded wildlife garden and a toddler area filled with play facilities.

DERWENT WALK COUNTRY PARK & DERWENTHAUGH PARK
Swalwell, Gateshead Visitors' Centre

at Thornley Woodlands 01207 545 212 and Swalwell 0191 414 2106. Over 300 acres of woodlands, riverside meadow and bridleways.

GIBSIDE 18TH CENTURY
Landscape Garden
near Rowlands Gill, Gateshead

01207 541 820 £6.50 adults, £4 children. Cared for by the National Trust, this is one of the North's finest landscapes, a Georgian forest garden with many walks through woodland and along the riverside. There are several outstanding buildings including the Palladian Chapel and the newly conserved Stables. Gibside is the former home of the Bowes-Lyon family.

JESMOND DENE
Off Jesmond Road, Newcastle
M *Jesmond*

A narrow wooded valley that follows the river Ouseburn between South Gosforth and Jesmond Vale, the Dene has recently underwent some major changes as part of a £6 million investment by the council. There is also a new state of the art visitor centre and a new cafe located at Millfield House. Improvements have also been made to the wider park including new path surfacing, fencing and railings. One thing that hasn't changed is the fact that the Dene remains one of the most beautiful spots in Newcastle.

LEAZES PARK
Richardson Road, Newcastle
0191 278 3080 **M** *St. James*

This beautiful park first came into being in 1873 and became the first public or people's park created on Tyneside for the purposes of exercise and recreation. Over the last decade or so, the park has been carefully, and lovingly, restored to its original, and former, glory. Visitors can now enjoy it in all its splendour with an array of impressive features including reproductions of the two major ornate gateways reconstructed from period photographs. The Jubilee Gates were originally installed to commemorate the Diamond Jubilee (60 years) of the reign of Queen Victoria. The 16,500km2 lake has also been totally restored with rowing boats being made available for hire at weekends and during school holidays. The bandstand has been exactly recreated from historic records and events are held in it over the summer months which can be viewed from the completely rebuilt terrace. The terrace and its statuary have been reproduced using the remains of the originals to create new moulds. The listed bust of Alderman Hamond, who is a key figure in the history of the park, is a centre piece to the terrace and at the rear there is a memorial garden for the 15th/19th Hussars.

SALTWELL PARK
Saltwell Road, Gateshead
0191 433 7000

Through historic research, this beautiful park has been restored to its former 19th century splendour. Opened in 1876 to provide a haven of peace and tranquillity, it's a Grade II Park and Garden of Special Historic Interest and contains 12 listed buildings, the main one being the mansion Saltwell Towers, which is a mix of several styles including Gothic, Elizabethan and French. After undergoing a massive restoration programme, the towers are just one of the restored jewels of the park and now house the popular visitors' centre.

Saltwell Park is laid out as a series of 'garden rooms' in different styles. In a short walk, users experience a wide variety of styles - going from open meadow, to formal Italianate gardens and then to a woodland glade.

TOWN MOOR
Off The Great North Rd, Newcastle
M *Haymarket*
The Town Moor is one of the features that make Newcastle special, with acres upon acres of open space providing a green heart to the city. It has a history as pasture land dating back to the 12th century and its land tenure and use is regulated by its own Act of Parliament. In late June The Town Moor also plays host to 'The Hoppings' Europe's largest travelling fairground.

WATERGATE FOREST PARK
near A1 off Whickham Highway, Lobley 0191 460 4696
Reclaimed site of the former Watergate Colliery extensively landscaped with trails and paths through heather moorland, wildflower meadows, lakeside, woodlands and coppices.

ALBERT PARK
Linthorpe Road, Middlesbrough, 01642 829319
Open 7.30am to dusk (varies with time of year). This has been described as the "green lung" of Middlesbrough, and by does it breathe fresh air into the area. It was first opened in 1868 and it was the site for the formation of the original Middlesbrough Football Club. Since then, it has been a much loved family park, with facilities including tennis courts, a lake with rowing boats and two play parks: one for the ankle-biters and one for the adults!

BILLINGHAM BECK
Valley Country Park 01642 360376
Open daily 8.30am-4pm in winter and open until

9pm in the summer. The original purpose of this country park in 1992 was to serve as a local nature reserve, but the drained wetlands are posing environmental problems because the local wildlife is beginning to disappear from our countryside. Hopefully this will change because the wildlife compliments the colourful meadows and the many textures of the ponds and marshlands.

BURN VALLEY GARDENS
Burn Valley Gardens, Hartlepool, Tees Valley, 01429 523421
Burn Valley was opened in 1898 and it covers seven hectares of land. There are various activities in the park, such as a children's playground and a bowling green. There is a walkway which will take you through the family park and onto Ward Jackson Park. After the day is through, you'll be all parked out!

COWPEN BEWLEY WOODLAND PARK
01642 371633
The main attraction is the visitors' centre, which opened in 2000. Since then, the 300 acres of Woodland has thrived undisturbed by the cruelty of man.

FLATTS LANE WOODLAND COUNTRY PARK
Flatts Lane, Normanby, Middlesbrough, 01642 459629
Eston Hills will transform into Middlesbrough Mountains if you're on an exploration of the hills from Flatts Lane. If you believe that the best way in which to conquer the top is to start at the very bottom, then this is the challenge for you. (However, there are countryside volunteers at hand if you accidentally get lost on the way. phew!)

GUISBOROUGH FOREST AND WALKWAY
Pinchinthorpe, Guisborough, 01287 631132

The Guisborough Forest is near the Highcliff Nab, the Hanging Stone and Captain Cook's monument. There are many walking routes and trails for you to take if you are still hungry for the rural. If that doesn't fill you up, then the sublime views of Roseberry Topping will leave you stuffed and satisfied.

HEMLINGTON LAKE
Cass House Road, Hemlington, Middlesbrough 01642 596546
If the Animals of Farthing Wood were to take a camping holiday, they'd come here to hang out with the kingfishers, the swans and Britain's fastest declining mammal, the watervole. With 39 acres of land and a variety of wildlife amidst the lake, there's plenty to see. The many indoor facilities include an activity room, a tanning salon, a gym and various fitness classes. For the outdoorsy people, there are three football pitches, a skateboard park and canoeing facilities.

LINGFIELD COUNTRYSIDE CENTRE
Mount Pleasant Way, Coulby Newham, Middlesbrough 01642 577325
Weekdays 9.00am - 4.00pm plus weekends for events
This aims to promote the importance of the countryside and the environment in a town where cooling towers grow quicker than crops. There are various activities to partake in, such as an earth walk, a mini-beast hunt, orienteering, pond dipping and conservation work. The mini-beast hunt is mainly to discover what hides in the grass, but I'm sure we have all felt the mighty wrath of the midgy beast in our time.

PRESTON PARK
Preston Hall Museum and Park, Yarm Road, Eaglescliffe, Stockton-on-Tees, 01642 527375
The museum in this site is enveloped by 100 acres of rolling landscape, better known as

Preston Park. The park is home to an exotic bird aviary, a wildfowl pond and many riverside and woodland paths.

ROPNER PARK
Ropner Park, Stockton 01642 526871
Ropner Park makes an outstanding effort to give back to the community that has loved it for all these years. The restored water fountain is a focal point of the park because of its heart-warming history. Fisherman used to wash out the guts of their latest catch in the fountain, much to the locals disgust... but it is this humane touch of historical recollection that keeps Ropner Park in the heart of the locals.

ROSEBERRY TOPPING
Newton-under-Roseberry, North Yorkshire
01641 328901
If you think Helen Mirren looks good for her age, Roseberry Topping is 200 million years old! She has a few scars from the miners, but aside from that, she's still as strong as 100 million years ago.

ROSSMERE PARK
Hartlepool, Tees valley 01429 284124
Rossmere Park is in Hartlepool's urban centre and its four hectares of trees and flowerbeds work as a contrast to the halfpipe skateboard ramp and the aerial runway. It has a play area for the kids and a lake where you can feed the fowl. The park is a part of formal and informal sport and recreation, such as basketball, netball, tennis and even angling on the lake. The Wii is going to have stiff competition once the kids get a load of this.

SALTBURN VALLEY WOODLAND CENTRE
Valley Gardens, Saltburn-by-the-Sea, 01287 622408
This woodland centre blossoms because of its

excellent bird viewing area, its permanent and changing display panels and its orienteering course in the Valley Gardens. There is a Nature Club too, which is specifically aimed at 8-12yr olds to get them away from High School Musical and into the valley.

STEWART PARK
Ladgate Lane, Marton, Middlesbrough, 01642 300202
Open 7.30 am until dusk all year round, Stewart Park is a vast 120 acre plot of lakes, wild fowl, pet corners and The Captain Cook Birthplace Museum. It has two lakes and many domesticated animals, like fallow deer, highland cattle, llamas AND the all-important goats.

WARD JACKSON PARK
Elwick Road, Hartlepool, Tees Valley, 01429 262641
Ward Jackson Park is huge at 8.1 hectares and it was opened in 1883 to celebrate one of Hartlepool's greatest entrepreneurs, Ralph Ward Jackson. It is celebrated because of its collection of Victorian and Edwardian features, such as The Lodge House (1883), the bandstand (1901), the fountain (1902), and the clocktower (1925).

SUNDERLAND

BACKHOUSE PARK
Ryhope Road, Sunderland
Backhouse Park has been a landmark in Sunderland for over a century. It was owned by the Backhouse family and at that time was privy to a number of horticultural experiments, specifically as the seedbed for a unique strain of daffodil. The Friends of Backhouse are now in the process of aggressively developing the park into a safe haven for naturalists and education.

HERRINGTON COUNTRY PARK
Sunderland, 0191 534 8526

Herrington Country Park is a magnificent green site where visitors can enjoy delightful surroundings and a feast of events and activities. It has a contemporary children's play park, perfect haven for walking, picnics, model boating and cycle trails. Located near historic Penshaw Monument, just off the A19 and at the heart of the City of Sunderland.

MOWBRAY PARK
Burdon Road, Park Lane, 0191 219 3941
Open 7am until dusk.
Ⓜ *Park Lane*
Step inside the specially commissioned gates of Mowbray Park and experience a one-stop visitor attraction including the restored Victorian Park alongside the adjoining Museum & Art Gallery and Winter Gardens. The park holds also a children's playground and has an arrangement of events throughout the summer months. An intriguing array of artworks celebrate the city's connection with Lewis Carroll, who wrote his famous poem Jabberwocky while staying in the city.

ROKER PARK ROAD
Monkwearmouth, Ⓜ *Seaburn*
A municipal park opened to the public in 1880, making use of a deep natural ravine. Roker Park runs to about seven hectares next to the coast, on the northern boundary of Sunderland. The ornamental lake in the heart of the park, provided opportunities for a variety of activities including a model boating lake, two bowling greens and children's play facilities.

SUNDERLAND WINTER GARDENS
Sunderland Museum and Winter Gardens, Burdon Rd. 0191 553 23 23
Ⓜ *Sunderland*
Sunderland Museum & Winter Gardens combines a museum, art gallery, exhibition space and Winter Gardens to create a stunning visitor attraction in the heart of the city centre. The stunning Winter Gardens stimulate the

senses with over 2,000 flowers and plants brought together in a spectacular showcase of the world's natural beauty.

DURHAM

CASTLE EDEN DENE
Oakerside Dene Lodge, Stanhope Chase, Peterlee 0191 586 0004
Open: Footpaths open at all times. Lodge open for parties if booked in advance.
Cut deep into limestone, this is the largest of Durham's wooded coastal ravines and the North East's largest area of natural woodland. A National Nature Reserve with 12 miles of footpaths within its 500 acres, Castle Eden Dene is packed with over 450 different species of plant and many resident birds and mammals. Public events are held all year; call for details.

HARDWICK PARK
Sedgefield
01740 621 505
Open: All year.
Hardwick Park is a country park with a difference. The park has survived since the 1750s when its then owner, John Burdon, created a sprawling ornamental park. Come and admire the natural beauty of the lake, woodland and wildlife. The new Visitor Centre offers a modern retreat with café and interactive displays. Throughout the year there will be a variety of events for everyone to enjoy.

HOUGHALL GARDENS
East Durham and Houghall College, Stockton Road 0191 375 4700
Open: All year.
Set across 25 acres, the beautiful Houghall Gardens host a range of garden styles along with a country coffee shop. There is a small charge to obtain a worthwhile guide that will help you explore the arboretum, which contains some rare tree varieties as well as the National Collection of Whitebeams. Look out for the nearby Houghall Discovery Trail, a two-mile wooded track through the countryside.

OLD DURHAM GARDENS
Shincliffe Open: All year.
The old Durham hamlet in which these gardens are situated has a heritage stretching back to Roman times but the gardens themselves date from the early 17th Century. Formerly part of a mansion long since demolished, the gardens themselves had fallen into a poor state by the mid 1970s. Since then however, Durham City Council and a number of supporters have lovingly restored them back to their former glory.

BOTANIC GARDEN
Hollingside Lane, South Road
0191 334 5521
Open: Mar-Oct. 10am-5pm / Nov-Feb. 10am-4pm. Adults £4 / Concessions £3 / Children £1.50. Free to Durham students
A veritable rampage of colour in the summer and a great destination for sprawling around in when it's hot, the university-owned garden range includes a sculpture garden (including various former Bishops of Durham), a Japanese Bank, a butterfly house and a tropical rainforest. Written guides are available and there's also a glasshouse, a display of tropical insects and bugs, a visitors' centre and a coffee shop. Some plants are also for sale.

WHARTON PARK
Durham City Centre, behind train station
Open: All year.
Formed from part of the grounds of Dryburn Hall - the Wharton family residence - Wharton Park offers incredible views across Durham as well as including a Victorian-style conservatory, tennis courts and a kids' play area with swings. Disappointingly under-used but still utterly captivating.

What makes the north-east so special? It's not just the quality of what the cities and towns have to offer, but also their surrounding areas. We're right by the sea – the coastline is some of the most breathtaking in the UK – and our surrounding countryside – teeming with interesting villages, castles and other historical buildings of note – is simply stunning. Get off that beaten track!

Alnwich Gardens

TOWNS

ALNWICK

One of Alnwick's most stunning attractions is Alnwick Garden. This exciting venue features the Grand Cascade as its centrepiece, creating a series of spellbinding water displays. The Rose and Ornamental Gardens mix european garden design and superb planting but that's just the beginning. Attractions include the incredible Tree House (at 6,000sq feet, one of the largest in the world), the Labyrinth, the Serpent Garden and the Poison Garden where a mix of the unique and beautiful create an enchanted landscape where the imagination runs riot and the senses are stirred.

Another of the area's famous landmarks is Alnwick Castle, the film location for Harry Potter's Hogwart's School in the first two films and the Cate Blanchett film Elizabeth. This incredible medieval building now houses the world class restaurant The Sanctuary which is established itself as 'the' place for a unique dining experience. Northumberland has famed for its castles and as well as Alnwick Castle there are four others located nearby. As well as all this regal activity there's the fascinating Bailiffgate Museum and the legendary Barter Books, described by the New Statesman as 'The British Library of second-hand bookshops'. There's so much going on in and around Alnwick you may need a sabbatical rather than a day trip.

ALNWICK CASTLE

The Estate Office, Alnwick, Northumberland
01665 510777 24 hour information
01665 511100

Open: April-Oct daily 11am-5pm. Grounds open from 10am-6pm Adult £13, Conc. £10.40, Child £6, Under 5s free, Family ticket £34
The Alnwick Garden
On the B6341 (Leave the A1 north of Alnwick)
01665 511350
Open: Every day except Christmas Day. Summer: 10am-6pm. Winter: 10am-4pm.
The Garden's shop, restaurant and cafes are open during Garden opening hours. The Treehouse is also open for evening dining. Adult £11, Conc. £9, Children 16 and under (up to 4 per adult) £0.01 Assistance dogs only, these prices do not include the voluntary gift aid donation.

BAILIFFGATE MUSEUM

14 Bailiffgate, Alnwick, Northumberland
01665 605847

Open: April-Oct 10am-4pm every day. Nov-Easter 11am-4pm. Adults £2.50, Conc. £2, Children (under 16) free, under 5's free, Family ticket (2 + 1) £6.70 or (2+2) £7.60

Alnwick Castle

Belsay Hall

BARTER BOOKS
Alnwick Train Station
Alnwick, Northumberland
01665 604888
Open: Oct-Mar 9am-5pm daily except Thurs when the shop shuts at 7pm. April-Sept 9am-7pm daily. Closed Christmas Day.

CHILLINGHAM CASTLE
Alnwick, Northumberland 01668 215 359
Open: April-Oct 12pm-5pm for tearoom, ground, garden, and castle. Closed Saturdays. Open Nov-April by appointment.
Adult £8.50, Conc. £7.50, Child £4, under 5s free, family ticket £21. Assistance dogs only.

DUNSTANBURGH CASTLE
Craster - near Alnwick Northumberland 01665 576231
Open: April-Sept 10am-5pm daily. Oct 10am-4pm daily. Nov-Mar 10am-4pm daily.
Adult £4, Child £2.40.

EDLINGHAM CASTLE
Edlingham (between Rothbury and Alnwick) Alnwick, Northumberland 0870 333 1181
Access. Free.

WARKWORTH CASTLE
Warkworth, Alnwick Northumberland 01665 711423
Open: April-Sept 10am-5pm daily. Oct 10am-4pm daily. Nov-Mar 10am-4pm Hermitage open April – Sept 11am-5pm Wednesdays and Sundays.
Castle prices: Adults £4.80, Children £2.90, Conc. £4.30, Family ticket £12.50. Hermitage: Adults £3.20, Children £1.90, Conc. £2.90

BARDON MILL
Bardon Mill is one of a collection of pretty hamlets situated almost exactly halfway between Newcastle and Carlisle. There's a lot to see and do in the area, which is best known for its proximity to the Roman Wall. The fascinating Vindolanda Roman Fort site is just up the road and recent excavations have uncovered numerous buildings and some of the most unusual and well-preserved artifacts from the Roman world. After visiting the site itself head for the Roman Army Museum where you can view Roman boots, shoes, armour, jewellery and coins. Green fingered visitors to Bardon Mill should pop into the Errington Reay Pottery, a family run operation, which was established in 1878 and continues to produce quality earthenware pots with a uniquely textured finish. Once you've selected a few pots for the garden you should visit the Bowes Hotel next door for a drink or two and perhaps one of their reasonably priced meals. There's plenty of accommodation to suit all pockets around Bardon Mill but for those on a tight budget Once Brewed Youth Hostel is just the ticket. This purpose built centre is well placed for easy access to all Bardon Mill and the surrounding area has to entertain visitors.

BOWES HOTEL
Bardon mill, Hexham, Northumberland 01434 344237

ROMAN ARMY MUSEUM
Chesterholm Museum, Bardon Mill, Hexham, Northumberland
Roman Army Museum 016977 47485
Open: March 10am-5pm. April-Sept 10am-6pm. Oct 10am-5pm. Closed Dec to early Feb.
Adult £5, Student/OAP £4.25, Child £2.75, Family (2+2) £14.

ERRINGTON REAY POTTERY
Bardon Mill, Hexham Northumberland 01434 344245
Open: Daily 9.30am – 5.00pm
Once Brewed Tourist Information Centre
Military Road, Bardon Mill
Hexham, Northumberland
01434 344396

ONCE BREWED YOUTH HOSTEL MILITARY ROAD
Once Brewed, Northumberland
0845 371 9753
Adult: £ 16.40, Under 18s: £12.50.

VINDOLANDA
Accessible by foot from Bardon Mill and only a short detour is walking the Wall.
01434 344277
Open: March 10am-5pm. April-Sept 10am-6pm. Oct 10am-5pm. Closed from Dec to start of Feb.   Adult £6.25, Student/OAP £5.20, Child £3.75, Family £18.

BARNARD CASTLE
The historic market town of Barnard Castle was built in the imposing shadow of Bernard Balliol's castle which is not to be confused with Bowes Castle, a Norman Keep situated in nearby Bowes and dating from 1087. Other town attractions include the picturesque ruins of Egglestone Abbey, the dramatic nearby spectacle of High Force Waterfall and the extraordinary Bowes Museum. Housed in a replica 18th century French chateau, the museum has a magnificent collection of European art, design artefacts, and even a two-headed calf. It also has the country's finest collection of Sevres porcelain. The highlight though must be the beautiful silver swan automaton, which performs twice daily - check with the museum for exact times. And if this isn't enough you could visit Barnard Castle on a Wednesday and catch the market itself.

BOWES CASTLE
Bowes, Near Barnard Castle
County Durham 01833 638212
Open Access. Free.

BOWES MUSEUM
Barnard Castle 01833 690606
Open: Daily 10am-5pm.
Adults £9, Conc. £8.

EGGLESTONE ABBEY
Barnard CastleCounty Durham
0191 269 1200
Open: daily 10am-6pm. Free.

HIGH FORCE WATERFALL
Forest-in-Teesdale
Middleton-in-Teesdale
Barnard Castle 01833 622209
Open: Mon-Sun 11am-5.30pm. Adult £1.50, conc. £1, Children free

BELSAY
Belsay is a small village that lies seven miles north- west of Ponteland and 14 miles north-west of Newcastle. The 19th century mansion is a building of european importance, and the accompanying 14th century castle and 17th century manor house serve to place much of the region's history in context. Belsay is also noted for its fine gardens - particularly the romantic quarry with its dramatic collection of evergreens and exotic plants. There's also a gift shop and a tea-room to rest your feet in. For a more rustic outdoor experience visit Bolam Country Park - a favourite with twitchers and famed for its beautiful mute swans.

BELSAY HALL, CASTLE AND GARDENS
NW of Newcastle on A696
Belsay, Northumberland
01661 881 636
Open: April-Oct 10am-5pm daily. Nov 10am daily. Dec- Mar 10am-4pm Mon & Thurs, Friday, Sat & Sun
Adult £7.50, Conc. £6.80, Kids £4.50, Family £19.50.

BOLAM COUNTRY PARK AND VISITOR CENTRE
Access from C156/155
Nr. Belsay 01661 881 234
Open: Visitor Centre: 10.30am-4.30pm. Weekends, Bank holidays and school holidays from 12.00pm-3.30pm.

Bowes Museum

High Force

CHOLLERFORD

Chollerford is home to Chester's Fort, one of the largest forts on Hadrian's Wall. Chester's houses the extensive Clayton Collection of altars and sculptures from the wall. There's also the remains of a military bathhouse; one of the best examples of Roman building in the country. Visitors can find out more in the museum attached to the fort. Just next door to this historical gem is Chester's Walled Garden. This two-acre 18th century garden is sheltered on three sides by woodland and open on the fourth to stunning views of the Tyne Valley. For 200 years the garden provided the fruit and vegetables for Chester's House but it is now laid out as a unique herb garden. Don't forget to take a peek at the Roman Garden where the Roman's favourite herbs are planted – a fascinating glimpse into the culinary, medicinal and religious habits of the time. If you're staying in the area or even if you just fancy a bite to eat, head to The George Hotel. This 17th century hotel is built on the banks of the Tyne and has a great spa and pool that can be used by day visitors as well as guests.

CHESTERS FORT AND MUSEUM
Chollerford, on B6318
01434 681379
Open: April–Sept daily 10am-6pm. Oct-March

10am–4pm daily
Adult £5, Conc £4.50, Child £3.
The George Swallow Hotel
Chollerford, Northumberland
0870 050 20 20

CORBRIDGE

Corbridge, so named because when the Romans saw the bridge crossing the Tyne to the village they shouted 'Cor! Bridge!' Or perhaps that's just another piece of Roman Wall hearsay. Either way, this village falls decidedly into the pretty (some may say twee) camp. However, the abundance of tearooms, art shops and cottages gives way nicely to a rather unexpected interiors shop called RE: which sells 'REscued and REstored found objects from around the world'. And very stylish they are too. Also worth a visit whilst in Corbridge is Aydon Castle. This fortified 13th century manor house (converted to a farmhouse in the 17th century) has often been the setting for major films including Ivanhoe and Elizabeth. Other features on the list of things to do and see in and around Corbridge are the Corbridge Roman Site Museum and the delightful Dilston Physic Garden, a mere half mile up the road.

RE: SHOP
Bishops Yard, Main Street
Corbridge, Northumberland
01434 634567
Open: Tues-Fri 10am-5pm, Sat 10.30am-5pm, Sundays 12pm-4pm

AYDON CASTLE
Corbridge 01434 632 450
Open: April–Sept 10am-5 pm except Tue and Wed.
Adult £3.80, Conc. £3.40, Child £2.30.

CORBRIDGE ROMAN SITE MUSEUM
Corbridge, Northumberland 01434 632349
Open: April-Sept 10am-5.30pm daily. Oct 10am-4pm daily. Nov-Mar 10am-4pm Wed-Sun.
Adult £5, Conc. £4.50, Child £3.

DILSTON PHYSIC GARDEN
Dilston Mill House, Dilston Nr. Corbridge
Northumberland Tel: 01434 608129
Open: April- Adult £4, Conc. £3, under 12s free

COWSHILL
Cowshill's main claim to fame is Killhope Lead Mining Museum. This restored and complete lead mining operation boasts a most impressive 32ft water wheel. Visitors can walk down the original tunnel of the Park Level Mine and discover working conditions of 19th century miners, with superb guided talks. Surrounded by good walking areas, there's also a cafe if you need refreshment to restore your constitution. 'Santa in the Mines' at the beginning of December is a big hit with the kids. We recommend you dress warmly – Cowshill is 1500 feet above sea level and a bit nippy even at the height of summer.

KILLHOPE LEAD MINING MUSEUM
Cowshill, Upper Weardale
01388 537505
Open: April-Nov 10.30am –5.00pm daily.
Surface only: Adult £7, Conc £6.50, Child (4-16) £4,under 4s free but not allowed into the Mine.
Mine included: Adult £8.75, Conc. £7, Child (4-16) £4.50.

HAYDON BRIDGE
Haydon Bridge is a small town with a few decent pubs and shops. The main attraction is Hadrian's Wall World Heritage Site, Vercovicium which, as well as the site itself, boasts an impressive museum where visitors can see the site recreated in all its glory.

Segedunum Roman Fort Museum & Baths

Washington Old Hall

HOUSESTEADS ROMAN FORT (VERCOVICIUM)
Hadrian's Wall, Haydon Bridge
Hexham, Northumberland
01434 344363
Open: April-Sept 10am-6pm daily.
Oct-Mar 10am-4pm. Adult £5, Conc. £4.50 Child £3.

HEXHAM
Hexham is a pleasant market town situated about 20 miles west of Newcastle and well served by local rail services. It's the home of some fine old buildings including the Abbey and Moothall whilst the newly refurbished Border History Museum is well worth a visit. Also check out the wonderful Queen's Hall Art Centre, which plays host to music, exhibitions, theatre and a whole lot more beside. The market itself takes place every Tuesday selling home produce, clothes, bedding, pots and pans etc. If you time your visit carefully you could stock up on homewares and have a flutter later on as Hexham is also home to Northumberland's only racecourse.

BORDER HISTORY MUSEUM
Old Gaol, Hallgate
Hexham, Northumberland
01434 652349
Adults £3.95, OAP £3.20, Child £2.10, Family £10.50. Open: April-Sep 11am-4.30pm Tues to Sat. Feb, March, October and Nov open Tues and Sat only 11am-4.30pm.
10am-4pm. Open other times by arrangement.

HEXHAM ABBEY
Beaumont Street, Hexham
01434 602031
open 9.30-5pm.

HEXHAM RACECOURSE
The Riding, Hexham, Northumberland
01434 606881

QUEEN'S HALL
Beaumont Street, Hexham
01434 652 477
Box office open: 10am-4pm Mon-Sat, plus open one hour before performance start times in evenings.

JARROW
Jarrow is a town dripping in history. There was a Roman fort here in the first century, and by the fifth the site was occupied by the Anglo-Saxons. A mere 1300 years ago the Venerable Bede arrived and created the rich legacy that is celebrated today at Bede's World. Here you can discover the exciting world of the Venerable Bede, early Europe's greatest scholar, who lived and worked in the monastery of Wearmouth. Attractions include an interactive 'Age Of Bede' exhibition in the stunning museum building and an Anglo-Saxon demonstration farm, with rare breeds of animals and reconstructed timber buildings. Bede's World also has a medieval herb garden, gift shop, café and a lively and wide-ranging programme of events and temporary exhibitions. Jarrow's more recent history includes the famous Jarrow Crusade of 1936 when people marched to London to protest against the mass unemployment in Britain.

BEDE'S WORLD
Church Bank, Jarrow, Tyne & Wear
0191 489 2106
Open: Apr-Sep 10am-5.30pm Mon-Sat, 12pm-5.30pm on Sun. Adults £5.50, Kids and Conc. £3.50, Family Ticket (two adults and two children) £13.50.

ST. PAUL'S CHURCH AND MONASTIC SITE
Church Bank Jarrow 0191 489 7052
Open: Mon – Sat 10am-4pm. Sun 2.30pm-4pm.

KIELDER WATER & FOREST PARK

Home to northern Europe's largest man-made lake, England's largest forest and officially the country's most tranquil spot, Kielder Water & Forest Park is not to be missed. Nature lovers, water sports enthusiasts, explorers, walkers, cyclists, artists, families... anyone looking to escape, set their own agenda and create new experiences will delight in everything the park has to offer. The forest itself is one of the main attractions featuring mile upon mile of purpose-built trails including forest walks for all the family and dedicated mountain bike tracks. There's also Lakeside Way, a unique, multi-user trail suitable for walkers, runners, cyclists, push chair and wheelchair users and horse riders, which opened in 2009. The trail encircles Kielder Water stretching for 26 miles. A haven for wildlife – explorers can expect to encounter deer, otters, badgers, bats and rare breeds of birds including the first breeding ospreys in Northumberland in 200 years. Famed for having the darkest night skies in England thanks to minimal light pollution, Kielder Water & Forest Park is a star gazers' heaven and the Observatory offers exciting opportunities for those with an interest in learning more about the night sky. There's also an abundance of contemporary art and architecture in this striking rural setting including the new giant forest head, Silvas Capitalis. With plenty of picnic spots and places to eat throughout the park, visitors are spoilt for choice when it comes to spending a day trip, weekend break or holiday in the most tranquil area in England.

KIELDER WATER & FOREST PARK
Kielder, Northumberland
Call: 01434 220 616
Most facilities open from Feb to Dec.

MIDDLETON-IN-TEESDALE

The London Lead company arrived in Mickley in 1815 and the effects of the prosperity it brought with it are still clearly on show today in this pretty Victorian village. Venture out of the village itself and visit nearby High Force. The highest waterfall in England is well worth a visit and is also adjacent to one of the most attractive sections of the Pennine Way long distance footpath, wellies a must...

HIGH FORCE
alongside B6277
nr. Middleton-in-Teesdale, Co. Durham.

ROTHBURY

Rothbury is one of the prettiest Northumbrian villages sitting as it does alongside the river with the dramatic Simonside hills framing the view behind. Four miles east of Rothbury is Brinkburn Proiry. This 12th century priory was carefully restored in the 19th century and is one of the best examples of early Gothic architecture in the north. Founded in 1135 by Augustinian canons, the building stands in a beautiful setting in a loop of the river Coquet. If you visit the priory in early July you may be lucky enough to catch the Brinkburn Music Festival. This series of classical concerts and workshops is held annually in the priory which, as well as having beautiful surroundings has pretty impressive acoustics.

A little closer to Rothbury village is Cragside House. This beautifully maintained Victorian estate was built for Lord William Armstrong (of Vickers-Armstrong fame) and was the first building ever to be lit by hydro-electricity.

BRINKBURN PRIORY
Nr. Rothbury, Morpeth, Northumberland
01665 570628
Open: April-Sept 11am-4pm Mon, Thurs, Fri, Sat and Sun
Adult £3.30, Conc. £3, Child £2

CRAGSIDE HOUSE AND GARDENS
Rothbury, Morpeth, Northumberland
01669 620333
House Open: March-April, late April – May, June – July, Sept - Oct 1pm-5pm. Early April- late April, late May- June, late July – Sept, Oct 11am- 5pm. Daily except Mon
Gardens, estate, shop and restaurant: March- Oct 10.30am- 5pm, daily except Mon. Nov- Dec 11am- 4pm, Tues- Sun.

WALLSEND
Wallsend centre itself can't really be described as a beauty spot. There's a high street just far enough away from Newcastle to keep busy and bustling and there's a reasonably pretty park too. However, it is what Wallsend marks rather than what it is that makes it special and this is, of course, the end of the Roman wall. Segedunum Roman Fort stands on the banks of the Tyne, the last outpost of Hadrian's Wall. £9 million has brought the fort back to life with superb hands-on displays, the only reconstructed Roman bath-house in the country and a fabulous viewing tower.

SEGEDUNUM ROMAN FORT MUSEUM AND BATHS
2 Buddle St., Wallsend, Newcastle
0191 236 9647
Open: April-Oct 10am-5pm daily, Nov-Mar 10am-3pm daily. Closed Christmas day, Boxing day and New Years day.
Adults £4.50, Conc. £2.70, under 16s free.

WASHINGTON
The ancient ancestral home of George Washington - Washington Old Hall – was built in this town in the 17th century. The Old Hall is beautifully furnished in pieces from the same period, providing a fascinating insight into how the first President of the United State's family may have lived. Outside are immaculately maintained gardens featuring the scented plants and herbs of the time.

The Great Hall is also available for weddings and private functions – a venue sure to lend any occasion an upmarket air. A Washington attraction with very different appeal is Washington Wetlands Centre. The centre is set in 100 acres of stunning wetland and woodland on the River Wear and is a major conservation success story providing as it does a home to hundreds of rare and endangered ducks, geese and swans, plus a colourful breeding colony of Chilean Flamingos.

WASHINGTON OLD HALL
The Avenue, District 4, Washington
0191 416 6879
Open: Mid March-Start Nov 11am-5pm Sun-Wed. Garden 10am-5pm. Tea Room 11am-4pm.
Adults £5.50, Kids £3.50, Family £14.50

WASHINGTON WETLANDS CENTRE
The Wildfowl & Wetlands Trust
District 15, Washington, Tyne and Wear
0191 416 5454
Open: Apr-Oct 9.30am-5.30pm. Nov-Mar 9.30am-4.30pm. Adult £8.45, Conc. £6.50, Child £4.25, Family £20.91 (Two adults and two children).

COASTAL TOWNS

The north-east is blessed with some of the most beautiful coastline and intriguing history in Britain. Below we outline some of the many delights to be found by the sea.

BAMBURGH
Bamburgh is the ancient capital of Northumbria and is well known for the imposing figure of its castle, which stands on the cliff edge overlooking the Farne Islands. A truly magnificent sight, this colossus towers above the lovely village of Bamburgh on a basalt crag. The castle houses a fine collection of artefacts and is surrounded by wonderful sandy beaches that attract hundreds of campers to the area each

year. Notable Bamburgh characters include Grace Darling, the local girl who, along with her father, rescued shipwrecked sailors in a small open boat at the height of a storm in 1838. The Grace Darling Museum commemorates her achievement.

BAMBURGH CASTLE
Bamburgh 01668 214 515
Open: Late Feb- Oct 10am-5pm daily. Nov – Feb 11am- 4.30m weekends only.
Adult £8.50, Senior £7.50, Child £4, Children under 5s free, family £21 (2 adults and 3 children).

GRACE DARLING MUSEUM
Bamburgh, Northumberland
01668 214 910
Open: Easter–Oct 10am-5pm, Oct- Easter 10am-4pm daily Closed 24-27 Dec and New Years day. Adult £2.75, Conc. (over 60s and 5-16 year olds) £1.75, family £7.25 (2 adults and 3 children)

BERWICK-UPON-TWEED
This historic border market town has changed hands between the Scottish and the English 14 times and is soaked in the bloody history of these fierce exchanges. Visit the Regimental Museum, Tweed Main Guard and Ramparts or Berwick Castle to immerse yourself fully in the battles of the past. And if all that history proves a little too violent, Berwick and the surrounding area has stunning beaches and countryside in spades. Particularly popular with campers, there are loads of sites to choose from but one of our favourites is Beachcomber Campsite in nearby Goswick for its friendly atmosphere and its generous tent spacing policy. Also well worth the trip up to this border town is The Maltings; an arts centre and theatre in the heart of Berwick staging contemporary pieces as well as more traditional shows. The Berwick Gymnasium Gallery meanwhile stages some great exhibitions.

BEACHCOMBER CAMPSITE
Goswick Sands, Berwick-upon-Tweed
01289 381217
Adult £8.50 per night, Child £4 per night, serviced pitch £20. Prices are for high season (spring bank holiday and 29th June – 2nd Sept), reduced prices outside these dates.

BERWICK CASTLE
Berwick-upon-Tweed
Northumberland
01289 2691200/ 0870 3331181
Open access at any reasonable time. Free.
Berwick Gymnasium Gallery
The Parade, Berwick-upon-Tweed
01289 304 535

MALTINGS THEATRE
AND ARTS CENTRE
Eastern Lane, Berwick-upon-Tweed
01289 330999

REGIMENTAL MUSEUM
The Barracks, The Parade
Berwick-upon-Tweed
01289 301869
Open: April-Sept 10am-5pm Wed-Sun. Closed: 1st Oct–31st March.
Adults £3.80, Conc. £3.40, Child (under 16) £2.30 Children under 5 go free.

TWEED MAIN GUARD
Palace Street, Berwick-upon-Tweed
Northumberland
01289 308005 (evenings)
Open: Mon-Fri 10pm-5pm.
Adult £3.80, Conc. £3.40, Child £2.30

TWEED RAMPARTS
Berwick-upon-Tweed
Open access at any time. Free.

DRURIDGE BAY

One of the finest stretches of coastline in the country with a nature reserve, lake, water sports, cafe, visitors' centre, kids' play area, woods and meadows. The bay spans a huge area from the old village of Hauxley in the north to Cresswell in the south. The Country Park is a big favourite with wildlife enthusiasts and the views are simply stunning - take a flask, lie back and enjoy.

DRURIDGE BAY COUNTRY PARK
Red Row, Morpeth, Northumberland
01670 760968
Open all year. Toilets and information open 9.30am-4.30pm. Café, shop and display rooms open April – Sept, weekends, bank holidays and school holidays 11am – 4pm.
Closed to vehicles at night.

HOLY ISLAND

Originally known as Lindisfarne and often described as 'The jewel of the Northumberland Coast', Holy Island is only accessible across a causeway at low tide. In the seventh century it was one of the great seats of Christian learning in western europe and was where the beautiful Lindisfarne Gospels were written. Lindisfarne Castle is a Tudor fort converted to a house by the architect Edwin Lutyens for Edward Hudson, founder of The Country Life magazine.

If you're a bit of a film buff you may wonder where you've seen it before... That's right, it doubled as Donald Pleasance's house in Polanski's "Cul-De-Sac" and in the Millennium episode of the series 'Cold Feet'. The ruined Lindisfarne Priory was established by St.Aidan. When the corpse of St. Cuthbert was discovered undecayed in 698AD, Lindisfarne became one of the holiest shrines in Christendom. For 1300 years, it has been a place of pilgrimage and considered the birthplace of Christianity in Britain. There's also a museum exhibiting artefacts from excavations as well as a gift shop. Make sure you have a tide timetable - at high tide the causeway linking Holy Island to the Northumbrian coast is submerged and the island is cut off from the mainland.

LINDISFARNE CASTLE
Holy Island 01289 389 244
Mar-Oct open Tues-Sun. Opening times depend on the tides - please always phone in advance. Castle and garden: Adult £6.95, Child £3.50, Family £17.40. Garden only: £1.30, children free.

St Marys Lighthouse

Lindisfarne

LINDISFARNE PRIORY AND MUSEUM
Holy Island 01289 389 200
Open: April-Sept 9.30am-5pm daily. Oct 9.30am- 4pm daily. Nov-Jan 10am –2pm Sat-Mon, Feb-Mar 10am-4pm daily. Adult £4.80, Conc. £4.30, Child £2.90.

NORTH SHIELDS

North Shields is a bustling town with good travel links from other coastal towns and Newcastle centre. Those with a nostalgic streak should visit the Childhood Memories Toy Museum, which exhibits toys from every era. There's something slightly creepy yet oddly comforting about the mix of Tiny Tears dolls from the 1980s and highly unsavoury Gollywogs from the 1880s. For more avant garde exhibitions head to The Globe Gallery. The Globe has an innovative and continuous programme of contemporary art, often giving valuable and much needed space to graduating students and other up and coming artists. Other North Shields attractions include the Stephenson Railway Museum where you can explore the history of railways from steam to coal to electricity through interactive media and 'hands-on' exhibits. There's also the chance to re-live the days of the steam railway and take a ride on a real steam train.

CHILDHOOD MEMORIES TOY MUSEUM
Palace Building, Grand Parade
North Shields 0191 259 1776
Open: April-May 10.30am-5.00pm weekends only, June-Sept 10.30am-5.00pm Tues-Sun except bank holidays, Sept-Nov 10.30am-5.00pm weekends only. Adults £1.50, Child/Conc.75p

GLOBE GALLERY
97 Howard St, North Shields
0191 259 2614
Open: 11.30am-5.00pm Tues-Sat. 11am-2pm Sunday. Free

STEPHENSON RAILWAY MUSEUM
Middle Engine Lane, North Shields
0191 232 6789
Open: from 2rd April weekends, bank holiday Mondays and school holidays from 11am-4pm, open at different times over Bank Holidays, School Holidays and Christmas contact Museum for further details. Museum admission is free. Train rides: Adult £2.20, Conc. £1.10, family £5.50.

ROKER

As well as the fabulous St. Peter's beach, for many, one of Roker's main attractions is the 200 berth Marina complex, which offers up all sorts of thrilling water-based sports from sailing and canoeing to pleasure fishing and river cruising. Heritage fans and art lovers visiting the area should also check out St. Andrew's Church; designed by Edward Prior one hundred years ago and much inspired by the Arts and Craft Movement.

ST ANDREWS CHURCH
Talbot Road, Roker 0191 516 0135
Sunderland Marine

ACTIVITIES CENTRE
North Dock, Roker, Sunderland
0191 514 4721 Open: 24/7

SALTBURN

Sitting high over the sea, Saltburn retains all the traditional charm of a Victorian seaside resort including colourful Italian gardens and walks through wooded glens. It also has the oldest water balanced cliff tramway in Britain, linking the town with the pier 120 feet below. Visit nearby Deepdale and the Cleveland Ironstone Mining Museum to gain an insight into how the industrial revolution affected the area.

CLEVELAND IRONSTONE MINING MUSEUM.
Deepdale, Skinningrove
Saltburn-by-the-Sea 01287 642877
Open: April-Oct 1.00pm-3.30pm daily.
Please note that as this Museum is staffed by volunteers it is recommended that you call first to confirm opening times and prices

THE ITALIAN GARDENS
Valley Gardens, Saltburn
Open: All year daily dawn to dusk.
Admission free.

SEABURN
Seaburn is renowned for its wonderful, sandy beaches and was a popular holiday haunt of artist LS Lowry who captured many of its wonderful sights on canvas. Today it's the home to the Sunderland International Airshow, which takes place every August, attracting hundreds of thousands of fans keen to get a glimpse of some of the stars of the skies.

SUNDERLAND INTERNATIONAL AIR SHOW
Seaburn, Free

SEAHOUSES
This tiny fishing harbour has more to offer the weary traveller than many much larger towns. A Farne Island boat trip is a must. Check out the seal and bird colonies as you hit the waves. There are guides available and cruises to Holy Island can be arranged too. When you return ruddy cheeked and with frozen fingers check in to The Olde Ship Hotel. With locally caught seafood on the menu, seafaring paraphernalia at every turn and a welcoming real fire this hotel offers the perfect sanctuary on stormy nights.

ISLAND BOAT TRIPS
Seahouses 01665 720 308
Various boat trips available, contact the company for further details and for information on sailing times and prices

THE OLDE SHIP HOTEL
Main Street, Seahouses 01665 720200

SOUTH SHIELDS
South Shields is home to the Arbeia Roman Fort. This is one of the few Roman sites where you can actually watch excavations in progress throughout the summer months. There is a fine reconstruction (full size) of the fort's West Gate, and on some of the special event days you can sample Roman food or watch re-enactments of training. Other local treats include the 1871 Souter Lighthouse, (the first ever electrically powered lighthouse) and the South Shields Museum and Art Gallery.
The town also boasts more than its fair share of curry houses – perfect for when you've had your fill of historical visits. For a more unusual dining experience venture a half mile up the coast to The Marsden Grotto. This restaurant/bar is built into the cliff itself and offers unbroken views of the dramatic North Sea below.

ARBEIA ROMAN FORT AND MUSEUM
Baring St, South Shields
0191 456 1369 South Shields
Open: April-Oct 10.00am-5pm Mon-Fri, 1pm-4pm Sat, 2pm-5pm Sunday. Free.

MARSDEN GROTTO
Coast Road, Marsden, South Shields
0191 455 6060

SOUTER LIGHTHOUSE
Coast Road, Whitburn 0191 529 3161
South Shields
Open: Mar-Oct 11am-5pm daily except Friday.

SOUTH SHIELDS MUSEUM AND ART GALLERY
Ocean Road 0191 232 6789
South Shields
Open: Mon-Fri 10am-4pm, Sat 11am-4pm,
Closed Dec 19-Jan 8.

TYNEMOUTH
This smallish seaside town is full of charm
and character and it is well worth paying a
visit on weekends when a very popular market
is held in the Metro station. Up for grabs are
antiques, books, plants, cakes, clothes and
records: in fact anything and everything. The
most famous aspects of the town however
are Tynemouth Priory and Castle, both of
which are steeped in the history of religion
and war. For activities with kid-appeal the
Blue Reef Aquarium is a winner. Enjoy close
encounters with graceful sharks and rays and
stroll among the colourful inhabitants of coral
reef in a spectacular underwater tunnel. Over
30 naturally-themed undersea habitats are
home to an amazing variety of aquatic life.
After all that sightseeing you may be in need
of refreshment so head to Marshall's fish
and chip shop for the crispiest batter and
the flakiest cod in miles.

MARSHALLS FISH AND CHIPS
(The Fryery by the Priory)
33 Front Street, Tynemouth

TYNEMOUTH PRIORY AND CASTLE
0191 257 1090 Tynemouth
Open: April – Sept 10am –5pm daily.
Oct –Dec 10am-4pm Thurs – Mon. Jan- March
10am-4pm Thurs – Mon.
Adult £4.50, Conc. £4.10, Child £2.70,
family £11.70.

BLUE REEF AQUARIUM
Grand Parade, Seafront
Tynemouth,
0191 258 1031
Open: 10am-6pm daily.
 Adults £8.30, Children £5.95, Under 3s free,
Senior/students £7.20, Family tickets £26.50
(2+2)/£31.50 (2+3)

WHITLEY BAY
Whitley Bay has something of a party
reputation with plenty of bars tempting the
frolicsome and carefree to jump on a Metro
and head for 'Whitley' to let their hair down
(see Newcastle pubs section for more on
these). For those searching for high jinx,
a good time is guaranteed. Candyfloss,
ice-cream and fruit machines are also
very much the order of the day. St. Mary's
Lighthouse attracts many visitors to the town
as it is one of the few lighthouses to allow
the public full access. The views from the
top are pretty impressive too. Surrounding
the building is a nature reserve – perfect
for soggy ankles and happy kids who will
be fascinated by the rock-pool inhabitants.
Also worth checking out is the totally rebuilt
Whitley Bay Playhouse which has had £8
million splashed out on it and plays host to
popular plays, musicals and bands.

ST. MARY'S LIGHTHOUSE AND WETLAND
St. Mary's Island, Whitley Bay
0191 2008650
Opening times vary according to tides and
weather conditions. Call for details.
Adults £2.30. Conc. £1.20, family £5 (2 adults
and 2 children)

WHITLEY BAY PLAYHOUSE
Marine Avenue, Whitley Bay
0844 277 2771

White exploring the north-east it always pays to have a good base and the region has scores of hotels and bed and breakfasts in which to moor your boat. From the gorgeously hip to the cheap and cheerful, you're sure to find something to suit.

Hotel Du Vin

THE ADELPHI HOTEL
63 Fern Avenue, Jesmond
0191 281 3109
M *West Jesmond*
Single £39.50
Double £60.00
£10 per child over 5

BACKPACKERS INN
0191 340 7334
51 Grainger Street,
Newcastle
M *Central Station*
From £17.95

BENTLEYS
425 Westgate Road
0191 273 3497
Single £25-£30
Double £50-£60

THE BRIGHTON
49 Brighton Grove,
Fenham
0191 273 3600
Single £25-30
Double £40 - £60 per room
Triple £60-£90 per room
Family £60-£100 per room

BRITANNIA HOTEL
Newcastle Airport,
Ponteland
0191 401 9988
Airport
Rooms from £51

CAIRN HOTEL
97-103 Osborne Rd,
Jesmond
0191 281 1358
M *West Jesmond*
Single from £45
Double from £60
Family £90

THE CALEDONIAN HOTEL
64-68 Osborne Road,
Jesmond
0191 281 7881
M *West Jesmond*
Single £55-£110
Double £65-£120
Family £75-£130

CLIFTON HOUSE HOTEL
46 Clifton Road, (off
Grainger Park Road)
0191 273 0407
Single (including breakfast)
from £29
Double (including breakfast)
from £59
Family (including breakfast)
from £85

THE CARLTON COMFORT INN
82-86 Osborne Rd.
Jesmond
0191 281 3361
M *West Jesmond*
Single £45-£55
Double £65-£85

COPTHORNE HOTEL
The Close, Quayside
0191 222 0333
M *Central Station*
Rooms from £95-£180

COUNTY THISTLE
Neville Street, Newcastle
0191 232 2471
M *Central Station*
Single from £60
Double from £85

CORNERHOUSE
Heaton Road, Newcastle
0191 265 9602
Single £49.00
Double/Twin £59.00
Family £69.00

CUMBERLAND ARMS
James Place Street,
Ouseburn, 0191 265 6151
Single £60
Double or twin £70 per room
per night. Family room £90

DERWENT PARK (CAMPING/CARAVAN)
Rowlands Gill Tyne &
Wear
01207 543 383
Touring caravans £17.50
Two Man Tents only £12.50

ELEPHANT ON THE TYNE
Riverside Park,
Gateshead
0191 495 0282
Single £39.50 . Double
£55-£75. Family £80

THE GEORGE HOTEL
88 Osborne Road,
Jesmond, 0191 281
4442 M *West Jesmond*
Single £40
Double £60
Triples £90
Family £90 - £120

GREY STREET HOTEL
Grey Street, Newcastle
0191 230 6777
M *Monument*
Rooms £145-£189

HOLIDAY INN NEWCASTLE CITY
1 Waterloo Square, Newcastle
0870 400 9070/
0191 224 6850
M *Monument*
Rooms from £65

JACKSON HOUSE
88 Fern Avenue, Jesmond
0191 2813129
M *West Jesmond*
£95-£185

MALMAISON
Quayside, Newcastle
0191 245 5000
M *Manors*
Rooms from £120 upwards, check hotel for special promotional rates

MATFEN HALL COUNTRY HOTEL & GOLF COURSE
Maften, Newcastle
01661 855708
Single £90-£150
Double £99-£275

VILLAGE HOTEL & LEISURE CLUB
Cobalt Business Park, West Allotment, Newcastle Upon Tyne, Tyne and Wear
0191 270 1414
£65 - £115

NEWCASTLE MARRIOTT GOSFORTH PARK
High Gosforth Park, Ncle
0191 236 4111
Rooms from £99

NEWCASTLE MARRIOTT
Metrocentre, Gateshead
0191 493 2233
Rooms from £99

NOVOTEL
Ponteland Road, Kenton
0191 214 0303
M *Bankfoot*
£65 upwards

THE OSBORNE HOTEL
13-15 Osborne Rd, Jesmond
0191 281 3385
M *West Jesmond*
Single £45, Double £65
Triple £90, Family £105

ROYAL STATION HOTEL
Neville Street, Newcastle
0191 232 0781
M *Central Station*
Single from £69
Double from £79

RYTON PARK COUNTRY HOTEL
Holburn Lane, Ryton
0191 413 3535
Single from £65
Double from £79
Twin from £95

SHAFTESBURY GUEST HOUSE
245 Prince Consort Road, Gateshead
0191 478 2544
Single £30 , Twin £46
Family £68

THE STABLES LODGE GUEST HOUSE
South Farm, Lamesley
0191 492 1756 From £74

SWALLOW IMPERIAL HOTEL
Jesmond Road, Jesmond
0191 281 5511
M *Jesmond*
Doubles and twin from £65 - £150

PREMIER INN MILLENIUM BRIDGE
City Road, Quayside
0191 232 6533 **M** *Manors*
From £69 a night

PREMIER INN AT NEWCASTLE AIRPORT
Ponteland Road, Newcastle
0870 1977 190
M *Airport*
rom £57

TRAVEL LODGE NEWCASTLE CENTRAL
4 Forster Street, Quayside,
0871 984 6164
M *Manors*
Rooms from £51.30

VERMONT HOTEL
Castle Garth, Newcastle
0191 233 1010
M *Central Station*
Rooms from £120 (£65 per person)

WATERSIDE HOTEL
48-52 Sandhill, Quayside
0191 230 0111
M *Central Station*
Twin/Double £69

TEES VALLEY

CRATHORNE HALL HOTEL
Crathorne, Near Yarm
01642 700 398
Single from £77 including breakfast
Double from £87 including breakfast

THE GRAPES
Scaling Dam,
Saltburn-by-the-sea
01287 640 461
Single £40-£45
Double £50-£60

HALL GARTH HOTEL
Cortham Mundeviell,
Darlington
0870 609 6131
Prices are from £69 for a double but vary seasonally

HARDWICK HALL HOTEL
Sedgefield, Co. Durham
01740 620 253
Single £110-£180
Double £135-£215

BEST WESTERN MIDDLESBROUGH
Marton Road,
Middlesbrough
01642 817 638
Single from £45
Double from £55

HUNLEY HALL HOTEL
Brotton, Saltburn
01287 676 216
Single from £45
Double from £85

JUDGES COUNTRY HOUSE HOTEL
Kirklevington Hall,
Kirklevington, Yarm
01642 789 000
Single from £145
Double from £175

BEST WESTERN PARKMORE HOTEL
Yarm Road, Eaglescliffe,
Stockton-on-Tees
01642 786 815
Singles from £79.50
Double/Twin from £99.50

RUSHPOOL HALL
Saltburn Lane,
SALTBURN-BY-THE-SEA
01287 624 111
Single £90
Double / twin room from £135
Family £155

THE SPA HOTEL
Saltburn Bank, Saltburn
01287 622 544
Single from £39.50
Double from £70
Family of 3 from £80
Family of 4 from £90

STAINCLIFFE HOTEL
The Cliff, Seaton Carew,
Hartlepool
01429 264 301
Single £55
Double £70

THISTLE HOTEL
Fry Street,
Middlesbrough
0871 3769 028
Rooms from £50

BEST WESTERN WALWORTH CASTLE HOTEL
Walworth, Darlington
01325 485 470
Single from £69
Double from £79

SUNDERLAND

THE BALMORAL GUESTHOUSE
3 Roker Terrace, Roker
0191 565 9217
Single from £23
Double from £40

BRAESIDE HOLIDAY GUEST HOUSE
26 Western Hill,
Sunderland
0191 565 4801
M University
Rooms from £25-£38

GEORGE WASHINGTON GOLF & COUNTRY CLUB
Stone Cellar Road,
High Usworth,
Washington
0191 402 9988
Room only (double or single) from £50

HOLIDAY INN WASHINGTON
Emerson,
District 5, Washington
0871 9429 084
Room only(double, single or family) from £69

THE PROMENADE
1-2 Queen's Parade,
M *Seaburn*
0191 529 2919

Single £20
Double £39
Family £55

LEMONFIELD HOTEL
Sea Lane, Seaburn
0191 529 3018
Rooms from £25

BEST WESTERN ROKER HOTEL
Roker Terrace
0191 567 1786
0191 567 8221
Single (including breakfast) from £78
Double (including breakfast) from £95

SUNDERLAND MARRIOT HOTEL
Queen's Parade, Seaburn
0191 529 2041
Double from £90

PREMIER INN
Wessington Way, Castletown
0191 5489 384
Rooms from £29

TRAVELODGE HOTELS LTD
Low Row, Sunderland
0871 984 6050
Rooms from £56

DURHAM

THE BAY HORSE INN
Brandon Village
0191 378 0498
Single Room £40 Inc breakfast
Double Room £50 Inc breakfast

Family Room of 3 - £65
Family Room of 4 - £75

THE BEAMISH MARY INN
No Place, Stanley
0191 370 0237
Single from £25 (including breakfast) Double £50 (including breakfast)

BOWBURN HALL HOTEL
Bowburn
0191 377 0311
Single room only from £38
Double room only from £45

DURHAM MARRIOTT
Old Elvet
0191 386 6821
Prices vary according to Season

THE HONEST LAWYER HOTEL
Croxdale Bridge, Durham
0191 3783780
Single £53.50
Double £60-£110

THE GABLES HOTEL
59 Front Street, Haswell, Plough
0191 526 2982
Single: - £50-56
Double: without bathroom - £64-72
Family Room (3 people) - £96

HIGH FORCE HOTEL
Forest-in-Teesdale, County Durham
01833 622 222
Single £40
Double £80

KINGSLODGE HOTEL
Waddington Street
0191 370 9977
Single room only from £60
Double room only from £75
Family room only from £95 (4 people)

PETERLEE LODGE HOTEL
Bedeway, Peterlee
0191 586 2161
Single (including breakfast) from £30
Double (including breakfast) from £40

BARCELO REDWORTH HALL HOTEL
Redworth, County Durham
01388 770 600
From £56.50 per person

THREE TUNS HOTEL
New Elvet
0191 386 4326
Single from £50
Double from £60

The Tourist Information Centres that you'll find situated in the main towns and cities across the north-east are the ideal place to call in to make the most of your time here. The helpful staff have a wealth of knowledge and the centres are jam-packed with information.

NEWCASTLE/GATESHEAD

TOURIST INFORMATION CENTRE
*@ Gateshead Old Town Hall
Gateshead, Old Town Hall, West Street,
Gateshead, Tyne and Wear, NE8 1HE*
Tel: +44 (0)191 478 4222 / 477 5380
Email: tourism@gateshead.gov.uk
Opening hours are Mon-Sat 10am-4pm
Closed Mondays

TOURIST INFORMATION CENTRE
@ GATESHEAD CENTRAL LIBRARY,
*Gateshead Central Library Prince
Consort Road, NE8 4LN
Tel: +44 (0)191 433 8420
Fax: +44 (0)191 477 7454
Minicom: +44 (0)191 478 2060*
Email: enquiries@gateshead.gov.uk
Open: Mon-Fri 9am-7pm , Wed 9am-5pm Sat
9am-1pm, Closed Sundays & Bank Holiday
Mondays

NEWCASTLE TOURIST
INFORMATION CENTRE
*City Centre, 8/9 Central Arcade, Market
Street, NE1 5BQ.*Tel: +44 (0)191 277
8000
Email: tourist.info@newcastle.gov.uk
Open: Mon-Fri 9.30am-5.30pm
Sat 9am-5pm.
Sundays & Bank Holidays 10-4pm

NORTH SHIELDS TOURIST
INFORMATION CENTRE
*Unit 18, Royal Quays Outlet Village
Coble Dene, North Shields, NE29 6DW
Tel: +44 (0)191 200 5895*
Email: ticns@northtyneside.gov.uk
Open: Mon-Sat 9am-4.30pm;
Sun 9.30am-4.30pm.

WHITLEY BAY TOURIST
INFORMATION CENTRE
*Park Road, Whitley Bay, NE26 1EJ
Tel: +44 (0)191 200 8535*
Email: ticwb@northtyneside.gov.uk
Open: Mon, Tues, Thurs-Sat – 9.30am-5pm
(Closed for lunch 12.30pm-1.30pm)
Closed Wednesday & Sunday

DURHAM

BISHOP AUCKLAND TOURIST
INFORMATION CENTRE
*The Town Hall, Market Place, Bishop
Auckland, County Durham, DL14 7NP
Tel: +44 (0)1388 604 922 / 602 610
Fax: +44 (0)1388 604 960*
Open: Mon-Fri 10am-5pm. Sat 9am-4pm
Closed Sunday & Bank Holiday

SUNDERLAND

SUNDERLAND TOURIST
INFORMATION CENTRE
*City Library & Arts Centre, 2nd Floor,
Fawcett Street, Sunderland, SR1 1RE
Tel: +44 (0)191 553 2000
Fax: +44 (0)191 553 2003*
Email: tourist.info@sunderland.gov.uk
Open: Monday-Friday: 9.30am-5pm;
Saturday: 9.30am-4pm
Closed Sunday & Bank Holiday

SOUTH SHIELDS TOURIST
INFORMATION CENTRE
*Museum and Art Gallery,
Ocean Road, South Shields, NE33 2HZ
Tel: +44 (0)191 454 6612
Fax: +44 (0)191 454 6612*
Email: museum.tic@southtyneside.gov.uk
Open: Mon-Fri 10am-5pm, Sat 11am-4pm
Closed Sunday

TEES VALLEY

HARTLEPOOL TOURIST INFORMATION CENTRE & ART GALLERY
Church Square, Hartlepool, TS24 7EQ
Tel: +44 (0)1429 869 706
Fax: +44 (0)1429 523 408
Email: hpooltic@hartlepool.co.uk
Open: Tuesday-Saturday 10am-5pm
Closed Sunday & Monday

MIDDLESBROUGH TOURIST INFORMATION
Town Hall Box Office, Albert Road,
Middlesbrough, TS1 2QQ
Tel: +44 (0)1642 729700 / 729 729
Fax: +44 (0)1642 729935
Email: tic@middlesbrough.gov.uk
Open: Monday-Wednesday 10am-5pm,
Thursday 10am-8pm, Friday 10am-4.30pm,
Saturday 9am-1.30pm.
Closed Sundays & Bank Holidays

NORTHUMBERLAND

ALNWICK TOURIST
Information Centre
2 The Shambles, Alnwick NE66 1TN
Tel: +44 (0)1665 511 333
July-August: Mon–Sat, 9am-5.30pm, Sunday
10am-4pm November-April: Mon-Saturday
9.30am-4.30pm, Closed Sunday.
Spring & Autumn: 9.30am-5pm, Sunday
10am-4pm

BERWICK-UPON-TWEED TOURIST INFORMATION CENTRE
106 Marygate, Berwick-upon-Tweed,
Tel: +44 (0)1289 330733
Fax: +44 (0)1289 330448
Email: tourism@berwick-upon-tweed.gov.uk
April-October: Mon-Sat 10am-5pm; (June-October) Sundays 11am-3pm.
November-March: Mon-Sat 10am-4pm;
Closed Sunday

HEXHAM TOURIST
Information Centre,
Wentworth Car Park,
Wentworth Place, Hexham, NE46 1QE
Tel: +44 (0)1434 652220
Fax: +44 (0)1434 652393
April-September: Mon-Sat 9.30am-5pm.
Sun 11am-4pm.
October-March: Mon-Sat 10am-4pm. Closed
Sundays.

TOURIST INFORMATION

www.thecrackmagazine.com

211

Metro Student Cards mean money for you, with cheaper travel around Tyne and Wear.

nexus.org.uk/metro @My_Metro 🅑

The north-east is easily accessible so we thought we'd detail the best ways of getting here by road, rail and air as well as the best ways to move around the region.

Way out
Lift

Alarm

NEWCASTLE

AIR Airport Newcastle Airport is located only 15-20 minutes from the city centre. There are regular and frequent air services from European cities along with connections from major international cities around the world, plus UK and Ireland direct schedule services. For more information and details of scheduled routes: Tel: 0871 882 1121 or visit: www.newcastleairport.com

RAIL Central Station Direct train services operate from most cities in Britain to Central Station, which is served by Great North Eastern Railways, Virgin Cross Country and Regional Railways. Journey times are 3hr 45min from London and 1hr 30min from Edinburgh. National Rail enquiries: Tel: 0845 748 4950, Train Tracker: Tel: 0871 200 4950 or visit www.nationalrail.co.uk

ROAD The A1(M) runs from the North to the South and passes close by Newcastle Gateshead.

SUNDERLAND

AIR Airport At some 20 miles away, Newcastle Airport is the nearest to Sunderland. There are good Metro links directly to Sunderland town centre or it's approximately a thirty five minute drive. For more information and details of scheduled routes: Tel: 0871 882 1121 or visit: www.newcastleairport.com

RAIL Sunderland Sunderland can be reached by taking a train to Newcastle (1hr 50min hours from Edinburgh and taking a connection from there to Sunderland (20 mins). There is now a direct train from Sunderland to London (3hr 40min). National Rail enquiries: Tel: 0845 748 4950, Train Tracker: Tel: 0871 200 4950 or visit www.nationalrail.co.uk

ROAD From the A1(M), northbound and southbound, take the junction at Washington Services for the A1231 (Sunderland).

DURHAM

AIR There are regular domestic and international flights from both Newcastle Airport (35 minutes drive from Durham) and from Durham Tees Valley Airport (45 minutes drive). For more information and details of scheduled routes: Newcastle Airport: Tel: 0871 8821 121 or visit: www.newcastleairport.com
Durham Tees Valley Airport: Tel: 0871 2242 426 or visit: www.durhamteesvalleyairport.com

RAIL Durham is served by the British Rail main East Coast Inter-City route. There is a frequent high speed service between London and Scotland, stopping at Durham. National Rail enquiries: Tel: 0845 748 4950, Train Tracker: Tel: 0871 200 4950 or visit www.nationalrail.co.uk

ROAD Both the Al(M) and A19 are easily accessed from Durham city centre, providing fast road links to the rest of the north-east and the UK road network.

TEES VALLEY

AIR Durham Tees Valley Airport is less than half an hour's drive from Middlesbrough. Scheduled passenger flights run to British and European destinations. For more information and details of scheduled routes: Tel: 0871 2242 426 or visit: www.durhamteesvalleyairport.com

RAIL Arriva Trains Northern services operate to Middlesbrough with connections at Durham, Newcastle, Sunderland and Hartlepool. There are also daily Transpennine Services from York, Leeds, Manchester and Liverpool. National Rail enquiries: Tel: 0845 748 4950, Train Tracker: Tel: 0871 200 4950 or visit www.nationalrail.co.uk

ROAD Middlesbrough is at the intersection of the A19 (north-south) and A66 (east-west) major trunk roads, putting it within an hours drive of Newcastle, Sunderland and York.

GETTING AROUND

THE METRO

Tyne and Wear Metro has been rated as one of the country's most efficient modes of transport and carries over 40 million passengers a year. It is an ideal way to get to and from the airport as well as coastal areas and Sunderland. The Metro trains have room for wheelchairs and buggies and have comfortable seating. Many stations have real-time platform indicators (telling you how many minutes before the next train arrives), help points, CCTV, payphones and a high standard of accessible information as well as improved lifts and escalators. Tickets are purchased via ticket machines at the Metro stations. Look out for Metro DaySaver tickets.

BUSES

Bus services in Newcastle Gateshead are frequent and there are a wide variety of special travel tickets available: Network Travel tickets save you time, money and the inconvenience of buying individual tickets. They offer unlimited journeys within Tyne and Wear and are available for weekly, two weekly, four weekly and annual travel. They are valid on Metro, Shields Ferry, buses, and Newcastle to Sunderland Rail line. Day Rover gives you all the freedom to travel, all day – wherever you want, anywhere in Tyne and Wear. Tickets are available to purchase from most Metro ticket machines and from the bus driver. It's easy to use – all you do is show the driver or inspector your ticket when you board. Then just travel as much as you like on bus, Metro, the Sunderland to Blaydon rail line, and the Shields Ferry. The North

East Explorer Ticket - The ticket you need if you want to combine journeys on an Arriva bus with journeys on buses operated by other bus companies or the Tyne and Wear Metro.

NEXUS TRAVELSHOPS

Nexus Travelshops offer assistance with everything from obtaining local travel tickets through to booking day excursions, mini-break coach trips and national holidays. Nexus Travel Shops can be found at: Four Lane Ends Metro Station; Gateshead, Bus/Metro Interchange; Heworth Metro Station; Newcastle, Central Station; Newcastle, Haymarket Metro Station; Newcastle, Monument Metro Station; North Shields Metro Station; South Shields, Fowler Street and Sunderland, Park Lane.

TRAVELINE: For all your local travel enquiries call Traveline on 0871 200 2233. Lines are open 7am - 9pm daily (except Christmas Day and providing a 'reduced hours' service on Boxing Day and New Year's Day). You can also check their website: www.traveline.org.uk which provides timetable and fare information for all local bus, Metro, train and ferry journeys throughout the north-east.

THE METRO STUDENT CARD

The Metro is ideal for students - there are Metro stations located near to all the main university and college campuses and many of the halls of residences. With a Metro Student Card you get unlimited travel in the zones chosen.
All Zones: £48.50 (4 Week) £410 (Annual)
Inner Newcastle: £31 (4 Week) £290 (Annual)
Inner Sunderland: £31 (4 Week) £290 (Annual)
A further discounted card is available for students aged 16-18. £9.5- (1 week) £32.50 (4 week).
For more information visit www.nexus.org.uk/metro or any Nexus Travelshop.

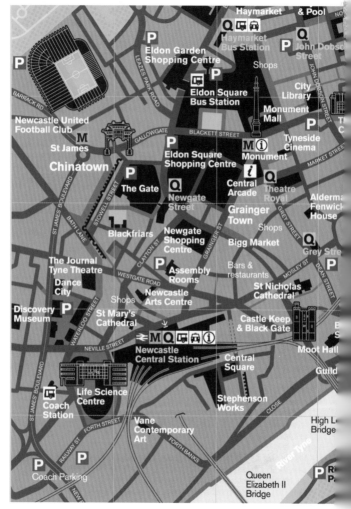

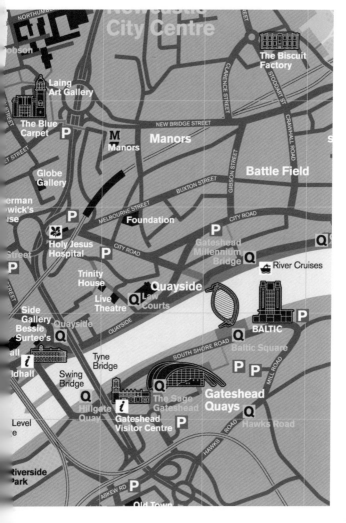

Newcastle
City Centre

NORTHUMBE

Jobson

The Biscuit
Factory

Laing
Art Gallery

STODDART ST

CLARENCE STREET

CRAWHALL ROAD

The Blue
Carpet

P

NEW BRIDGE STREET

M
Manors

Manors

Globe
Gallery

GIBSON STREET

Battle Field

erman
wick's
se

BUXTON STREET

MELBOURNE STREET

P

Foundation

CITY ROAD

Holy Jesus
Hospital

P

CITY ROAD

Gateshead
Millennium
Bridge Q

Q

Street

P

River Cruises

Trinity
House

Quayside

Live
Theatre

Q Law
Courts

Side
Gallery

Q

Quayside

QUAYSIDE

Q

BALTIC

P

Bessie
Surtee's

Baltic Square

all

i

SOUTH SHORE ROAD

P P

ldhall

Tyne
Bridge

MILL ROAD

Swing
Bridge

Q

Q

Gateshead
Quays

Hillgate
Quay

i

The Sage
Gateshead

Q

Level
e

Gateshead
Visitor Centre

P

Hawks Road

HAWKS ROAD

ASKEW RD

P

Riverside
ark

Old Town

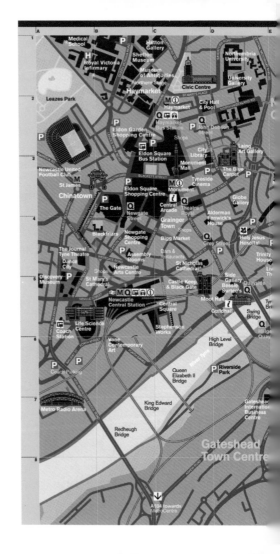

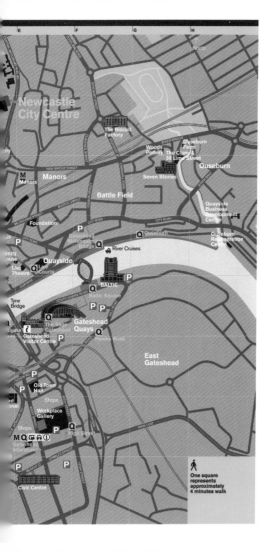

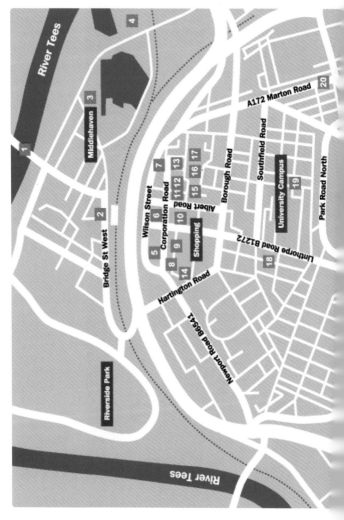

River Tees

4

3 Middlehaven

1

2 Bridge St West

Riverside Park

River Tees

Wilson Street

Corporation Road

7

13

11 12

5 6

15 16 17

10

Albert Road

9

8

Shopping

14

Hartington Road

Borough Road

A172 Marton Road

Southfield Road

University Campus

19

Linthorpe Road B1272

18

Newport Road B6541

Park Road North

20

MIDDLESBROUGH MAP

1. Transporter Bridge and Visitor Centre
2. Railway Station
3. Middlehaven
4. Middlesbrough Football Club
5. Hillstreet Shopping Centre
6. Dundas Shopping Centre
7. Thistle Hotel
8. Bus Station
9. Spectra-txt

10. The Mall Shopping Centre
11. Middlesbrough Town Hall
12. Tourist Information Centre
13. The Empire
14. Captain Cook Square Shopping Centre
15. Centre Square
16. mima and 'Bottle of Notes'
17. Central Library
18. Psyche

19. University of Teesside
20. Baltimore Hotel
21. Dorman Museum
22. Albert Park
23. Chadwicks Guest House
24. Clairville Stadium
25. Highfield Hotel
26. Grey House Hotel

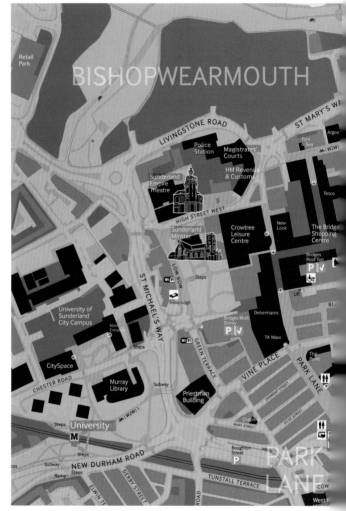

SUNDERLAND MAP

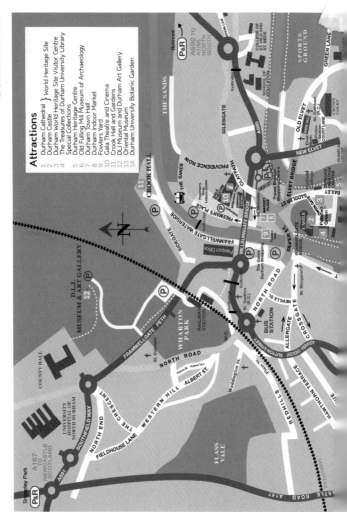

Attractions

1 Durham Cathedral ⎫ World Heritage Site
2 Durham Castle   ⎬
3 Durham World Heritage Site Visitor Centre
4 The Treasures of Durham University Library
   Special Collections
5 Durham Heritage Centre
6 Old Fulling Mill Museum of Archaeology
7 Durham Town Hall
8 Durham Indoor Market
9 Fowlers Yard
10 Gala Theatre and Cinema
11 Crook Hall and Gardens
12 DLI Museum and Durham Art Gallery
13 Oriental Museum
14 Durham University Botanic Garden